Doing Your Research Project

A Guide for First-time Researchers

SIXTH EDITION

Judith Bell
with Stephen Waters

Open University Press
McGraw-Hill Education
McGraw-Hill House
Shoppenhangers Road
Maidenhead
Berkshire
England
SL6 2QL

email: enquiries@openup.co.uk
world wide web: www.openup.co.uk

and Two Penn Plaza, New York, NY 10121-2289, USA

First published 1987
Second edition published 1993
Third edition published 1999
Fourth edition published 2005
Fifth edition published 2010
First published in this sixth edition 2014

A catalogue record of this book is available from the British Library

ISBN-13: 978-0-335-26446-9
ISBN-10: 0-335-26446-8
eISBN: 978-0-335-26447-6

Library of Congress Cataloging-in-Publication Data
CIP data applied for

Cover and internal illustrations by Clare Wood

Typeset by SRNova Private Limited, India

Printed in Great Britain by Bell & Bain Ltd, Glasgow

Brief Table of Contents

Detailed Table of Contents

Acknowledgements

I have been helped throughout the preparation of all six editions of this book by the interest of friends, colleagues and former research students who have given strong support in often difficult times.

I am particularly grateful to **Stephen Waters**, an outstanding former research student. Stephen has supported me in the writing of this edition with invaluable work on reading, drafting and updating chapters and his collaboration has been a real asset. He also contributed the new Chapter 8, 'Using social media in research', to this sixth edition, which provides an introduction to how social networks can be harnessed to enhance the research process.

Brendan Duffy, another exceptional former student, wrote Chapter 7. 'The analysis of documentary evidence', included in this and earlier editions. I am very grateful for his continued contribution.

My thanks to **Gilbert Fan**, Singaporean-based former postgraduate student of the University of Sheffield, who permitted me to quote parts of his MEd literature review in Chapter 6 and to **John Richardson** and **Alan Woodley**, both of the British Open University, who have again given me permission to quote from their journal article, 'Another look at the role of age, gender and subject as predictors of academic attainment in higher education' (Richardson and Woodley 2003).

I would also like to acknowledge the contributions of two friends, **Jan Gray**, who provided the narrative inquiry sections in Chapter 1, and **Katie Waterhouse**, who supplied the 'Top ten guide to Internet searching' in Chapter 5. My thanks to you both.

In my experience, I have found that good librarians generally know everything about most things and so I 'persuaded' **Richard Pears**, co-author of *Cite Them Right* (Pears and Shields 2013) and faculty support librarian at Durham University library, to read and comment on Chapter 5 ('Literature searching') when I drafted it for the fifth edition. He commented in great detail and also brought me up to date about online search facilities in libraries – and a great deal more. My apologies for this imposition Richard, but also my thanks.

Long-suffering **Fred Bell** once again took on the boring task of reading all the scripts and checking that the figures, tables, graphs and the like matched the texts. As usual he winced at what he regarded as some of my oversimplifications and 'unscientific' language, but I have long since learnt which of his complaints and objections to ignore and which to accept with gratitude.

My continuing gratitude to **Michael Youngman**, formerly of the University of Nottingham, who devised the question types in Chapter 8, which have eased the burden of many research students who are in the early days of designing questionnaires and interpreting the results. The generous assistance and support he invariably gave to many struggling PhD students, including me, made the difference between our dropping out altogether and actually finishing.

I have always enjoyed **Chris Madden**'s mazes, which have appeared on the front cover of all editions of this book. Unfortunately, Chris was unable to contribute to the cover in this edition but I thank him for his previous drawings, and welcome our new illustrator, **Clare Wood**, whose new interpretation of the research maze stays true to Chris's original concept. I can still smile (or sometimes even laugh out loud) at the pictures of distraught researchers going down blind alleys, attacking their laptops, losing patience and wondering why they ever started on the research in the first place. Yes. Been there; done that! However, the overall image is of students who managed to negotiate the maze and, having overcome the difficulties experienced by all researchers, are seen to be leaving it deliriously happy, in academic dress, holding their diplomas on high, throwing their mortarboards in the air and going forth to do more and even better research. The book would not be the same without the maze.

Nor could this sixth edition have been produced without all of your support and encouragement. To you all, my grateful thanks.

Judith Bell

Introduction

Doing Your Research Project is intended for those of you who are about to undertake research for what I refer to as a '100-hour project', an undergraduate dissertation or a postgraduate thesis. This new sixth edition follows the same tried-and-tested format as the previous five editions. It has, however, been thoroughly revised and updated throughout, reflecting developments in research practice and in the fast-paced world in which we operate as students, faculty members and researchers. In particular, Stephen Waters, contributing author to this edition, has updated the book by adding content on using social media in research and written a new chapter (Chapter 8) on the subject. You will also find a number of new features in this edition to help you navigate through your research project:

- New chapter introductions provide 'at a glance' lists of the key concepts and new ideas you will come across when you read each chapter.
- New 'Dead End!' boxes highlight potential risks or research problems, to help you to avoid the common pitfalls that can lead you to a dead end in the research maze!
- New key terms boxes appear in each chapter linked to a glossary, providing the first-time researcher with a guide to core concepts and research vocabulary.
- Fully revised chapter checklists now appear at the end of all chapters, reminding you of best research practice and helping you work through the research process step by step.
- Fully updated further reading sections provide 'jumping off' points to extend your learning about research methods and techniques.
- Comprehensive references provide further sources that will prove invaluable to you as you progress through your project and develop your skills as an academic researcher.

Regardless of the topic or your discipline, the problems facing you will be much the same. You will need to select a topic, identify the objectives of your study, plan and design a suitable methodology, devise research instruments, negotiate access to institutions, materials and people, collect, analyse and present information, and, finally, produce a well-written report. Whatever the size of the undertaking, techniques have to be mastered and a plan of action devised that does not attempt more than the limitations of expertise, time and access permit.

Large-scale research projects will require sophisticated techniques, and often statistical analysis, but it is quite possible to produce a worthwhile study with a minimum of statistical knowledge. We all learn how to do research by actually doing it, but a great deal of time can be wasted and goodwill dissipated by inadequate preparation.

This book aims to provide you with the tools to do the job, to help you to avoid some of the pitfalls and time-consuming false trails that can eat into your time allowance, to establish good research habits and to take you from the stage of selecting a topic through to the production of a well-planned, methodologically sound and well-written final report or thesis – ON TIME. There is, after all, little point in doing all the work if you never manage to submit!

No book can take the place of a good supervisor, but good supervisors are in great demand, and if you can familiarize yourself with basic approaches and techniques, you will be able to make full use of your tutorial time for priority issues.

YOU ARE HERE

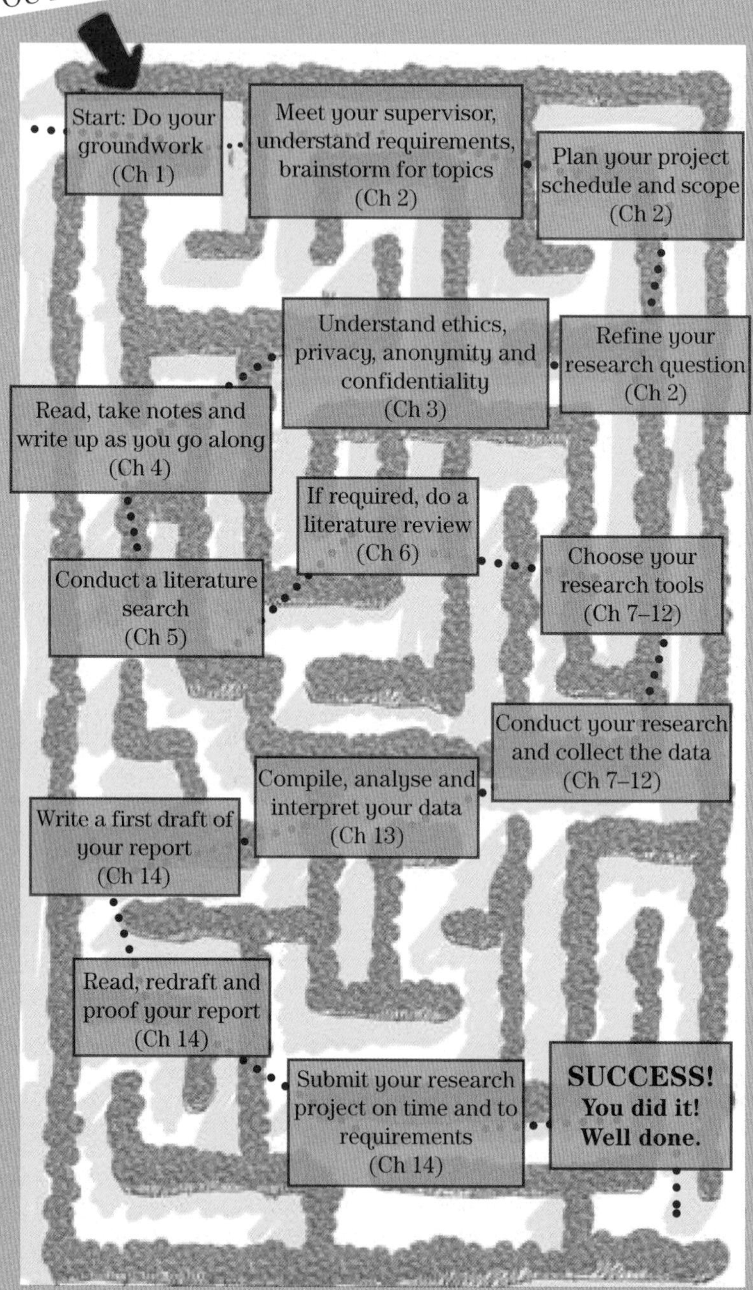

Start: Do your groundwork (Ch 1)
Meet your supervisor, understand requirements, brainstorm for topics (Ch 2)
Plan your project schedule and scope (Ch 2)
Refine your research question (Ch 2)
Understand ethics, privacy, anonymity and confidentiality (Ch 3)
Read, take notes and write up as you go along (Ch 4)
Conduct a literature search (Ch 5)
If required, do a literature review (Ch 6)
Choose your research tools (Ch 7–12)
Conduct your research and collect the data (Ch 7–12)
Compile, analyse and interpret your data (Ch 13)
Write a first draft of your report (Ch 14)
Read, redraft and proof your report (Ch 14)
Submit your research project on time and to requirements (Ch 14)
SUCCESS! You did it! Well done.

PART I

Preparing the Ground

As a first-time researcher, you are probably a little daunted by the task ahead of you. Not only are you faced with deciding what or who you are going to research but how you are going to collect data, what to do with it when you have got it, and how to write up your findings. As the maze on the front cover suggests, the path ahead is unlikely to be direct and you will take many twists and turns and go down a few blind alleys before you reach your goal. I understand how you might be feeling – after all, I was once in the same position myself. I wrote this book to act as your guide through the maze of research and to give you advance warning of possible dead ends and pitfalls so that you avoid making the same mistakes as I once did. We all learn by making mistakes and experiencing failure – but it is much less painful to learn from other people's errors and avoid making the same mistakes that they did!

The first part of the book sets out the range of research methods and approaches that you have at your disposal and considers what you need to do before you begin to collect your data. Chapter 1 takes you through the advantages and disadvantages of each research method, providing essential information to enable you to decide which is the most appropriate for collecting your data. If you have yet to decide on the focus of your research, that's fine – you can always come back to Chapter 1 later.

Chapter 2 looks at planning and structuring your research and how you might make notes during this process. While writing the report seems a long way off right now, it is important to be able to visualize how the report will be organized and to appreciate how it might look when completed. As you will see, there is far less variation between the format of research reports than you might think, and understanding how you should present your research is important from the outset.

Ethical considerations are reviewed in Chapter 3. Even experienced researchers, who begin with the best of intentions, sometimes come across ethical issues they failed to see or appreciate. The issues of anonymity and confidentiality are examined, and Stephen Waters explains how his intention that the participants in his insider study of his own institution should remain anonymous was undermined by his lack of foresight when the report was written up. Luckily, the research report was not adversely affected and participants kindly overlooked what could have been a potential problem, as their identities were unintentionally revealed. We would rather you did not depend on luck but avoid such problems occurring in the first place.

Part 1 also devotes a significant amount of space to how you manage information, how you organize references and avoid plagiarism – using other people's words and ideas as your own. It asks important questions about whether you will understand notes you have made today in the future. Even if you have a good memory, will you really be able to go back to a specific page in a book to retrieve a quotation that you have forgotten to write out in full? The answer is almost certainly that you will not, and thus it is important to get into the habit of making detailed notes from the start – on everything, even if you think you will never use it. While careful note-taking is time-consuming, it will save hours, perhaps days, of work later in your research when you would otherwise have to retrace your steps before setting out on your research journey again.

Whatever your research topic, it is highly unlikely that you will be the first person to have researched the area, although the specific focus of your research may be original (and if you are a PhD student, this will be essential). Chapters 5 and 6 concentrate on how to find relevant literature on your research topic and how you should go about writing a review of the literature you find. This will help you to put your research in the context of previous investigations and will enable you to compare your findings with those of researchers who have gone before you. A literature review should also give you a valuable insight into the advantages and disadvantages of previous research and enable you to build on researchers' successes and help you to avoid similar problems.

I do not claim to be able to offer you an untroubled path through the research maze. Nevertheless, I hope that this book will be a useful guide along the way. However challenging your research journey, I know what a great learning experience it is and how immensely rewarding completing a research project can be. I wish you well as you set out on your journey.

1 Approaches to Research

INTRODUCTION

This chapter provides you with an overview of the various approaches you might take to your research project. It offers brief summaries of the different research styles and methodologies, and further reading to help you to understand the approach your own research might take. In this chapter, you will find:

- An explanation of the difference between quantitative and qualitative research.
- An overview of action research, case study, survey and experimental approaches, their advantages and limitations.
- An introduction to ethnographic research, grounded theory and narrative theory.
- Detailed further reading lists on each of the main approaches described so that you can do preparatory reading before beginning your project.

Key terms

The following key terms are highlighted on the pages shown below. You will find a definition for each term in the glossary at the back of the book.

Quantitative	9	Survey	14
Qualitative	9	Experiment	15
Action research	10	Ethnography	17
Case study	11	Grounded theory	18
Theoretical sampling	18	Narrative inquiry/stories	21

Styles of research

It is perfectly possible to carry out a worthwhile investigation without having detailed knowledge of the various approaches to or styles of research, but a study of different approaches will provide insight into different ways of planning an investigation and, incidentally, will also enhance your understanding of the literature. One of the problems of reading research reports and reading about research reports is the terminology. Researchers use terms and occasionally jargon that may be incomprehensible to other people. It is the same in any field, where a specialized language develops to ease communication among professionals. So, before considering the various stages of planning and conducting investigations, it may be helpful to consider the main features of certain well-established and well-reported styles of research.

Different styles, traditions or approaches use different methods of collecting data, but no approach prescribes or automatically rejects any particular method. **Quantitative** researchers collect facts and study the relationship of one set of facts to another. They use 'numerical data and, typically ... structured and predetermined research questions, conceptual frameworks and designs' (Punch 2005: 28). They therefore use techniques that are likely to produce quantified and, if possible, generalizable conclusions. Researchers adopting a **qualitative** perspective are more concerned to understand individuals' perceptions of the world. They doubt whether social 'facts' exist and question whether a 'scientific' approach can be used when dealing with human beings. Importantly, Punch draws our attention to one important distinction, which is that 'qualitative research not only uses non-numerical and unstructured data but also, typically, has research questions and methods which are more general at the start, and become more focused as the study progresses' (Punch 2005: 28). There are occasions, however, when qualitative researchers draw on quantitative techniques, and vice versa. It will all depend on what data the researcher requires.

Classifying an approach as quantitative or qualitative, ethnographic, survey, action research or whatever, does not mean that once an approach has been selected, the researcher may not move from the methods normally associated with that style. Each approach has its strengths and weaknesses, and each is particularly suitable for a particular context. The approach adopted and the methods of data collection selected will depend on the nature of the inquiry and the type of information required.

It is impossible in the space of a few pages to do justice to any of the well-established styles of research, but the following will at least provide a basis for further reading and may give you ideas about approaches you may wish to adopt in your own investigation.

Action research and the role of practitioner researchers

Action research is an approach that is appropriate in any context where 'a problem involving people, tasks and procedures cries out for solution, or where some change of feature results in a more desirable outcome' (Cohen *et al.* 2011: 344). It is not a method or a technique. As in all research, the methods selected for gathering information depend on the nature of the information required. It is applied research, carried out by practitioners who have themselves identified a need for change or improvement, sometimes with support from outside the institution; other times not. The aim is 'to arrive at recommendations for good practice that will tackle a problem or enhance the performance of the organization and individuals through changes to the rules and procedures within which they operate' (Denscombe 2010b: 12).

Lomax (2007: 158, 169) provides a series of useful questions for action researchers under the headings of 'purpose', 'focus', 'relations', 'method' and 'validation'. Under the 'purpose' heading, she asks:

- Can I improve my practice so that it is more effective?
- Can I improve my understanding of this practice so as to make it more just?
- Can I use my knowledge and influence to improve the situation?

Under 'method', she asks whether the action researcher can collect 'rigorous data' that will provide evidence to support claims for action. These and similar questions can serve as a starting point for action research but when the investigation is finished and the findings have been considered by all participants, the job is still not finished. The participants continue to review, evaluate and improve practice. The research involves 'a feedback loop in which initial findings generate possibilities for change which are then implemented and evaluated as a prelude to further investigation' (Denscombe 2010a: 126). Denscombe goes on to argue that, while generalizations are unlikely to emerge from findings of 'practice-driven and small-scale' research, it:

> "should not lose anything by way of rigour. Like any other small-scale research, it can draw on existing theories, apply and test research

propositions, use suitable methods and, importantly, offer some evaluation of existing knowledge (without making unwarranted claims). It is the rigour, rather than the size of the project or its purpose, by which the research should be judged."

(Denscombe 2010a: 134)

There is nothing new about practitioners operating as researchers, but as in all 'insider' investigations, difficulties can arise if dearly held views and practices of some participants are challenged, as can happen if the research evidence appears to indicate that radical changes are needed if progress is to be made. The participatory nature of action research means there is a question as to who owns the research and its outcomes:

> "Who is in charge? Who calls the shots? Who decides on appropriate actions? Who owns the data? These and similar issues need to be worked out sensitively and carefully by the partners to *ensure that there are shared expectations about the nature of participation* in action research."

(Denscombe 2010a: 131)

Denscombe also reminds us that:

> "Because the activity of action research almost inevitably affects others, it is important to have a clear idea of when and where the action research necessarily steps outside the bounds of collecting information which is purely personal and relating to the practitioners alone. Where it does so, the usual standard of ethics must be observed: permissions obtained, confidentiality maintained, identities protected."

(Denscombe 2010a: 132)

Of equal or, perhaps, even greater importance is that before the research begins, everyone involved must know why the investigation is to take place, who will see the final report, and who will have responsibility for implementing any recommended changes.

Case study

Even if you are working on a 100-hour project over a three-month period, the **case study** approach can be particularly appropriate for individual researchers because it provides an opportunity for one aspect of a problem to be studied in some depth. Of course, not all case studies have to be completed in three months, or even three years. For example, a study by Francis *et al.* (1994) of what led to the closure of a large psychiatric hospital took five years to complete.

Sadly, you will have to wait until you are head of research in your hospital, local authority, university or government department before you will be in a position to undertake and to obtain the funding for such a venture, so, for the time being, be realistic about the selection of your case study topic. Yin reminds us that 'case studies have been done about decisions, about programmes, about the implementation process, and about organizational change. Beware these types of topic – none is easily defined in terms of the beginning or end point of the case.' He adds that 'the more a study contains specific propositions, the more it will stay within reasonable limits' (Yin 1994: 137). Good advice and worth following.

Case studies may be carried out to follow up and to put flesh on the bones of a survey. They can also precede a survey and be used as a means of identifying key issues that merit further investigation, but are usually carried out as free-standing exercises. Researchers identify an 'instance', which could be the introduction of a new way of working, the way an organization adapts to a new role, or any innovation or stage of development in an institution. Evidence has to be collected systematically, the relationship between variables studied (a *variable* being a characteristic or attribute) and the investigation methodically planned. Though observation and interviews are most frequently used, no method is excluded.

All organizations and individuals have their common and their unique features. Case study researchers aim to identify such features, to identify or attempt to identify the various interactive processes at work, to show how they affect the implementation of systems and influence the way an organization functions. These processes may remain hidden in a large-scale survey but could be crucial to the success or failure of systems or organizations.

Critics of case study

Critics of the case study approach draw attention to a number of problems and/or disadvantages. For example, some question the value of the study of single events and point out that it is difficult for researchers to cross-check information. Others express concern about selective reporting and the resulting danger of distortion. A major concern is that generalization is not always possible, though Denscombe (2010a: 60) makes the point that, 'The extent to which findings from the case study can be generalized to other examples in the class depends on how far the case study example is similar to others of its type.' He illustrates this point by drawing on the example of a case study of a small primary school. He writes that: 'this means that the researcher must obtain data on the significant features (catchment area, the ethnic origins of the pupils and the amount of staff turnover) for primary schools in general, and then demonstrate where the case study example fits in relation to the overall picture' (Denscombe 2010a: 61).

In his 1981 paper on the relative merits of the search for generalization and the study of single events, Bassey used the term 'relatability' rather than 'generalizability'. In his opinion 'an important criterion for judging the merit of a case study is the extent to which the details are sufficient and appropriate for a teacher working in a similar situation to relate his decision-making to that described in the case study. The relatability of a case study is more important than its generalizability' (Bassey 1981: 85). He considers that if case studies 'are carried out systematically and critically, if they are aimed at the improvement of education, if they are relatable, and if by publication of the findings they extend the boundaries of existing knowledge, then they are valid forms of educational research' (1981: 86)

Writing about an education case study in 1999, Bassey amends or rather adds to his 1981 thoughts. He recalls that:

> "Previously I had treated the concept of generalization (of the empirical kind, that is) as a statement that had to be absolutely true. This is the sense in which physical scientists use the term. It is the basis of their concept of scientific method ... in which a hypothesis stands as a generalization (or law) only if it withstands all attempts at refutation. I argued that there were very few generalizations (in this absolute sense) about education – and even fewer, if any, that were useful to experienced teachers."
>
> (Bassey 1999: 12)

He makes it clear that he still holds to this view as far as scientific generalizations (of the absolute kind) are concerned but now acknowledges that there are two other kinds of generalization that can apply in the social sciences, namely, statistical generalizations and 'fuzzy' generalizations:

> "The statistical generalization arises from samples of populations and typical claims that *there is an x per cent or y per cent chance* that what was found in the sample will also be found throughout the population: it is the quantitative measure. The fuzzy generalization arises from studies of singularities and typical claims that *it is possible, or likely, or unlikely that* what was found in the singularity will be found in similar situations elsewhere: it is a qualitative measure."
>
> (Bassey 1999: 12)

The pros and cons of case study will no doubt be debated in the future as they have been in the past. It's as well to be aware of the criticisms but, as I said at the beginning of this section, case study can be an appropriate approach for individual researchers in any discipline because it provides an opportunity for one aspect of a problem to be studied in some depth. You will have to decide if it suits your purpose or not.

Survey

It would be nice to have a clear, short and succinct definition of **survey** but as Aldridge and Levine (2001: 5) point out, 'Each survey is unique. Therefore, lists of do's and don'ts are too inflexible. A solution to one survey may not work in another.' Moser and Kalton (1971: 1) agree that it would be pleasant to provide a straightforward definition of what is meant by a 'social survey' but make it clear that 'such a definition would have to be so general as to defeat its purpose, since the term and the methods associated with it are applied to an extraordinarily wide variety of investigations'. They continue by giving examples of the range of areas that might be covered by a survey:

> "A survey may be occasioned simply by a need for administrative facts on some aspects of public life; or be designed to investigate a cause–effect relationship or to throw fresh light on some aspect of sociological theory. When it comes to subject matter, all one can say is that surveys are concerned with the demographic characteristics, the social environment, the activities, or the opinions and attitudes of some group of people."
>
> (Moser and Kalton 1971: 1)

The census is one example of a survey in which the same questions are asked of the selected population (the population being the group or category of individuals selected). It aims to cover 100 per cent of the population, but most surveys have less ambitious aims. In most cases, a survey will aim to obtain information from a representative selection of the population and from that sample will then be able to present the findings as being representative of the population as a whole. Inevitably, there are problems in the survey method. Great care has to be taken to ensure that the sample population is truly representative. At a very simple level, that means ensuring that if the total population has 1000 men and 50 women, then the same proportion of men to women has to be selected. But that example grossly oversimplifies the method of drawing a representative sample and, if you decide to carry out a survey, you will need to consider what characteristics of the total population need to be represented to enable you to say with fair confidence that your sample is reasonably representative.

In surveys, all respondents will be asked the same questions in, as far as possible, the same circumstances. Question wording is not as easy as it seems, and careful piloting is necessary to ensure that all questions mean the same to all respondents. Information can be gathered by means of self-completion questionnaires (as in the case of the census), by using an online survey tool such as Survey Monkey (see Chapter 9) or face-to-face by an interviewer. Whichever method of information gathering is selected, the aim is to obtain answers to the same questions from a large number of individuals to not only enable the researcher to describe, but also to compare, to relate one characteristic to another and to demonstrate that certain features exist in certain categories.

Surveys can provide answers to the questions 'What?', 'Where?', 'When?' and 'How?', but it is not so easy to find out 'Why?'. Causal relationships can rarely, if ever, be proved by the survey method. The main emphasis is on fact-finding, and if a survey is well-structured and piloted, it can be a relatively cheap and quick way of obtaining information, particularly if you use online web-based survey software, such as survey monkey, to send your questionnaires by email.

The experimental style

It is relatively easy to plan **experiments** that deal with measurable phenomena. For example, experiments have been set up to measure the effects of using fluoridated toothpaste on dental caries by establishing members of a control group (who did not use the toothpaste) and an experimental group (who did). In such experiments, the two groups, matched for age, sex, social class and so on, were given a pre-test dental examination and instructions about which toothpaste to use. After a year, both groups were given the post-test dental examination and conclusions were then drawn about the effectiveness or otherwise of the fluoridated toothpaste. The principle of such experiments is that if two identical groups are selected, one of which (the experimental group) is given special treatment and the other (the control group) is not, then any differences between the two groups at the end of the experimental period may be attributed to the difference in treatment. A causal relationship appears to have been established. It may be fairly straightforward to test the extent of dental caries (though even in this experiment the extent of the caries could be caused by many factors not controlled by the experiment) but it is quite another matter to test changes in behaviour.

Experiments may allow conclusions to be drawn about cause and effect, *if* the design is sound, but large groups are needed if the many variations and ambiguities involved in human behaviour are to be controlled. Even allowing for the collection of data in online surveys or via a questionnaire in an email attachment, both of which can be delivered to a large population in a matter of minutes, large-scale experiments are expensive to set up and take more time than most students working on 100-hour projects can devote. Tests that require only a few hours (for example, to test short-term memory or perception) can be very effective, but in claiming a causal relationship, great care needs to be taken to ensure that all possible causes have been considered.

It is worth noting at this point that ethical issues are associated with experimental research. Permission to conduct the research must be obtained from the heads of institutions or units concerned and from the participants themselves, all of whom must be fully informed about what is involved. Proposals may have to be considered by ethics committees and/or research committees in order to ensure that research participants will not come to any harm as a result of the research. It is particularly important to seek parents' permission if children are to participate in the research. If your research brings you into contact with children or vulnerable adults, you must have Disclosure and Barring Service (DBS) clearance. Either you or the organization that is supervising your research must apply for a criminal records check to confirm that you have not been convicted of a crime involving young people under the age of 18 or against adults who are vulnerable. It can take several weeks for you to receive your certificate, so make sure that you leave plenty of time for it to arrive before beginning to collect your data.

Some research has to be approved by ethics committees. Check with your supervisor. If you intend to collect data from young people under the age of 18 or from vulnerable adults, you must obtain Disclosure and Barring Service (DBS) clearance to prove that you have no criminal offences against these groups. Make sure you leave plenty of time before starting your research to obtain your certificate.

Cohen and colleagues object to the principle of 'manipulating' human beings. They write that:

> "notions of isolation and control of variables in order to establish causality ... may be appropriate for a laboratory, though whether, in fact, a social situation ever *could become* the antiseptic, artificial world of the laboratory or *should become* such a world is both an empirical and moral question ... Further, the ethical dilemmas of treating humans as manipulable, controllable and inanimate are considerable."
>
> (Cohen *et al.* 2000: 212)

Quite so, though ethical issues have to be considered in all research, regardless of the context. If you decide to undertake an experimental study, ask for advice, consider any implications and requirements – and be careful about making claims about causality.

Ethnography and the ethnographic style of research

Brewer defines **ethnography** as:

> "The study of people in naturally occurring settings or 'fields' by methods of data collection which capture their social **meanings** and ordinary activities, involving the researcher participating directly in the setting, if not also the activities, in order to collect data in a systematic manner but without meaning being imposed on them externally."
>
> (Brewer 2000: 6)

Ethnographic researchers attempt to develop an understanding of how a culture works and, as Lutz points out, many methods and techniques are used in that search:

> "Participant observation, interview, mapping and charting, interaction analysis, study of historical records and current public documents, the use of demographic data, etc. But ethnography centres on the participant observation of a society or culture through a complete cycle of events that regularly occur as that society interacts with its environment."
>
> (Lutz 1993: 108)

Participant observation enables researchers, as far as possible, to share the same experiences as the participants, to understand better why they act in the way they do. However, it is time-consuming and so is often outside the scope of researchers working on 100-hour projects or on time-limited Master's degrees. The researcher has to be accepted by the individuals or groups being studied, and this can mean doing the same job, or living in the same environment and circumstances as the participants for lengthy periods.

Time is not the only problem with this approach. As in case studies, critics point to the problem of representativeness. If the researcher is studying one group in depth over a period of time, who is to say that group is typical of other groups that may have the same title? Are nurses in one hospital (or even in one specialist area) necessarily representative of nurses in a similar hospital or specialist area in another part of the country? Are canteen workers in one type of organization likely to be typical of all canteen workers? Critics also refer to the problem of generalization but, as in the case study approach, if the study is well-structured and carried out, and makes no claims that cannot be justified, it may well be relatable in a way that will enable members of similar groups to recognize problems and, possibly, to see ways of solving similar problems in their own group.

The grounded theory approach

Glaser and Strauss (1965, 1968) developed the **grounded theory** approach to qualitative data analysis in the 1960s during the course of a field observational study of the way hospital staff dealt with dying patients. So what does it involve? Strauss tells us that:

> "The methodological thrust of the grounded theory approach to qualitative data analysis is toward the development of theory, without any particular commitment to specific kinds of data, lines of research, or theoretical interests. So, it is not really a specific method or technique. Rather it is a style of doing qualitative analysis that includes a number of distinct features, such as theoretical sampling, and certain methodological guidelines, such as the making of constant comparisons and the use of a coding paradigm, to ensure conceptual development and density."
>
> (Strauss 1987: 5)

He defines **theoretical sampling** as: 'sampling directed by the evolving theory; it is a sampling of incidents, events, activities, populations, etc. It is harnessed to the making of *comparisons* between and among those samples of activities, populations, etc.' (Strauss 1987: 21).

The theory is not pre-specified. It emerges as the research proceeds (hence 'theoretical' sampling). Over the years, there have been some adjustments to the original 1960s approach to grounded theory, but the principles remain much the same, which are that theory evolves during actual research by means of the analysis of the data. Punch agrees but considers that 'grounded theory is not a theory at all. It is a method, an approach, a strategy whose purpose is to generate theory from data … The theory will therefore be grounded in data' (Punch 2005: 155).

At first sight, this seems straightforward enough, but as Hayes makes clear:

> "The process of conducting grounded theory research isn't just a matter of looking at the data and developing a theory from it. Instead, it is what researchers call an **iterative** process – that is, a cyclical process in which theoretical insights emerge or are discovered in the data, those insights are then tested to see how they can make sense of other parts of the data, which in turn produce their own theoretical insights, which are then tested again against the data, and so on."
>
> (Hayes 2000: 184)

She continues by reminding us that:

> "The theory which is produced using a grounded theory analysis may sometimes be very context-specific, applying only in a relatively small number of situations; but because it is always grounded in data collected from the real world, it can serve as a very strong basis for further investigations, as well as being a research finding in its own right."
>
> (Hayes 2000: 184)

Most grounded theory researchers will begin with research questions but they do not start with a hypothesis, nor do they begin their investigation with a thorough review of the literature relating to their topic. They build up theory from their data and they do not wait until all data are collected before they begin the analysis stage. Instead, analysis takes place as the data are collected. The researcher examines the findings of an interview or of participant observation and then proceeds to the analysis of those findings before any other data are collected. As the research proceeds, there will be more data collection and more analysis and so on until 'theoretical saturation' is reached, which is the stage at which 'further data produce no new theoretical development. Saturation is necessary to ensure that the theory is conceptually complete' (Punch 2005: 214–15).

Miles and Huberman have some reservations about the principle that coding and recording are over when the analysis appears to have run its course, when all the incidents can be readily classified, when categories are 'saturated' and sufficient numbers of 'regularities' have emerged. They warn us to 'be careful here' because:

> "Fieldwork understanding comes in layers; the longer we are in the environment, the more layers appear to surface, and the choice of when to close down, when to go with a definitive coding system or definitive analysis can be painful. That choice may be dictated as much by time

> and budget constraints as on scientific grounds. When those constraints are relaxed, saturation can become a vanishing horizon – just another field trip away, then another . . ."
>
> (Miles and Huberman 1994: 62)

Glaser (1992) has also expressed some concern at the way grounded theory has developed over the years, in particular the use of code and retrieve software, such as NVivo, which generates theory from qualitative data on grounded theory lines. He considers that more subtle procedures are required to tease out the layers of meaning that emerge, and this cannot be achieved by narrow analytical procedures.

More recent developments include the identification of more sophisticated criteria for grounded theory studies. For example, Charmaz (2008: 230–1) outlines four key criteria for considering the rigour and quality of a grounded theory study. These criteria provide a solid framework for any researcher when reviewing their own grounded theory study.

The analysis of grounded theory data is, to me at least, quite complex. It requires the researcher to identify concepts, codes, categories and relationships in order to bring order to the data, and the time taken to become skilled at identifying and applying them is considerable. I confess that I find the level of abstraction and the language used, which appear to be implicit in grounded theory, difficult to absorb. However, that is no more than my perception of the difficulty of teasing out those layers of meaning. Many colleagues and former students whose views I respect and who have successfully completed research based on a grounded theory approach disagree with me. They tell me that the software can cope with the layers and the complexity perfectly well. So, all I can say is that before you decide to commit yourself to a grounded theory approach, read as widely as time permits and, as always, take advice before you finally decide how to proceed.

Narrative inquiry and stories

The use and interpretation of narratives and in particular the acceptance of stories as valuable sources of data is well established in qualitative research, although perhaps less represented in books on research methodology than other sources. **Stories** are certainly interesting and have been used for many years by management consultants and others who present examples of successful (and unsuccessful) practice as a basis for discussion as to how successful practice might be emulated and disasters avoided.

What has always taxed me has been how information derived from storytelling can be structured in such a way as to produce valid research findings. It took an experienced group of postgraduate and postdoctoral students who had planned their research on **narrative inquiry** lines to sort me out and to explain precisely what was involved. I was not even sure what narrative inquiry actually meant and so, always believing the best way to find out is to ask an expert, I asked one member of the group, Dr. Janette Gray, to tell me. She wrote as follows:

> "It involves the collection and development of stories, either as a form of data collection or as a means of structuring a research project. Informants often speak in a story form during the interviews, and as the researcher, listening and attempting to understand, we hear their 'stories'. The research method can be described as narrative when data collection, interpretation and writing are considered a 'meaning-making' process with similar characteristics to stories (Gudmunsdottir 1996: 295). Narrative inquiry can involve reflective autobiography, life story, or the inclusion of excerpts from participants' stories to illustrate a theme developed by the researcher. A narrative approach to inquiry is most appropriate when the researcher is interested in portraying intensely personal accounts of human experience. Narratives allow voice – to the researcher, the participants and to cultural groups – and in this sense they can have the ability to develop a decidedly political and powerful edge."
>
> (Gray 1998: 12)

Colleagues to whom I had spoken and who had successfully adopted a narrative inquiry approach to one or more of their research projects had always made it clear that stories were not merely used as a series of 'story boxes' piled on top of one another, with no particular structure or connecting theme. The problem I had was in understanding how such structures and themes could be derived. Jan's explanation was as follows:

> "All forms of narrative inquiry involve an element of analysis and development of theme, dependent on the researcher's perspective. Stories share a basic structure. The power of a story is dependent on the storyteller's use of language to present an interpretation of personal experience. The skill of the narrative researcher lies in the ability to structure the interview data into a form which clearly presents a sense of a beginning, middle and an end. Even though the use of story as a research tool is a relatively new concept in the social sciences, historically story has been an accepted way of relating knowledge and developing self-knowledge. One of the major strengths of such a means

of conducting inquiry is the ability to allow readers who do not share a cultural background similar to either the storyteller or the researcher to develop an understanding of notices and consequences of actions described within a story format. Narrative is a powerful and different way of knowing . . ."

"Data collection for narrative research requires the researcher to allow the storyteller to structure the conversations, with the researcher asking follow-up questions. So a narrative approach to the question of how mature-age undergraduates perceive their ability to cope with the experience of returning to study would involve extended, open-ended interviews with mature-aged students. This would allow the students to express their personal experience of the problems, frustrations and joys of returning to study. It might also involve similar 'conversations' with other stakeholders in their education – perhaps family members; their tutors and lecturers – to provide a multiple perspective of the context of the education of mature-aged undergraduates."

(Gray 1998: 2)

Jan added that 'the benefit of considerate and careful negotiation will be a story allowing an incredibly personal and multi-faceted insight into the situation being discussed'. I am sure this is so. I have become convinced of the value of this approach and that stories can in some cases serve to enhance understanding within a case study or an ethnographic study. However, narratives can present their own set of problems:

"Interviews are time-consuming and require the researcher to allow the storytellers to recount in their own way the experience of being (or teaching) a student. This may not emerge in the first interview. Until a trust relationship has developed between researcher and storyteller, it is highly unlikely that such intimate information will be shared. Such personal involvement with the researcher involves risks and particular ethical issues. The storytellers may decide they have revealed more of their feelings than they are prepared to share publicly and they may insist either on substantial editing or on withdrawing from the project."

(Gray 1998: 2)

Problems of this kind can arise in almost any kind of research, particularly that which is heavily dependent on interview data, but the close relationship needed for narrative inquiry can make the researcher (and the storyteller) particularly vulnerable.

When asked in 2009 what had changed in terms of narrative inquiry as a methodology, Jan responded:

"The last decade has seen a broadening of the theoretical basis of narrative inquiry to include a deeper appreciation of the impact of context on any interpretation of a participant's 'story'. This includes an acknowledgement of the need to consider the complex interactions between the personal, professional and social contexts within which the participant situates their story. Further, there has been a significant change in the international, multi-disciplinary recognition of narrative inquiry as a rigorous methodology focused on developing an understanding of personal and professional experience. For interested researchers, Clandinin (2007) provides a comprehensive rationale for the theoretical positioning of narrative inquiry as a methodology."

(Gray 2009: 1)

Online diaries in the form of blogs (short for 'web logs': see Chapters 8 and 11), which combine self-reflection with content in the form of a narrative, can provide a rich source of information in narrative enquiry. In addition, YouTube and the professional video platform Ted contain vast archives of autobiographical reflections, interviews and presentations that may also be relevant to your research area.

That the narrative approach carries with it a number of potential difficulties, especially for first-time researchers, and researchers operating within a particularly tight schedule, does not mean that it should be disregarded when considering an appropriate approach to the topic of your choice. Far from it – but as is the case with all research planning, I feel it would be as well to discuss the issues fully with your supervisor before deciding what to do, and if possible to try to find a supervisor who is experienced, or at least interested, in narrative inquiry.

Which approach?

Classifying an approach as ethnographic, qualitative, experimental – or whatever – does not mean that once an approach has been selected the researcher cannot move from the methods normally associated with that style. But understanding the major advantages and disadvantages of each approach is likely to help you to select the most appropriate methodology for the task in hand. This chapter has covered only the basic principles associated with different styles or approaches to research. This should suffice – at any rate until you have decided on a topic and considered what further information you need to obtain.

Always consult the library catalogue *and* the librarians and take advantage of what the library has in stock or is able to obtain from another library, preferably without cost, and make sure you know which online facilities are provided by the library and/or your department.

Laying the Groundwork Checklist

After reading this chapter you should:

1. Understand the main approaches to research.	At this stage, you will start to build an understanding of research methods, their characteristics and advantages and disadvantages.	☑
2. Understand the difference between qualitative and quantitative research.	You will be able to describe what each means to another student.	☑
3. Start to build your research vocabulary.	Understand research terms, including ethnographic research, action research, grounded theory and narrative theory.	☑
4. Extend your understanding of research methods.	Use the suggested further reading suggestions at the end of the chapter to develop your knowledge of techniques that appear most relevant to your research topic.	☑
5. Focus on specific methods that interest you.	Consider how the various research methods work in practice, and how they could be applied to your area of study.	☑
6. Reach a point where you feel ready to approach the planning stages of your own project.	Once you understand the basics, you are now in a position to plan your own project. Proceed to Chapter 2…	☑

Further reading

Action research, case study, survey, experimental style, ethnography, grounded theory and narrative have been dealt with very briefly in this chapter and many general books about research methods will also include sections relating to all seven of these approaches. One of the most helpful is:

Denscombe, M. (2010) ***The Good Research Guide for Small-scale Social Research Projects*** **(4th edn). Maidenhead: Open University Press.**
Part 1 provides clear accounts of the advantages and limitations of surveys, case studies, Internet research, experiments, ethnography, phenomenology, grounded theory, action research and mixed methods research. Helpful checklists are provided at the end of main sections. Denscombe also includes sections on quantitative and qualitative research.

Quantitative and qualitative research

Brett Davies, M. (2007) ***Doing a Successful Research Project: Using Qualitative or Quantitative Methods.*** **Basingstoke: Palgrave Macmillan.**
This useful book considers the differences between qualitative and quantitative research in the context of surveys, questionnaires, sampling, interviewing – and much more.

Punch, K.F. (2005) ***Introduction to Social Research: Quantitative and Qualitative Approaches*** **(2nd edn). London: Sage.**

Case study

Bassey, M. (2007) Case study, in A.R.J. Briggs and M. Coleman (eds) ***Research Methods in Educational Leadership and Management*** **(2nd edn). London: Sage.**

Cohen, L., Manion, L. and Morrison, K. (2011) ***Research Methods in Education*** **(7th edn). Abingdon: Routledge.**

Yin, R.K. (2014) ***Case Study Research: Design and Methods*** **(5th edn). London: Sage.**
This book covers all aspects of case study method, from definition, design and data collection to data analysis in just about every discipline. Also covers data computer-assisted coding techniques – and much more. Examples of actual case studies are referred to in Yin's (2012) companion volume, *Applications of Case Study Research* (3rd edn). London: Sage.

Survey research

Aldridge, A. and Levine, K. (2001) *Surveying the Social World: Principles and Practice in Survey Research*. Buckingham: Open University Press.

Fogelman, K. and Comber, C. (2007) Surveys and sampling, in A.R.J. Briggs and M. Coleman (eds) *Research Methods in Educational Leadership and Management* (2nd edn). London: Sage.

Roberts, B. (2002) *Biographical Research*. Buckingham: Open University Press.
Chapter 6 considers oral history; Chapter 7 deals with narrative, in particular narrative analysis; Chapter 9 concentrates on biographical research.

Sapsford, R. (2006) *Survey Research* (2nd edn). London: Sage.
This book provides useful examples of theoretical and practical aspects of survey research and includes examples of using materials on the Internet.

The experimental style

Hayes, N. (2000) *Doing Psychological Research: Gathering and Analysing Data*. Buckingham: Open University Press.
Chapter 3, 'Experiments', provides useful information about causality in experiments.

Ethnography and the ethnographic style of research

Brewer, J.D. (2000) *Ethnography*. Buckingham: Open University Press.

Crang, M. and Cook, I. (2007) *Doing Ethnographies*. London: Sage.
Crang and Cook base this book on their own fieldwork experience. This book is particularly useful for first-time ethnographers.

Lutz, F.W. (1993) Ethnography: the holistic approach to understanding schooling, in M. Hammersley (ed.) *Controversies in Classroom Research* (2nd edn). Buckingham: Open University Press.
This excellent chapter relates mainly to ethnographic research in education, but also has valuable advice about any type of qualitative research.

Neyland, D. (2007) Organizational Ethnography. London: Sage.
This book takes us through the history of ethnography. Neyland discusses a wide range of procedures, from research design to data analysis, and provides interesting examples of organizational ethnography at work.

The grounded theory approach

Charmaz, K. (2011) Grounded theory methods in social justice research, in N.K. Denzin and Y.S. Lincoln (eds) *The Sage Handbook of Qualitative Research* (4th edn). London: Sage.
This chapter has several very helpful aspects for a beginner researcher. For example, throughout the chapter excerpts from research data illustrate the more abstract descriptions of data analysis.

Punch, K.F. (2005) *Introduction to Social Research: Quantitative and Qualitative Approaches* (2nd edn). London: Sage.
I particularly like Chapter 8 ('Design in qualitative research'). Section 8.5, pp. 155–62 provides a brief but useful and clear section on the meaning and analysis of grounded theory. Chapter 8 also includes sections on case study, ethnography and other approaches.

Narrative inquiry and stories

Clandinin, D.J. (2007) *Handbook of Narrative Inquiry: Mapping a Methodology*. Thousand Oaks, CA: Sage.
This handbook provides a comprehensive overview of all aspects of narrative inquiry as a methodology. Part IV is particularly helpful in illustrating the power of narrative-based research within the professions.

Clough, P. (2002) *Narratives and Fictions in Educational Research*. Maidenhead: Open University Press.
Peter Clough provides interesting 'fictional' stories to demonstrate the use of narrative in reporting research, and discusses the potential merits and difficulties of such an approach.

Goodson, I.F. and Sikes, P. (2001) *Life History Research in Educational Settings: Learning from Lives*. Buckingham: Open University Press.
This book explores reasons for the popularity of life-history research in education, though many of the examples considered are likely to have similar application to researchers in other disciplines.

Roberts, B. (2002) *Biographical Research*. Buckingham: Open University Press.
Chapter 6 considers oral history; Chapter 7 deals with narrative, in particular narrative analysis; Chapter 9 concentrates on ethnography and biographical research.

2 Planning the Project

INTRODUCTION

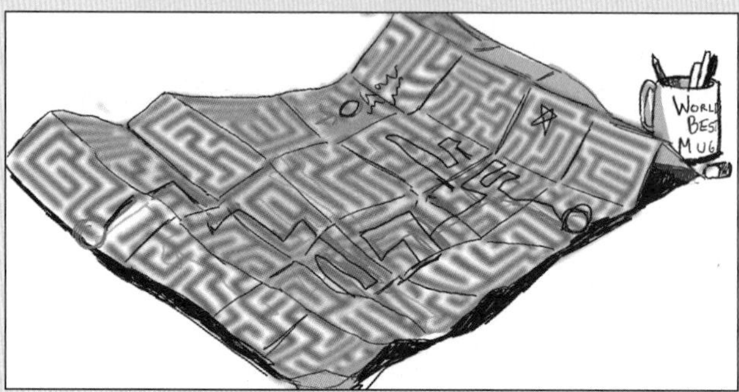

This chapter provides you with a step-by-step approach to planning your project. It begins by identifying the purpose of the study and taking you through the initial groundwork stages. This includes developing a hypothesis, making your first attempts at writing a question and planning a schedule. The crucial supervisor–student relationship is also covered. In this chapter, you will find:

- Getting started – pointers for kick-starting your thought processes, generating ideas and focusing on a productive and achievable research topic.
- Advice on identifying the purpose of the study – thinking critically about what your research is going to achieve.
- How to plan your schedule – planning a realistic timetable for your work, and sticking to it!
- A guide to the supervisor–student relationship – understanding the expectations on both sides, establishing a professional relationship with your supervisor and what to do if things go wrong.
- Suggestions for keeping a research diary and advice for writing as you go along.

Key terms

Selecting a topic

Selecting a topic is more difficult than it might seem. With limited time at your disposal, there is a temptation to select a topic before the groundwork has been done, but try to resist it. Prepare well and you will save time later. Your discussions and inquiries will help you to select a topic which is likely to be of interest, which you have a good chance of completing, which will be worth the effort and which may even have some practical application later on.

Many researchers in areas such as education, social science and health are directly concerned with the practical outcomes of research and, in particular, the improvement of practice in their organization. The aim is not only to gain more understanding of the present but to use this knowledge to act more effectively in the future. This is not to deny the importance of research that may have no immediate practical outcome. Eggleston provides a timely reminder of the importance of longer-term objectives and of the need to look beyond current practices. To restrict research to current practices would, in his opinion, lay it 'open to the charge that its sole function was to increase the efficiency of the existing system in terms of accepted criteria and deny it the opportunity to explore potentially more effective alternatives' (Eggleston 1979: 5).

Clearly there will always be a need to explore potentially more effective alternatives to existing provision. But after 100 hours of study, you are unlikely to be in a position to make recommendations for fundamental change to any system. Whatever the size and scope of the study, however, you will always be required to analyse and evaluate the information you collect and, in some cases, you might then be in a position to suggest desirable changes in practice.

Discuss possible practical outcomes with your supervisor and ask whether the department has any guidelines for the selection of topics and the preparation of research briefs. Consider what the emphasis of your study is to be. Is applicability to be important or is your study to have different aims?

Getting started

You may be assigned a topic to research, but in most cases you will be asked to select a topic from a list or to decide on a topic yourself. You may have an idea or a particular area of interest that you would like to explore. You may have several ideas, all equally interesting. Write them down:

> *Something to do with mature students?*
> *Stress at work?*
> *The effectiveness (or otherwise) of the research methods/introduction to using social media in research/introduction to the library course?*
> *Supervision of research projects?*
> *Teamwork in an accident and emergency department?*
> *Questioning in the classroom?*
> *Supervision of placements?*
> *Starting up a business?*
> *The role of social media in reporting the news?*

These are all possible topics but before a decision can be made about which to select, some work needs to be done. Think about what might be involved in each topic and which will be likely to maintain your interest. If you become bored with a topic, the time will drag unmercifully and the likelihood is that the quality of your research will suffer. Talk to colleagues and friends about your initial ideas. They may be aware of sensitive aspects of certain topics that could cause difficulties at some stage, or they may know of other people who have carried out research in one or more of your topics who would be willing to talk to you. If you are hoping to carry out the research in your own institution, then another very good reason for discussing possible topics with colleagues is that you will probably be asking for their support and collaboration: early consultation is essential if you are to avoid difficulties later.

Google your topic to see if similar research has already been conducted. Although there are other search engines such as Bing and Yahoo, I refer to Google throughout this book in recognition of the fact that it is the market leader of search engines. Some supervisors prefer you to write your research topic in the form of a question and I have also found this helpful when carrying out a Google search. Try similar keywords or synonyms related to your question. For example, for the topic 'How do houses built before 1900 contribute to global warming?', 'houses' could be replaced by 'homes' and 'built before 1900' could become 'pre-1900' or 'in the eighteenth century'.

If you are on Twitter, it may be worth entering keywords related to your research topic in the search feature. Yes, it may be a long shot, but it may also lead to a contact who is researching the same topic as you or who may know someone who is. It is well worth the short time that it will take to look through the search results.

If you have a LinkedIn profile, write an update about the research you are doing on your home page and ask if anyone else is researching the same area. If you are a member of any LinkedIn networks, do the same there too. If you don't have a LinkedIn account or belong to any networks, you might consider setting one up to connect with people who are working in the same research field. LinkedIn is a network for professional people and will give you the opportunity to present your profile as a researcher, to connect with other researchers and to share ideas (see Chapter 8).

Try to reduce your list of research topics to a choice of two – one likely to be of main interest and the second to fall back on if your preliminary investigations throw up problems. Let's say you decide you would be particularly interested in the topic of mature students, but that stress comes a close second. It will have become clear to you that 'something to do with mature students' requires more focusing before you can proceed. So far, you have been thinking in general terms but now you need to start the process of trying out ideas and asking yourself questions.

Start with your first choice (mature students) and begin to make notes of your ideas. If you prefer a digital record, you can use the note-making tool that may have come free with your smartphone or tablet. You can also download a version of Microsoft's OneNote, which is free for web and mobile apps and compatible with both iOS and Android, or EverNote, which is the most versatile and capable and works on Mac OS, Windows or Blackberry and which is free with a storage limit. Apart from text, both platforms can store images, web pages, photos and files. OneNote can also store audio notes and video clips. Both EverNote and OneNote can be accessed offline and have features that enable you to identify your notes with tags and organize them into different categories so that you can easily find them. Write 'mature students' in the middle of the paper or screen and link to it all the questions, doubts, theories and ideas you can think of. Insert arrows, if necessary, to link one idea or query with another. Write quickly and write as you think. If you decide to wait until your thoughts are in better order, you may (and probably will) have forgotten what you thought of first. It doesn't matter how illegible and disorganized your chart is at first so long as you can understand your own notes. You can put your ideas in order later. This first shot is for you, not other people.

The purpose of this exercise is to help you to clarify your thoughts and to try to decide what you actually *mean* by each statement and each question. It will give you ideas about refining the topic so that you will not be attempting to do research into everything there is to know about mature students, but into one precise aspect of the topic. It will give you clues as to whether this topic is likely to be too complex for you to complete in your timescale, or whether it might prove impossible because you would require access to confidential information that in all probability would not be forthcoming.

Your first shot will be a mess but that doesn't matter. Your second attempt will be far more focused and you will be on the way to making a fairly firm decision about which aspect of your topic to investigate. Incidentally, don't throw away your first or your second attempts until after your research is complete, examined and/or your work is published. You may need to refer to first shots and early drafts at some stage, so start a 'reject' or a 'trash' file.

Consider your priorities. For example, if you have decided that you would be interested in investigating barriers to learning among mature undergraduates, draw together the various items on your first and second thoughts charts into a list of questions on your selected topics, eliminating overlaps or rejects, and adding any other thoughts that occur to you as you write. At this stage, the order and wording are not important. You are on the way.

The purpose of the study

Start with the purpose of the study. It might be difficult at this stage to provide the exact wording but it's important to know why you want to carry out this research. Think about it. Write down your ideas. Ask yourself questions and make a note of any prompts about the likely sub-questions. Be critical. *The purpose of this study is* ... what?

- *To identify any barriers to learning for mature students?* Meaning of 'barriers'? Why do I need this information and how will I find it? Ask students? Ask a sample of students who started their degree course straight from school for comparison? Any differences? Any differences between mature students who experienced no barriers and those who did?
- *To identify any differences between the performance of mature and younger students?* How judged? Degree classification of former students? Would need access to statistics. Any data protection issues?

Each question raises other issues. Ask yourself:

- *What do institutions mean by 'mature'? What do I mean by 'mature' and 'older'?* Need to think of synonyms for 'mature'. Over

21, 25, 30, 60? Age at registration? Age at graduation? Need to get this sorted. How will I find out? Will I be given access to records? Are the records paper-based or online/in databases or both?

- *Which mature students?* Those who graduated since the university was established? In the last three years? All students in the university, in one department, in one subject area, one group? Need to think.
- *Which institutions/faculties/departments/groups are to be included in this investigation?* Need to ask supervisor's advice about how to go about obtaining permission. Is one institution/department/subject area/group sufficient – or feasible? Would it be acceptable for me to concentrate on mature students on my course?
- *Has any research been done already on this topic?* Need to go to the library to find what has already been written about mature students and see what those researchers said about the definition of 'mature' – and other things. Supplement work in the library with a search on Google and use LinkedIn and Twitter to explore whether other researchers have carried out research in this area.

These questions will give you and your supervisor or tutor some idea of where you are heading. You're still at the *what* stage (the *how* stage comes later), but each stage continues to be a process of refining and clarifying so that you end with a list of questions, tasks or objectives that you can ask, perform or examine. These will become what Laws *et al.* (2013: 52) describe as *researchable questions*, which will take you a major step forward in the planning of your project.

Hypotheses, objectives and researchable questions

Many research projects begin with the statement of a **hypothesis**, defined by Verma and Beard as:

> "A tentative proposition which is subject to verification through subsequent investigation. It may also be seen as the guide to the researcher in that it depicts and describes the method to be followed in studying the problem. In many cases hypotheses are hunches that the researcher has about the existence of relationship between variables."
>
> (Verma and Beard 1981: 184)

This definition is taken a step further by Medawar, who writes:

> "All advances in scientific understanding, at every level, begin with a speculative adventure, an imaginative preconception *of what might be true* – a preconception which always, and necessarily, goes a little way (sometimes a long way) beyond anything which we have logical or factual authority to believe in. It is the invention of a possible world, or of a tiny fraction of that world. The conjecture is then exposed to criticism to find out whether or not that imagined world is anything like the real one. Scientific reasoning is therefore at all levels an interaction between two episodes of thought – a dialogue between two voices, the one imaginative and the other critical; a dialogue, if you like, between the possible and the actual, between proposal and disposal, conjecture and criticism, between what might be true and what is in fact the case."
>
> (Medawar 1972: 22)

Thus hypotheses make statements about relations between variables and provide a guide to the researcher as to how the original hunch might be tested. If we hypothesize, because our conjecture suggests it may be so, that age (one variable) has an influence on degree results (another variable), then we can attempt to find out whether that is the case – at least among the individuals in our sample. The results of the research will either *support* the hypothesis (that age does have an influence on degree results) or will *not* support it (age has no influence on degree results).

Small-scale projects of the kind discussed in this book will not require statistical testing of hypotheses often required in large-scale sample surveys. Unless your supervisor advises otherwise, a precise statement of objectives and a list of researchable questions are generally sufficient. The important point is not so much whether there is a hypothesis, but whether you have carefully thought about what is and what is not worth investigating. It may be permissible to make modifications to objectives or changes to the questions as the study proceeds, but that does not obviate the need to identify exactly what you plan to do at the outset. Until that stage has been achieved, it is not possible to consider appropriate methods of data collection, so it's now time to check the following items.

Working title and the project outline

Select a *working title* – 'Barriers to learning' or 'Mature students'? Either will do for the time being. You're almost ready to produce the project outline for discussion with your supervisor, but just go through the stages once again:

- Are you clear about the *purpose of the study*? Are you sure about it? Do you think it's really worth doing?
- Have you decided on the *focus of the study*?
- You have not yet *identified your sample*. Discussion with supervisor required and then permissions sought. You're not there yet.
- You've been through all your *key questions* (several times now) and know what your priorities are. There will almost certainly be adjustments as the research continues, but never mind.
- You have begun to consider *what information* you might need to be in a position to answer your questions. More work needed, but you've made a start.
- You have not yet begun to consider *how* you might obtain this information, but once the focusing is finished, you can begin to consider possible ways and means. Remember that you can't assume you will be allowed to interview people or give them a questionnaire to answer. You have to clear official channels and obtain permission.

There are still some decisions to be made, but you're ready to produce the first draft of your project outline for discussion with your supervisor. Before you do, think about your submission date. Think about *time*. What are your chances of completing your provisional plan in your allocated time? You are not going to be living in isolation with only a laptop and your mobile for company for the duration of your research, away from work commitments, family responsibilities and holidays. They all need to be taken into account in your time plan. I make plans all the time and I live by lists. I don't always succeed in keeping to them, but at least their presence is enough to remind me about what still needs to be done and to nag me when I am thinking about all the things I'd rather do than get back to the writing.

Timing

There is never enough time to do all the work that appears to be essential to do a thorough job, but if you have a handover date, then somehow the work has to be completed in the specified time. It is unlikely you will be able to keep rigidly to a timetable, but some attempt should be made to devise a schedule so that you can check progress periodically and, if necessary, force yourself to move from one stage of the research to the next.

If you have to complete more than one project in the year, it is particularly important to produce a list or a chart indicating the stage at which all data should have been collected, analysed and drafts produced. Delay on one project means that the timing for the second and third will be upset. It is immaterial whether you produce a list *or* a chart, but some attempt at planning progress should be attempted.

One of the most common reasons for falling behind is that reading and associated research takes longer than anticipated. Books and articles have to be located, and the temptation to read just one more book or to do one more search online is strong. At some stage a decision has to be made to stop reading and researching and start writing, no matter how inadequate the coverage of the subject is. Forcing yourself to move on is a discipline that has to be learnt. Keep in touch with your supervisor about progress. If things go wrong and you are held up on one stage, there may be other ways of overcoming the problem. Talk about it. Ask for help and advice *before* you become weeks out of phase with your timetable, so that you have a chance of amending your original project plan.

The project outline is for guidance only. If subsequent events indicate that it would be better to ask different questions and even to have a different aim, then change while there is time. You have to work to the date specified by the institution, and your supervisor and external examiner will understand that.

Make sure that you draw up a timetable for your research and put deadlines into your calendar. Don't underestimate the amount of time that reading and background research will take. Try to stick to your timetable. If a task takes longer than you thought, reset your deadlines and work to the new timetable.

Supervision

I cannot emphasize enough the importance of establishing a good working relationship with your **supervisor**. Few researchers, inexperienced *and* experienced, can go it alone and expect to produce quality research. There are exceptions of course – aren't there always? Somebody told me once about a PhD student who made it clear that he did not need a supervisor and had no intention of attending any research tutorials. He was advised that this would be very unwise and that his chances of succeeding without support were very slight. He persisted and eventually submitted a thesis that proved to be a work of outstanding quality and depth. His external examiner had no doubt in recommending that it was a clear pass. There is a problem with this approach, namely that few people can aspire to such single-mindedness and brilliance. Most of us really do need a supervisor in whom we have confidence, with whom we can share our thinking, who is willing to advise and to give an honest view about our drafts, and that applies regardless of whether we are working on a 100-hour project, an undergraduate or a postgraduate degree.

Student–supervisor relationships

I have occasionally heard students complain that they are getting a raw deal from their supervisors, and in some cases they may have been right – though not always. Supervisors are only human. Most will also be lecturing, supervising other students and carrying out their own research. Time is generally in short supply and some friends who are heavily committed with supervision have suggested to me that I give the impression that they should be available at all hours to see students on demand who might wish to discuss any aspect of their work, regardless of the time of day, the time involved and the frequency of such requests. Not so. A reasonable balance has to be struck, though I realize that the big question is what 'reasonable' means to both sides.

Perhaps, not surprisingly, interviews with students and with supervisors reveal a wide variation in supervisory practice (Bell 1996; Phillips and Pugh 2000). The majority of students appear to have enjoyed very positive relationships with supervisors. Their comments were on the lines of 'very helpful'; 'taught me what research was all about'; 'could not have done this without her'; and 'he made me believe I could do it, saw me through the bad times, read all my drafts carefully, was straight about what I had written and what more needed to be done'. However, when things went wrong, they went badly wrong, and students' comments were on the lines of 'could never get hold of him'; 'never returned my calls'; 'made me feel inadequate'; 'showed no signs of having read my drafts'; 'didn't seem to feel she had any responsibility for advising about my approach'; 'was only willing to see me once a term for a timetabled 20 minutes. He was always late but always finished on time. I had to travel 100 miles for these 10 minute meetings'; and 'went on study leave, never told me, and no-one was allocated to "take me over" at a crucial time in my research when I really needed help'.

Some of the supervisors mounted a vigorous defence. Regular telephone calls at 11 pm or later in spite of repeated requests not to call after 9 pm so exasperated one supervisor that he refused to release his number to his next batch of tutees. There were complaints about students not turning up for arranged meetings; demands for drafts to be read overnight; the assumption that supervisors should always be in their room and available for consultation whenever they were needed, and so on.

The point of raising these issues here is not to lay blame one way or the other but, rather, to consider ways of avoiding conflict if at all possible, and, only if reason does not prevail, to consider ways of resolving difficult situations.

Codes of practice for supervision

All universities now have (or should have) a code of practice for supervision. However, providing such a code is one thing, ensuring that everyone involved follows the guidelines is quite another. You should certainly be able to see the code of your university or organization in order to know what your and your supervisor's rights and responsibilities are. Some universities automatically provide a copy for students; others do not.

Most codes advise that supervisors and students should at an early stage clarify what 'supervision' actually means and what is reasonable for both to expect. Even where efforts are made to clarify rights and responsibilities, supervisor–student relationships do occasionally break down and if all efforts to improve the position fail, then the only thing to do is to request a change before depression and a feeling of hopelessness take over.

Change of supervisor

Achieving a satisfactory change may not be as easy as it might seem. One part-time student who was not getting on with her supervisor was desperate to change but the department was unable to find another supervisor who was willing to accept her. Having drawn a blank after following all the laid-down procedures, she decided to take action herself. She stood at the door of the postgraduate students' common room one lunch time and shouted, 'Is anybody here doing historical research?' When several hands went up, she asked what they thought of their supervisors and what their specialisms were. In desperation, she pleaded for an interview with the supervisor deemed by his students to be 'friendly, helpful, knowledgeable but tough' and who eventually, though somewhat reluctantly, agreed to take her on. They got on well and three years later she was awarded her PhD. Her advice to students in a similar position was:

> If you have justifiable concerns, talk about them and try to sort them informally. If that approach fails, go through the formal channels. In my case, neither approach produced the desired changes so I decided I had to take matters into my own hands. I didn't like doing what I did but I would never have completed with the first supervisor. He seemed to leave me feeling that I wasn't intellectually up to the research.

Most of the time, everything works well and supervisors are as anxious as their students that they should succeed, but if things go badly wrong, state your case clearly and fairly and don't give in.

Keeping records of supervisory tutorials

I firmly believe that records of supervisory tutorials should be kept by supervisors *and* by research students. Many of my colleagues disagree and claim this would be 'just another piece of unnecessary bureaucracy'. I am not speaking here of a large document that would require days, if not weeks, to produce, but a one-page form that has space for the date of the tutorial, a (very) brief note of issues discussed, targets set, if any, summary of comments given on drafts and on the general progress of the research, advice given and taken (or not taken) and the proposed date of the next meeting. Five minutes maximum at the end of the tutorial with a copy for the supervisor and for the student. If you create the form in Google Docs within Google Drive and editing permission is given to your supervisor, you can both edit the form online and access it from any browser. Changes are automatically saved, almost as quickly as either party makes them. This provides a useful record and reminder about what was said, promised and agreed (or disagreed), and acts as a log of progress. However, it also serves another purpose. Disputes have increased and it is in the interests of supervisors and students that there should be such an agreed record. Keeping records is not just another attempt at imposing yet another level of useless bureaucracy. It is good professional practice. If your supervisor considers such a record is unnecessary, keep your own.

Keep a dated record of your supervision sessions. Keep it to one side of A4 and summarize the actions you need to take before you meet your supervisor again.

The research experience

At its best, the supervisor–student relationship will ensure that your research experience is demanding, but also valuable, enjoyable and will result in the successful completion of your investigation – on time. As I have suggested earlier, only isolationist geniuses with plenty of time, a first-class library at their disposal and extensive Google search experience are likely to succeed – and there are not many geniuses around. Most of us need help, encouragement and supervisor expertise. As many first-time and experienced researchers have testified, a good supervisor is like gold dust, and by far the most valuable resource we have.

Writing as you go along and the research diary

Chapter 14, 'Writing the report', considers what should be included in the final report, but if you wait until the final stage before you begin to write, you will be in trouble. Writing should be ongoing, starting with your planning and topic selection and from then on, *as you go along*. Start with a personal **research diary**, research log or research notebook. This can be a hard copy notebook or your notes can be in digital form – whichever works best for you. Everyone has different ideas about what should go in and what should be left out. Keep your notebook with you at all times, or if you are working digitally, save your research diary file to whichever device you carry with you, and back it up elsewhere too. This document will track the progress of your research and be invaluable when you are describing the process of your research in your final report. Alternatively, use the note-making app or voice-recording tool on your Smartphone to make a record of your research, including any meetings that you attend with your supervisor or research participants. Don't forget to ask permission to make a recording and be prepared to say how you will guarantee its confidentiality.

I have no difficulty in deciding what should go into my research notes because I include everything (or almost everything). Rough notes, brief summaries of certain sections, target dates (and targets achieved or not achieved), dates of interviews, dates questionnaires were distributed (and returned). Names and telephone numbers of people I have spoken to or met. Records of names, addresses, telephone numbers, email addresses, good ideas I had in the middle of the night when I couldn't sleep, something I remembered when

I was on a bus. Difficulties experienced, advice to myself not to do something in this or that way again! A reminder about something I must ask the librarian. A note about how I might resolve the problem of . . . something or other. If I hadn't made a note of it at that time, in all probability I would have forgotten it the next day. A reference (new to me) that someone told me about when I was having a sandwich in the cafe. The times I left home to see someone and the times I returned, if I remember.

Every entry with a date. Do this tomorrow . . . Write this up before Thursday! Transfer this reference to the main list of references. I recall that one student considered my way of jotting down everything to be disorganized. I suppose it is, but I do flag or highlight items that need to be given further thought and, as I've already said and will continue to say throughout this book, we all have our own ways of working, so adopt ways of doing things that seem to work for you. As far as I'm concerned, the only rule is that *you start your diary as soon as you start your research, keep it going* and get into the habit of writing up small portions (with your comments) as you go along. Writing starts here and not when you are at the stage of writing the final report.

Planning the Project Checklist

1. Draw up a shortlist of topics.	Talk to colleagues, fellow students – anyone who will listen. Consult library catalogues, but briefly. Google your topic by asking questions about it. Bookmark interesting pages.	☑
2. Decide on a shortlist of two.	Select your first choice and keep the second in mind in case your first choice proves to be too difficult or not interesting enough.	☑

3. Make a list of first – and second – thoughts, questions or produce a chart or mind-map of ideas, possible problems – anything you can think of.	This is for your eyes only. The purpose is to help you to clarify your thoughts about which aspects of the topic are of particular interest or importance.	☑
4. Select the precise focus of your study.	You can't do everything, so you need to be clear about which aspect of the general topic you wish to investigate. Is your topic likely to be worth investigating? Think about it. The last thing you want is to be stuck with a topic that's going nowhere and which bores you to distraction.	☑
5. Make sure you are clear about the purpose of the study.	Give some thought to your sample. You need to consult your supervisor about which individuals or groups might be included.	☑
6 . Go back to your charts and lists of questions, delete any items which do not relate to your selected topic, add others which do, eliminate overlap and produce a revised list of key questions.	You are aiming to produce *researchable questions*. Watch your language! Are you absolutely clear about the *meaning* of the words you use. Words can mean different things to different people.	☑

7. Draw up an initial project outline. Check that you are clear about the purpose and focus of your study, have identified key questions, know what information you will require and have thought about how you might obtain it.	Check your submission date. Do you have enough time to carry out the research you have outlined – and to submit on time?	☑
8. Consult your supervisor at the stage of selecting a topic and after drawing up a project outline.	You don't want to get too far down the research road before you check that all is well. Make sure you discuss a suitable sample and find out who you need to approach for permissions.	☑
9. It's best to know about your institution's code of practice for supervision and what to do if the relationship with your supervisor breaks down.	Do your best to clarify any unclear areas of supervisor/student rights and responsibilities.	☑
10. Keep a brief record of what has been discussed, and agreed in supervisory tutorials.	It will help to remind you about what tasks and targets have been agreed.	☑

11. Remember that a good supervisor is like gold dust and by far the most valuable resource you have, so don't make unreasonable demands. If you're asked not to phone after 9 pm, please make sure you don't.	Unfortunately, very occasionally supervisor–student relationships break down. If you have justifiable concerns, try to talk about them and to sort out problems. If that fails, go through formal channels, state your case clearly and fairly and, if that fails, request a change.	☑
12. From the start of your research, get into the habit of writing everything down or making electronic notes or voice recordings.	And don't throw away or delete your drafts or recordings until your investigation has been submitted, assessed and/or published. You never know when you might need to refer to them.	☑
13. Start a research diary as soon as you start your research.	And get into the habit of writing up small sections as you go along. Writing begins here, rather than when you reach the stage of writing the report.	☑

Further reading

Brett Davies, M. (2007) ***Doing a Successful Research Project: Using Qualitative or Quantitative Methods*****. Basingstoke: Palgrave Macmillan.**
Brett Davies considers how to draw up a personal roadmap, planning and analysing qualitative data, sampling – and much more.

Cryer, P. (2006) ***The Research Student's Guide to Success*** **(3rd edn). Maidenhead: Open University Press.**

This book looks at the roles and responsibilities of supervisors ***and*** of research students and provides guidance about what to do if things do not go well.

Delamont, S., Atkinson, P. and Parry, O. (2004) *Supervising the Doctorate: A Guide to Success*. Maidenhead: Open University Press.
This is a book written for supervisors, but it is also full of helpful ideas and advice for students.

Eley, A. and Jennings, R. (2005) *Effective Postgraduate Supervision: Improving the Student–Supervisor Relationship*. Maidenhead: Open University Press.
The authors discuss the most frequently encountered difficulties in the student–supervisor relationship and offer realistic solutions to difficulties in 30 cases.

Fielding, N.G., Lee, R.M. and Blank, G. (2008) *The Sage Handbook of Online Research Methods*. London: Sage.
This handbook concentrates on online social research methods and the significance of the Internet as a research medium, considering research design, online surveys and the Internet as an archival resource.

Laws, S. with Harper, C. and Marcus, R. (2013) *Research for Development: A Practical Guide* (2nd edn). London: Sage.
Chapter 5 provides guidance about the processes involved in planning research, writing the brief, defining the research process, setting the research questions and hypothesis testing.

Rugg, G. and Petre, M. (2006) *A Gentle Guide to Research Methods*. Maidenhead: Open University Press.
This book covers a wide range of topics, including research design, data collection methods, statistics and academic writing – all with helpful examples.

Wolcott, H.F. (2009) *Writing Up Qualitative Research* (3rd edn). London: Sage.
Everything Wolcott has written is worth reading; his advice is excellent and if you can get hold of his book, read it from cover to cover! He is particularly good, as the title of this book indicates, on writing but also on planning.

3 Ethics and Integrity in Research

INTRODUCTION

This chapter considers the many ethical and moral dimensions involved in conducting a research project. It is your responsibility as a researcher to make sure that your project does not breach any legal boundaries and that it adheres to accepted ethical standards. This chapter will cover the following:

- Ensuring you follow any ethical guidelines drawn up by your institution and research setting, and that you understand your ethical responsibilities as a researcher.
- How to handle research contracts, codes of practice, protocols and the principle of informed consent.
- Where appropriate, taking account of the demands of ethics committees and preparing to meet their requirements.
- Understanding the meaning of 'confidentiality' and 'anonymity' and how they apply to the context in which you are carrying out your research. The application of these concepts to the online environment.
- Practical considerations about ethics in practice, including a case study that describes how the contributing author, Stephen Waters, tackled his first research project and the ethical issues he faced.
- Understanding the concept of intellectual property rights and the ethical and legal obligations relating to the ownership of ideas.

Key terms

It was once possible to plan and carry out a small piece of research with the permission of a head of department, principal of a college, head teacher of a school or an administrator without having to go through formal channels. The informal route will still apply for many 100-hour studies as long as whoever is in charge is convinced of your integrity and of the worth of your research. In most cases, your supervisor will be aware of any restrictions or legal requirements relating to your research, and will ensure that you have appropriate advice about procedures well before you begin to plan your data collection. However, you may not always be able to rely on your supervisor's knowledge. For example, if you work in one organization but are supervised somewhere else, the supervisor may not know what your organization's requirements are. If you live in Singapore or Kuala Lumpur but are registered for a higher degree in an Australian or British university, your supervisor may have no idea at all about the local rules, so it will be up to you to find out what is required. In particular, if you have any doubts about the ethics of your proposal, make sure you consult as widely as you can, discuss your concerns and do not proceed if you or your advisers have any misgivings.

Research contracts, codes of practice, protocols and the principle of informed consent

There is nothing new about research contracts and ethical guidelines. They have all been used in a variety of ways for many years. They may have been called something different and their use was on a less formal basis than now, but they existed. Lutz, writing about ethnographic research, advises researchers that:

> "it is undoubtedly necessary for every ethnographer to establish some type of 'contract' with the society to be studied. Such a 'contract' may include specifications about what records may and may not be examined; where the ethnographer may or may not go, when, and under what circumstances; which meetings may be attended and which are closed;

> how long the researcher will stay in the field; who (if anyone) has access to field notes, and even who has the right to review and/or approve the ethnography and its analysis prior to publication, or under what circumstances they may or may not be published at all."
>
> (Lutz 1986: 114)

This is good advice – but it is 'advice', not a 'requirement'. Today, many organizations and professional bodies, including the Medical Research Council, the Nursing and Midwifery Council, the British Sociological Association and the General Medical Council to name a few – have gone a long way in formalizing procedures and have produced their own ethical guidelines, research contracts, codes of practice and **protocols**, addressing such issues as deception regarding the purpose of investigations, encroachment on privacy, confidentiality, safety, care needed when research involves children – and much more.

Hart and Bond (1995: 198–201), writing about action research in health and social care, provide examples of different types of codes of practice or protocols that require researchers to ensure that participants are fully aware of the purpose of the research and understand their rights. Some of these are to be read out at the start of an interview, explaining that participation is voluntary, that participants are free to refuse to answer any questions and can withdraw from the interview at any time. Most promise confidentiality and anonymity, but as will be seen later in this chapter, it may be more difficult to fulfil such promises than might at first have been thought. Some suggest that respondents should be asked to sign a copy of the protocol form before the interview begins, indicating that they understand and agree to all the conditions. However, Hart and Bond argue that in their view:

> "It is not sufficient for the interviewer simply to read it [the protocol] out and then expect the respondent to sign … The respondent might justifiably feel anxious about signing anything, particularly at an early stage when the interviewer may be unknown to him or her. In our view it would be better to give the respondent time to read and re-read the protocol for himself or herself at his or her own pace, and to negotiate any additions or changes to it with the researcher. We would also recommend that the respondent should have a signed copy of the form as a record."
>
> (Hart and Bond 1995: 199)

This is sound advice. In my view, respondents should never be expected to sign any protocol form unless they have had time to read and consider the implications. All researchers will be aiming at the principle of **informed consent**, which requires careful preparation involving explanation and consultation before any data collecting begins (Oliver 2003: 28–30). If an interview is being conducted online, for example using Skype or other video conferencing software, the contract should have been sent in advance and the participant's agreement secured. If a signature is necessary, Docusign, electronic signature software, can be used to sign and return the contract online.

Bowling (2002: 157) also makes what is to me is an important and rarely considered point – namely, that in addition to ensuring that participants know exactly what will be involved in the research, the informed consent procedure 'reduces the legal liability of the researcher'. In these litigious times, it is as well to be sure you have done everything, not only to ensure participants' rights but also your own position.

Blaxter and colleagues summarize the principles of research ethics as follows:

> "Research ethics is about being clear about the nature of the agreement you have entered into with your research subjects or contacts. This is why contracts can be a useful device. Ethical research involves getting the informed consent of those you are going to interview, question, observe or take materials from. It involves reaching agreements about the uses of this data, and how its analysis will be reported and disseminated. And it is about keeping to such agreements when they have been reached."
>
> (Blaxter *et al.* 2006: 158–9)

Ethics committees

Ethics committees play an important part in ensuring that no badly designed or harmful research is permitted. Darlington and Scott consider they have:

> "an important gatekeeping role in all research involving human subjects and are likely to be extra vigilant in their consideration of proposals for research concerning any potentially vulnerable groups of people. Ethics committees have a duty to consider all possible sources of harm and satisfy themselves that the researcher has thought through all the relevant issues prior to granting permission to proceed."
>
> (Darlington and Scott 2002: 22–3)

Their gatekeeping role is not always welcomed. Reason and Bradbury reported some of the experiences of one of the researchers in the Midwives' Action Research Group (MARG). She stated that 'the Ethics Committee not only seems to fulfill an ethical role but also a gate-keeping role in hindering would-be researchers whose work doesn't fit the empirical-analytic framework and also which might reveal unpleasant truths about the setting' (Reason and Bradbury 2001: 295). The researcher felt that the committee members were trying to block her research, and asked 'What gives them the right to tell me which women I can or cannot have a conversation with on a voluntary basis for my research? Do they have a legal right? Or is it assumed power?' Well, they certainly have a right to tell researchers what they can do and what they can't. I don't know whether they are legal rights but ethics committees are powerful and if your submission is rejected, you won't be allowed to do the research at all. Happily, I have never known or heard of reports of ethics committees trying to block research. It's possible that some committee members may sometimes appear to be ... well, perhaps, rather overzealous in their requirements – at least to researchers who have been required to resubmit – but they have a duty to ensure that no sloppy, damaging or illegal research is allowed to slip through, and their requirements have to be met.

One complaint frequently levelled at ethics and research committees is the time taken to respond to submissions. Bowling (2002: 158) reports that researchers have been known to wait three to six months before receiving approval to proceed. Admittedly these delays have generally related to medical or other health-related topics where requirements are, and no doubt should be, stringent, but few committees are speedy – at least, as far as anxious researchers are concerned. They may meet infrequently but dates of meetings are generally known in advance and researchers will invariably have to submit applications well ahead of those dates. Everything takes time, so be aware of dates, and of possible delays.

These requirements and delays may be alarming if you are working on a 100-hour project, but unless you are concerned with medical or health-related research, you may not always be required to go through the ethics committee procedures. However, you will still have to conform to whatever vetting procedures your own organization, department and profession require, so make sure you know what they are.

Ethics and research committees often do their best to fast-track approval procedures for small studies but, even so, they will never rubber stamp a badly prepared submission, nor should they, so do your best to get your submission right. It's unlikely your first draft will be good enough, so make sure your supervisor sees it, take advice, obtain any guidelines provided by the committees and meet their requirements. Of course, there may be no requirements to submit anything to a committee. It may be quite sufficient if your supervisor gives you approval to proceed, but if you do find you have to wait for approval, there is a lot you can do, such as reading about and around your topic, carrying out a Google search, making notes, trying out different types of indexing and cataloguing systems, and thinking about ways in which your findings might become part of your literature review. You might spend time familiarizing yourself with your institution's library database, recording references and, all being well, considering the possible design of some of your proposed data collection instruments. What you can't do is begin to collect data and contact participants before written approval is received.

Confidentiality and anonymity

Not surprisingly, all the 'informed consent' statements and ethical guidelines I have seen mention **confidentiality** and **anonymity**. We all know what they mean, don't we? Well, do we? Is my 'confidentiality' likely to mean the same as yours? I regret to say that I have come across many broken promises of confidentiality and anonymity in research projects, and imprecision about what is meant by both terms can result in serious misunderstandings between researchers and participants. So, if you say that participants will be anonymous, then under no circumstances can they be identified. If you promise confidentiality, decide what you mean by that in the context of your investigation.

Sapsford and Abbott, writing about unstructured interviewing, remind us that 'interviewing is intrusive, but having your personal details splashed in identifiable form across a research project is even more intrusive'. They make it clear that in their view '*confidentiality* is a promise that you will not be identified or presented in identifiable form, while *anonymity* is a promise that even the researcher will not be able to tell which responses came from which respondents' (Sapsford and Abbott 1996: 318–19). These definitions are sound and, with appropriate acknowledgement, could be adopted in your own research. The implications of each can be significant. I discuss some of the issues in 'Selecting methods of data collection' in Part II of this book, but they are sufficiently important to be raised here also. If you promise anonymity to questionnaire respondents, then, as Sapsford and Abbott point out, that means that no one, *including you*, will know who has completed the questionnaire. As far as I am concerned, this means that no follow-up letters can be sent, no questionnaires can have coded numbers or symbols so that responses can be identified, and no other sneaky tricks of any kind can be used. If you feel you have to have the option of sending follow-up letters, then you must qualify your definition to respondents by saying something along the lines of, 'By "anonymity" in the context of this study, I mean that no one will see (your completed questionnaire/interview transcript) except me and all questionnaires and records will be shredded or deleted once the research is completed.' Is that what you mean? Think about it.

There may also be difficulties regarding confidentiality. If in your report you speak about the Director of Resources or the Head of English, you are immediately identifying the individual concerned. If you invent a pseudonym or a code, it might still be easy for readers who are in the know to identify the individual or institution concerned. I recall the anger of one school principal who was guaranteed confidentiality for his school but the way the report was written made it clear to the local community which school it was. No one minds being identified if the report is complimentary, but this particular principal was head of a school in an area of high deprivation that for some years had had a reputation for truancy and indifferent examination results. Great strides had been made and many improvements achieved in the two years before the research but, of course, long-term improvement takes time. His anger centred on the fact that he had been promised that the report would be written in such a way as to make it impossible for an individual school to be identified. His comment was that if any researcher came anywhere near his school in the future, they would be shown the door. So, watch your language and don't promise anything you can't deliver.

Safeguarding confidentiality and anonymity if disseminating information online

From time to time, a news story breaks about the loss of data – on a mislaid laptop or memory stick for example, or in confidential documents found in a bin. Most of us have, at one time or another, been rather careless. We might even have been unaware of the existence of rules and regulations relating to the security and dissemination of electronic data – or by any other method, come to that. Common courtesy and common sense might have seemed enough, but not any more. Now you must be fully aware of and observe individuals' rights of privacy in any research, in particular with respect to the storage, processing and dissemination of personal data.

As always, first check what guidelines are provided by your department and/or institution. It won't be sufficient to say that your supervisor, or someone else, told you it would be okay if you did that or did not do the other. You must obtain a copy of the guidelines and consult your supervisor if any item is unclear or if you have any queries about the interpretation of any item.

If you have time, particularly if you are involved in postgraduate research, it might also be helpful to consult any available published reports relating to the way information has been used in different cases. You might wish to consult the 1997 report of the Caldicott Committee review of patient-identifiable information. The review was commissioned because of concern about ways in which data about patients was used in the National Health Service (NHS) in England and Wales and the use of information technology to disseminate information. This is a very large, thorough and well-conducted review. Eighty-six flows of patient-identifiable information were mapped during the review and sixteen recommendations for the improvement of practice produced. It is easy to see how information stored electronically and transferred to other departments, hospitals or general practitioner (GP) clinics might easily become available to individuals and organizations who have no right to that information. The same concern might also be expressed about the way companies, hospitals, universities and individuals disseminate information about employees, students and, in the case of research programmes, participants – unless steps are taken to ensure no individual can be identified. If you have any concerns about maintaining the confidentiality of your participants, I recommend that you read this and more recent reports.

You should also be aware of the relevant sections of the Freedom of Information and Data Protection Acts, and the many clauses that relate to individuals' right to privacy and the processing of personal data. I am confident your supervisor will be able to advise you and to direct you to the appropriate documentation. However, if he or she is not available, ask around and if you are told that no guidelines exist, you might be asking the wrong person, so ask someone else. Ask your specialist and/or support librarian. Ask other students. Even if helpful guidelines do exist, and particularly if you are concerned with an extensive review or even a doctoral study, you may feel you need more detailed information provided by these two very detailed Acts. So, Google them and consult the 'processing of sensitive data' sections of the Freedom of Information and Data Protection Acts on the Internet or insert questions you would like answered in the search box.

If you decide you need more subject-specific information, you might see what your specialist research council has to offer. The Economic and Social Research Council (ESRC), for example, produces invaluable information and guidance about participants' rights and your responsibilities. I mention the ESRC because this is the area in which I work, but your research council might be the Medical Research Council, the Engineering and Physical Sciences Research Council, the Natural Environment Research Council, the Arts and Humanities Research Council – or whichever council relates most closely to your own topic.

The collection, storage, security and dissemination of data are your responsibility. You must carry out your research within the conditions of the Data Protection Act (http://www.open.gov.uk/dpr/dprhome.htm) and any other guidelines that relate to the people or organizations you are collecting information about.

Make a note in your **research diary** of any items you wish to return to later, but if you are working on a 100-hour project, then 100 hours, more or less, is all the time you have. Avoid becoming sidetracked by the wealth of research results that a Google search will unearth. Focus on those that are relevant to your research study and bookmark the page or make a note of the URL. Provided that you have used keywords effectively to focus your search, most search results that are relevant will be found on the first page, one of the main reasons why most people do not look beyond it. Search results that are within shaded boxes at the top of the first page and results on the right-hand side of the page are paid advertising (i.e. Google has been paid to rank the advert as high as possible via Google Adwords). Each time someone clicks on these adverts, the business or organization they promote pays Google. This is known as Pay-per-Click (PPC). These search results may be the most relevant for your research study, or they may not. You will need to decide this for yourself when you open them to read the content. Even if you are working on a three-year full-time PhD programme, you will only have three years, not the rest of your life, so be ruthless about rejecting search results that don't relate closely to the data or information you are hoping to find in your study. Remember also that an article found in a Google search will have references to related studies – some of those references may be what you are looking for, so allocate some time to following them up. Time to move on again.

Ethical research in practice, the problems of 'inside' research and personal codes of practice

Regardless of the requirements of your institution and of your supervisor, this will still be your research. Even if you are not obliged to conform to required codes of practice or to the demands of ethics or research committees, you will need to satisfy yourself that you have done everything possible to ensure that your research is conducted in a way that complies with your own ethical principles. This is the approach adopted by Stephen Waters, contributing author of this sixth edition and formerly a postgraduate diploma student and first-time researcher. At the time of his research study, he was a teacher of English in a high school and decided that he would like to undertake the research in his own institution. He was interested in investigating the role of his own Head of English (called Director of English). The Director had expressed interest in and support for the study, and this convinced Stephen that the topic would be worthwhile and would have a good chance of being successfully completed in the time allowed (effectively three months). He decided to produce his own personal code of practice which made clear the conditions and guarantees within which he felt he must work, in order to ensure his own and his school's integrity. The preparation proceeded on the following lines:

1. Informal discussion with the head teacher to obtain agreement in principle.
2. Refinement of the topic, statement of the objectives of the study and preparation of a project outline.
3. Discussion with his tutor and further discussion with the Director of English.
4. Minor adjustments made to the project outline and a consideration of the methods to be used.
5. Formal submission of the project outline to the head teacher, together with names of colleagues he wished to interview and the guarantees and conditions under which the research would be conducted.

The conditions and guarantees were presented as follows:

1 All participants will be offered the opportunity to remain anonymous.
2 All information will be treated with the strictest confidentiality.
3 Interviewees will have the opportunity to verify statements when the research is in draft form.
4 Participants will receive a copy of the final report.
5 The research is to be assessed by the university for examination purposes only, but should the question of publication arise at a later date, permission will be sought from the participants.
6 The research will attempt to explore educational management in practice. It is hoped the final report may be of benefit to the school and to those who take part.

So how did it go? This is what Stephen wrote after the project was completed:

> "I felt that presenting the guarantees formally was essential. As I was completely inexperienced in research, I had to assure the head teacher that the fieldwork would be carried out with integrity and convince him that he could place his trust in me.
>
> With hindsight, I should have exercised greater caution. Condition 3 could not be met in full since I later found that, although a proper check could be made to verify statements participants had made while being interviewed, there was insufficient time for them to proofread a full draft. Condition 4 was fulfilled but the cost proved to be prohibitive and I decided to eliminate this condition when other case studies were undertaken. This experience certainly alerted me to the danger of promising too much too soon.
>
> It was only when the time drew near for the findings of my research to be disseminated that I became aware of the two areas where the wording of my conditions of research was open to interpretation. The first was that, in promising confidentiality (Condition 2), I had not made it clear what the implications of releasing information would be. As there was insufficient time to produce a draft report, no one could check whether my interpretation of what they had said was fair. In any case, as the head teacher was the only person to hold a written copy of my guarantees, the respondents could only interpret the conditions under which they had agreed to participate from my verbal explanation. In retrospect, it would have been better to have provided a duplicated explanation of the written outline of my intentions. Teachers are busy people and it was unreasonable to assume that they would be able to remember a conversation which had taken place some time before their services were formally required. As it was, whether or not they

> remembered the guarantees, they were totally dependent on my integrity to present their views in a balanced, objective manner.
>
> More naively, until I was writing the report, I had not realized that identifying people by role may preserve the guarantee of anonymity for an outside reader, but it did not confer the same degree of obscurity for those within the school. Fortunately, my failure to clarify these points did not lead to problems – but it could have done."

Stephen learnt a great deal from his first experience of conducting an investigation. He felt he had made some mistakes at his first attempt and was uneasy because he had not been able to fulfil all the conditions and guarantees. He had prepared the ground very well but had not fully appreciated the time and effort involved in reporting back to colleagues and in producing copies of reports. He was concerned at his lack of precision in defining exactly what he meant by anonymity and confidentiality, and made quite sure that in subsequent investigations he clarified the position. He found it harder to know what to do about role conflict. He was a full-time teacher and a part-time researcher – a not unusual combination – and on occasions found it difficult to reconcile the two roles. There were definite advantages to being an 'inside' researcher. For example, he had an intimate knowledge of the context of the research and of the micropolitics of the institution, travel was not a problem and participants were easily reached. He knew how best to approach individuals and appreciated some of their difficulties. He found that colleagues welcomed the opportunity to air problems and to have their situation analysed by someone who understood the practical day-to-day realities of their task. On the other hand, he found interviewing some colleagues an uncomfortable experience for both parties. As an insider, he quickly came to realize that you have to live with your mistakes after completing the research. The close contact with the institution and colleagues made objectivity difficult to attain and, he felt, gaining confidential knowledge had the potential for affecting his relationship with colleagues. In the event, this did not seem to be the case, but he could foresee situations where problems might have arisen.

When he had successfully completed his diploma, Stephen was asked whether he felt it had all been worthwhile and whether he had any comments that might be helpful to others who were undertaking a research project for the first time. He wrote as follows:

> "I may have given the impression that my research was so fraught with difficulties that it was counter-productive. If so, it is because I wish to encourage the prospective inside-researcher to exercise caution and to

be aware of possible pitfalls. In reality, I enjoyed my research immensely and found that the experience of interviewing a cross-section of teaching staff provided me with a much greater working knowledge of the school's management practices. Indeed, my research was so absorbing that at times I found myself struggling to keep pace with my teaching commitments. I am certain, even with hindsight, that I could have done little to resolve this dilemma. I can honestly say that my research has made me more understanding of the problems confronting those responsible for running the school and has subsequently provided a great deal of thought about educational issues. If my research had not been practically relevant I would have felt concerned about the extent of my commitment to it. As it was, several recommendations which appeared in my first report have been taken up by the school; my third report on the role of the governing body in the curriculum was placed on the agenda of a governors' meeting in spring and many colleagues have been complimentary about the content of the case studies in general. If I had to choose one strategy that I would encourage prospective inside researchers to adopt, it would be to relate the research report to the pragmatic concerns of the institution. That might perhaps help to persuade colleagues that participation in research will be as beneficial to them as it is to the researcher."

Whether or not you relate your research to the pragmatic concerns of the institution depends on the nature of your task and your own special concerns, but whether you are an inside or outside researcher, whether you are full-time or part-time, experienced or inexperienced, care has to be taken to make no promises that cannot be honoured. When Stephen carried out his first piece of research, guidelines, protocols and research contracts were less common than they are today. He had to devise his own guarantees and conditions. Nowadays, most organizations have their own set of rules, not only about the conduct of research, but also about who owns what. Even so, you should still ensure that your research is conducted in a way that conforms to your own ethical principles and code of practice.

Be clear what you mean if you promise that your research will be confidential and that participants will be guaranteed anonymity. Don't assume that these terms have the same meaning for everyone. Even if names or roles of participants are not used in your research report, it may still be possible for readers to work out who you are writing about.

Codes of ethical practice relating to intellectual ownership/property

At one time, relatively little was heard about **intellectual property** or ownership. It was, and still is, customary in scientific and technological departments for supervisors' names to appear on joint papers, the decision about the positioning of the names having been decided by the supervisor and/or in accordance with common departmental or institutional practice. Where research has been sponsored by government agencies or commercial organizations, institutions generally have an agreement in place regarding intellectual property rights about which students are, or should be, informed at the start of their research, particularly if they have been recruited specifically to carry out some predetermined and pre-planned research. In some cases, students may be required to assign ownership of their intellectual property to institutions, to ensure that any potential patent or marketable findings are not lost, and so it is particularly important that everyone understands what this means. Is what students write the property of the institution, organization or research council that funded it? Is it the property of the researcher alone, or the joint property of the researcher and the supervisor? If jointly owned, whose name comes first in any published work? The question of the positioning of names may seem trivial, but the importance to all concerned cannot be underestimated. Universities in particular want their research students, and require their academic staff, to publish. Doing well in research assessment exercises brings not only recognition and prestige but also money – and all three count.

In hospitals and other health-related organizations, institutional property guidelines and rules have been in place for many years and advertisements that include responsibility for intellectual property are common for individual hospitals and for groups of hospitals, which seems to me not only to indicate the importance of this issue but also its complexity. Even where codes and guidelines are issued, disputes about ownership are still known to rage where students who consider they have done all the work find that their supervisor's and professor's names appear before theirs on published reports of the research.

The various codes of practice, guidelines and policies that are frequently provided by academic institutions and businesses, departments, hospitals and funding bodies should go some way to eliminating unethical practice and misunderstandings over ownership, just as I believe codes and protocols can help to eliminate similar unethical practice in issues relating to informed consent. No codes of ethical practice can resolve all problems, but they do at least clarify some of the major issues in this difficult area – and that is a start.

If you are a first-time researcher, the idea of asking to see your institution's or organization's guidelines relating to intellectual property rights may seem irrelevant. Even so, it might be interesting to find out what the guidelines say. You never know, your research may be outstanding and of sufficient interest to be considered for publication, and it's as well to know what your rights would be in that happy eventuality. It's always a good idea to be prepared for success.

Ethics and Integrity in Research Checklist

1. It is your responsibility to discover whether any restrictions or legal requirements relate to your research.	If you or your advisers have any doubts about the integrity of your proposal, don't proceed unless the issues are resolved.	☑
2. Many organizations now have ethical guidelines, codes of practice and protocols.	Make sure you know if such guidelines exist and conform to their requirements.	☑
3. Always aim for the informed consent of your participants.	And make sure that your participants' understanding of 'informed consent' is the same as yours. Remember that they should not be expected to sign a protocol form unless they have had time to read and consider the implications.	☑

4. If all proposed research has to be vetted by the ethics committee in your organization, make sure your submission is well thought out. Find out when the committees meet and allow time for your submission to be considered.	Consult, show your draft to your supervisor, talk to any students who have had their submission to the ethics committee rejected – or approved.	☑
5. Confidentiality and anonymity are generally promised to participants.	However, make sure you know what you *and* your participants mean by each.	☑
6. You must never break any promises to participants, so watch your language and never promise anything you can't deliver.	Thus if you promise anonymity, you can't send out follow-up letters. No tricks!	☑
7. Make sure you consult the guidelines of your department and institution on the dissemination of electronic information. Try to find time to read any reports that relate to participants' rights to privacy.	Consult the Data Protection and Freedom of Information Acts, your research council's guidance and any subject-specific reports that relate to individuals' right to privacy with respect to the processing of personal data.	☑
8. Regardless of the requirements of your institution and of your supervisor, this will still be your research, with your name.	Even if you are not obliged to conform to the required codes of practice, or to the demands of ethics and research committees, you should still ensure that your research is conducted in a manner that conforms to your own code of practice.	☑

9.	If you are carrying out research in your own institution or organization, do your best to let your colleagues know what you plan to do and how you hope they might be willing to help.	Don't be too ambitious. Consider how much time you are allowed in order to complete the research on time.	☑
10.	If you think you might wish to publish some of your findings at some stage, first make sure that you have obtained the permission of the people concerned.	Also make sure you have seen a copy of all codes of practice, protocols and guidelines relating to your organization and profession, in particular ethical guidelines relating to informed consent and to intellectual property.	☑
11.	You may think you own what you have written and thus can do as you like with any research report, article or book.	That might sometimes be possible, but not always, so check before you commit yourself.	☑
12.	No codes of ethical practice, protocols, guidelines and policies can solve all your problems, but they help.	They at least clarify some of the major issues. Don't forget to keep a record in your research diary of books, articles, URLs, names of people you consulted, mobile numbers, email addresses – anything you might need at a later date.	☑

Further reading

Blaxter, L., Hughes, C. and Tight, M. (2006) *How to Research* (3rd edn). Maidenhead: Open University Press.
Pages 157–62 provide a summary of the principles of research ethics.

Busher, H. and James, N. (2007) Ethics of research in education, in A.R.J. Briggs and M. Coleman (eds) *Research Methods in Educational Leadership and Management* (2nd edn). London: Sage.

Caldicott Committee (1997) *Report on the Review of Patient-identifiable Information*. London: Department of Health.

Cohen, L., Manion, L. and Morrison, K. (2011) Case studies, in *Research Methods in Education* (7th edn). Abingdon: Routledge.
Chapter 5, 'The ethics of educational and social research', provides 25 pages of sound advice.

Darlington, Y. and Scott, D. (2002) *Qualitative Research in Practice: Stories from the Field*. Buckingham: Open University Press.
See Chapter 2, 'Ethics and organisations'.

Data Protection Registrar (1998) *The Data Protection Act 1998: An Introduction* [http://www.open.gov.uk/dpr/dprhome.htm].
The sections relating to individuals' right to privacy with respect to the processing of personal data are particularly useful.

D'Cruz, H. and Jones, M. (2004) *Social Work Research: Ethical and Political Contexts*. London: Sage.
The emphasis of this book is on qualitative methodologies in social work research. I particularly like Chapter 3, which deals with procedures involved in producing good research questions. Chapter 4, which asks 'how does research contribute to knowledge: different ways of knowing', is also worth consulting.

Denscombe, M. (2010) *Ground Rules for Good Research: Guidelines for Good Practice* (2nd edn). Maidenhead: Open University Press.
Chapter 4 includes: codes of ethics, ethics approval, researcher integrity, protection of the interests of participants, security of the data, informed consent, Internet research and guidelines for good practice – all excellent.

Department of Health Research and Development includes information of interest to researchers and to public health and social

care workers, at https://www.gov.uk/government/organisations/department-of-health [Accessed 14 March 2014].

Farrell, A. (ed.) (2005) *Ethical Research with Children*. Maidenhead: Open University Press.
Farrell concentrates on early childhood research and the ethical issues involved.

Green, J. and Thorogood, N. (2013) *Qualitative Methods for Health Research* (3rd edn). London: Sage.
This book concentrates on examples of qualitative methodology in health research projects and on the design of ethical and feasible projects.

Greig, A.D., Taylor, J. and Mackay, T. (2012) *Doing Research with Children* (3rd edn). London: Sage.
The authors discuss many changes in research practice with children and provide extended guidance on research ethics.

Laws, S. with Harper, C. and Marcus, R. (2013) *Research for Development: A Practical Guide* (2nd edn). London: Sage.
Chapter 9 deals with ethics codes and responsibilities towards respondents.

Miles, M.B. and Huberman, A.M. (2014) *Qualitative Data Analysis* (3rd edn). Thousand Oaks, CA: Sage.
Chapter 3 explores ethics issues in analysis.

National Health Service National Patient Safety Agency at http://www.npsa.nhs.uk/
Facilitates and promotes ethical research within the NHS. It provides reviews, workshops, reports and much more.

Oliver, P. (2010) *The Student's Guide to Research Ethics* (2nd edn). Maidenhead: Open University Press.
Oliver clarifies research terminology, discusses the moral justification of research, areas of research that raise ethical issues, issues relating to the principle of informed consent, anonymity and confidentiality – and much more.

4 Reading, Referencing and the Management of Information

INTRODUCTION

This chapter provides you with guidance for managing the reading, note-taking and record-keeping aspect of the research process. You will be probably required to read a large volume of material in the course of your research project and this chapter provides guidance on maintaining an efficient and well-organized record-keeping system. In this chapter, you will find:

- Advice on focused and productive reading and on good note-taking, including using note-taking apps and related software.
- How to guard against plagiarism by being meticulous in recording detailed and accurate references during your research.
- Advice on getting to grips with referencing as the researcher's 'tools of the trade'.
- A brief guide to referencing books, journal articles, chapters in books and online sources.
- The importance of understanding the referencing guidelines of your institution.
- Using online tools such as Delicious, Mendeley, Dropbox, EndNote, RefWorks and Google to improve the management of information.

Key terms

Reading

Ideally, the bulk of your reading should come early on in the investigation, though in practice a number of activities are generally in progress at the same time, and reading may even spill over into the data collection stage of your study. If you're working to a strict timescale (and you will be, even if you have the luxury of being on a three-year full-time PhD programme), try to discipline yourself to ensure that reading doesn't take up more time than can be allowed. This is easier said than done because when you begin work on a topic, you're never sure what might be important and what might be irrelevant. Even if you're very disciplined about reading and resist the temptation to be led astray by some really interesting sounding books, articles or websites that may have nothing whatsoever to do with your topic, you'll still find it difficult to confine reading to precise time slots. It is rarely possible to obtain copies of all the books and articles at exactly the time you need them and there will always be new publications which may seem to be the answer to your prayers and which you consider just have to be read. As always, the one thing we always have to accept is that we can't do everything. We have to do the best we can in the time available – and not use 'more reading needed' as an excuse for not actually getting down to writing and everything else that needs to be done to progress the research!

Any investigation, whatever the scale, will involve reading what other people have written about your area of interest, gathering information to support or refute your arguments and writing about your findings. Reading as much as time permits about your topic may give you ideas not only about the research others have done but also about their approach and methods – and this is important, because everything you do from the start of your research will be preparation for the production of the final report.

Experience has shown that no matter how sophisticated we may consider ourselves to be as learners and researchers, we all need to be reminded about the importance of systematic recording. As soon as we begin to read, we begin to record and we have to include all the necessary detail. Keeping an accurate record of meetings, references, ideas and the 1001 activities that the lone researcher undertakes is a challenge. 'Next week', 'next month', 'one of these days', 'when I've got a minute' or 'when I've finished reading these 50 journal articles' won't do. We all think we'll remember, but after several weeks of reading, memory becomes faulty. After a few months, we may vaguely recall having read something some time about a particular topic, but when, where and by whom escapes us. After a longer period, the chances of remembering anything are remote.

Note-taking

In the past, researchers made notes in a notebook that was always with them and some, perhaps most, still do. The disadvantage of handwritten notes is that if the notebook is mislaid – or worse still, lost – the researcher's work is irretrievable. Handwritten notes are also fixed in the order in which they were made and, short of cutting out each entry (assuming you have written on one side of the page) and physically moving the notes around, this limits their flexibility. Notes recorded on a PC, laptop, mobile or tablet are far more adaptable.

Some note-taking platforms allow audio notes to be taken on your mobile and transcribed later. EverNote, Google Keep and OneNote are three personal favourites. All are available online and on mobile devices and can be synchronized across devices. EverNote and Google Keep are available on both Windows and IOS, while OneNote is part of Microsoft Office 365 as a paid version or is available free as a web app through Microsoft SkyDrive. Note-taking software and apps have significant advantages: the notes can be easily moved or copied; URL links to audio, video and image files can be saved as well as written notes; and, perhaps most importantly, most are saved in the cloud, enabling you to access and retrieve them from any device with an internet connection.

Note-taking and guarding against plagiarism

As you read, make notes of what seem to you to be important issues and highlight them. Be on the lookout for recurring themes, categories and keywords that will become increasingly important in your search for a structure or framework for your own research. Priorities (and issues) will inevitably change as your reading continues. You will in all probability abandon some of your early categories and identify others but keep a record, even of your early abandoned categories. You never know – they may crop up again in your later reading.

Take care with your note-taking. A particularly perceptive observation by an author may often illustrate a point you might wish to refer to, or even quote, at a later stage. Always make it quite clear in your notes which is the quotation and which is your paraphrase – otherwise, when you come to write up your project, you may find you are committing the sin of plagiarism.

Plagiarism is using other people's words as if they are your own. Remember that all sources have to be acknowledged, including paraphrases of other people's words and of other people's ideas. Plagiarism has become a major issue in schools and in further and higher education, as a result of the availability of model answers to examination and assignment questions online – usually for a fee. It seems that some people are now prepared to pay for 'a guaranteed A-grade essay' and blatantly submit the essay, or parts of it, as their own. This has become such a concern that plagiarism detection software, such as Grammarly, has been developed and now is regularly used, particularly in universities, to check examination and assignment texts.

Supervisors will be on the lookout for any examples in your drafts. Former colleagues tell me that the situation has become so blatant that sometimes, in coursework, students include paragraphs taken direct from an online article or a web page – and without any attribution. When challenged, the usual response is that everybody does it, so why can't they?

Easy access to vast amounts of online information may give the impression that it is public property. It isn't. Although open sharing on the Internet is gradually challenging our understanding of intellectual property and copyright, the legal position is that intellectual property and/or copyright is owned by the person, group or organization that produced the text, image or video. Unless the authors or creators of the content grant permission to quote it or use it, you need to acknowledge the source(s) of the information.

Most institutions now have guidelines on plagiarism, and make it clear that the penalties for infringement will be severe. These range from giving plagiarized work a fail grade to expulsion from the course. Guidelines are regularly updated, so make sure you have copies of the latest version and examine institutional and subject-specific codes of practice relating to academic and ethical standards. Of course, the best way to ensure you will never use other people's words or ideas as your own without acknowledgement is to be meticulous about your note-taking and to record exact details of references. Online tools that enable you to save references are covered later in this chapter and in Chapter 5, 'Literature searching'.

Plagiarism, or presenting someone else's words or ideas as your own, is a serious matter even if you do so unintentionally. You must acknowledge all sources, even if you don't use the person's exact words. It is important to keep detailed information about references and to make sure your notes tell you who said what and when. This includes information found online.

If you are making an exact copy of wording, add inverted commas at the beginning and end of the extract. Record author, chapter and page numbers or web page, show clearly if you have left out any word or words in the text by adding three full stops (or ellipsis), and file and label the extract where you know you will be able to find it, even if this requires some cross-referencing. If you prefer paper rather than, or in addition to, saving references online, you may prefer to photocopy the extract, adding details about the source in the usual way (library staff will advise about copyright regulations).

There's one more thing to bear in mind as you read and make notes – namely, the need to ask yourself whether you can trust what you read. This is always difficult, but ask yourself whether any other sources corroborate a particular source. What does the research/report/document actually say, and what evidence is provided to support the findings? What is known about the author? Do they have a LinkedIn profile? Are they on Facebook? If so, what does it tell you about them? Do you suspect bias? If so, why? Are sources fully referenced so that you can check them? Brendan Duffy considers all these questions and many more in 'The critical analysis of documents' section of Chapter 7. Before you begin any concentrated period of reading, refer to this chapter and section and devise your own 'authenticity' checklist.

I keep a record of everything I read, even sources that have proved to be of no interest or use to me. Other people don't and have made it clear to me that as far as they are concerned, it's pointless to keep records of useless sources and they are not going to clutter up their files with rubbish. They may well have a point and you may agree with them, but I tell myself there must have been some reason why I decided to look at the book or article in the first place. The title may have sounded interesting, or I might have read other works by the same author that left an impression on me. It would follow, then, that at some time in the future, the title may still sound interesting and the author may still be remembered as having produced quality work in another context. I might come across the reference a second time, and ask to borrow the book again. I might have asked for a copy on inter-library loan, and there may be costs involved with that. All this would be a waste of time and money, and in any investigation, whether small or large, there is never enough time to do everything that has to be done. A note to remind me why I decided the work was of no interest is enough to jog my memory and to enable me to abandon that particular line of enquiry. We all have our own ways of working and you will have to decide what your own particular practices are.

Referencing

In the early days of an investigation, it may seem enough to jot down a reference on the back of an envelope, but old envelopes thrown into a box will not provide a reliable resource, and the likelihood is that references will be incomplete and difficult to track down at a later stage. If you are only going to need half a dozen references, then scraps of paper may serve, but as your investigation proceeds, you will accumulate many sources of information and an orderly system of recording is essential from the day you start reading.

There are several perfectly acceptable ways of recording sources and other information. The **Harvard method of referencing** – that is, author's surname and date, which I use in this book – has a number of advantages over other methods. It avoids footnotes, which are awkward to deal with, and all sources mentioned in the text appear at the end of the report and not chapter by chapter. I have only recently discovered that even the Harvard author–date method, which at first sight appears to be fairly straightforward, should be referenced differently for many different sources. It does slightly worry me to think that I have been using the 'one style for most sources' approach for years. Clearly I must mend my ways.

I now know, thanks to Pears and Shields (2013: 11–83), that citing and referencing sources using the Harvard (author–date) style involves different referencing for books, journal articles, conferences, theses, virtual learning environments (VLEs) such as Blackboard, and reference organization and retrieval software such as CiteULike (www.citeulike.com), URLs, reports, legal material, government publications, EU publications, scientific and technical information. Then there is the reference manager, Mendeley (www.mendeley.com), and Zotero (www.zotero.org), the free software tool to help you *collect, organize, cite*, and *share* your research sources. More about these tools in Chapter 5.

I know I shall never remember all this and so, if I am to change my lazy ways, I shall need some readily available memory jogger. I am confident you will also need some citing and referencing guidelines.

Always start with where you are studying. It may well be that detailed guidelines are already available in your library. Check which referencing style your supervisor demands. Different supervisors (and different publishers) adopt different styles and your department or institution will almost certainly have a preferred 'house' style that you will be expected to adopt. However, if no guidelines are available and in the unlikely event of your supervisor saying you can adopt whichever style you wish, at least the following will give you a start.

If you look at the bibliographies or references sections at the end of several books, it is likely you will find different approaches, though each will require the same information.

For books

For books, you will need to provide the following:

- Author's surname and forename or initials
- Date of publication (in parentheses)
- Title of the book (underlined or *italics*) and which edition, if appropriate
- Place of publication
- Name of publisher

For example:

> "Bell, F. and Bell, J. (2014) *3000 Ways of Ruining Lancashire Hotpot* (3rd edn). Morecambe: Hotpot Publications."

As you see, this is the third edition of a book published in 2014 and so the number of the edition must be included. A new edition will incorporate a significant amount of upgrading and new writing, as does this edition of *Doing Your Research Project*, whereas a reprint is just what it says, namely, the production of more copies of the original publication. Only new editions need to be noted.

A word about punctuation. There is no reason why a full stop should appear after the title or '3rd edn'; you might prefer to use a comma or to leave a space. You might decide it would be better to indent the second line in order to make the author's name stand out more clearly. If you wish, you could put the author's name in capitals. Make up your mind and whichever approach you adopt, every single reference you record from then on must have the same format – but remember, always check your organization's guidelines before you start.

Where there are three or more authors of a book, the same format will apply as for one author, but there are one or two things to note. When sources are referred to (cited) in the text of your report, there is no need to include the full reference. It is sufficient to write 'As Bell and Bell (2014: 462) say. . .'. I like to have page numbers because without them it becomes time-consuming and sometimes impossible to find where the quotation appears in the book, though many authors omit them. Where books are produced in digital form as well as print, the search function usually makes it possible to find quotations much more easily. Until all books are produced in digital format, the inclusion of page numbers is very useful, both to you as a researcher and to readers of your research.

If you cite a source by three or more authors, then it's customary to use 'et al.' in the text for the second and subsequent names, though again, practice does vary. There is no full stop after 'et' because it is a complete Latin word meaning 'and', but there is after 'et al.' because 'al' is an abbreviation for 'alii' meaning 'others'. The full reference will appear in the alphabetic list of references at the end of your report. If an author or authors have more than one publication in the same year, then suffixes 'a' and 'b' should be added after the date of publication.

Let's move on. We have not yet covered all the referencing rules and regulations. There are certain differences if you are recording information about a journal article or a chapter in a book.

For journal articles

The author's surname, forename or initials and the date of publication are the same as for books but you are also required to give:

- Title of the article (sometimes in inverted commas, sometimes not)
- Title of the journal from which the article or chapter is derived (generally underlined or in *italics*, though again, not always)
- Volume number of the journal, the issue and page numbers

For example:

> "Spade, D. (2014b) Herbal remedies from the allotment, *The Review of Garden Diseases*, **99** (34): 30–3."

The volume number (**99**) is sometimes in **bold** type, the issue number (34) comes in brackets after the volume number, and this article was published in 2014 in the journal *The Review of Garden Diseases*. As the authors published an article earlier in the same year, the letter 'b' is added to the reference. The name of the journal is usually, though not always, in italics. Page numbers of journal articles (30–3) are always given.

For chapters in books

For a chapter in a book, something along the following lines would be appropriate:

> "Tapas, J.M. and Tortilla, F.D. (2014) 2000 ways of ruining good food, in F.D. Paella and J.M. Gazpacho (eds) *The Philosophy of Frying Pan Selection* (20th edn). Laujar: Guapa Publications."

This is a chapter in a book edited by Paella and Gazpacho and so (eds) is added after their names. After the 'in', the convention is that initials should be placed before rather than after the surnames of editors. Laujar is the place of publication and the name of the publisher is Guapa Publications. However, follow whatever convention your institution requires.

Citing online articles and other data and information

There are very many different ways of citing sources, depending on the type of source you are identifying. Find out what guidelines on referencing online sources are provided by your department, institution and/or library. Pears and Shields emphasize that the important points to remember are that:

> "You should aim to provide sufficient information for a reader to be able to locate your information source. As material on the Internet can be removed or changed, you should also note the date when you accessed/viewed the information – it might not be there in a few months' time. Remember to evaluate all Internet information for accuracy, authority, currency, coverage and objectivity. The ability to publish information on the Internet bears no relation to the author's academic abilities."
>
> (Pears and Shields 2013: 39)

Remember that if you make a record of electronic journal articles, in addition to giving the full reference details as above, you also need to indicate where the sources were obtained online. For example:

- Name of author
- Date of publication (in parentheses)
- Title of article (if appropriate), e.g. Can your genes really make you fat?
- Title of source in italics, e.g. *Psychology – and More Psychology*
- [Online]: Note that the word 'Online' is in square brackets
- Available from URL of website, e.g. www.psychologyandmorepsychology.com
- [Accessed on date]: Note square brackets, e.g. [Accessed 12 June 2014]

This is what the full citation would look like:

> Wurtman, J. (2014) Can your genes really make you fat?, *Psychology – and More Psychology* [Online]. Available at www.psychologyandmorepsychology.com [Accessed 12 March 2014].

Practice may very slightly but the main point is that sufficient information must always be provided so that other researchers are able to retrieve the article.

Some of the citations, particularly of electronic sources, are quite complex and if your library provides copies of referencing guides, make sure you consult them.

Creating, editing and storing references

Bibliographic software such as EndNote, ProCite and Reference Manager has many advantages for researchers. For example, EndNote gives us the facility to create, store, organize, retrieve and cite references and allows us to search and manage online bibliographic databases. Once we know how, we are able to produce our own bibliographies in various formats and, if we're clever enough, to insert graphics into text. Copyright and licensing restrictions may apply to some databases and electronic journals, which restrict what we are permitted to print but others will allow us to download items direct into our own records. We may even be able to access summaries of journal articles, texts of newspapers, dissertations, abstracts of doctoral theses, books and conference proceedings.

You may find that your library will provide you with access to and support for one or more databases. Many university libraries subscribe to Copac, which enables you to search the catalogues of over 70 libraries at once, including the UK national libraries, university libraries, and specialist libraries. Copac also enables you to save references and to export them to EndNote and Zotero. Depending on your software, you might also be able to save Copac records directly into the software from your web browser, or search Copac and download records from within your reference management software.

Never ignore the facilities that are on your doorstep, particularly if they come free. Many researchers are part-time, live or work some way from their main academic library (or are even based overseas), spend little or no time on campus and need to be able to access databases remotely. If you wish to have access to your institution's databases and other facilities at home, that may be possible. Many universities provide students with a username and a password, which provides access to all the institution's facilities, including the library catalogues and databases. Ask your supervisor what steps have to be taken. If she or he doesn't know, or says home access is not permitted, look further. Always look further. Ask one of the librarians. I always believe librarians know everything, and they generally do. They will know the rules and will tell you what is involved.

In an ideal world, you would familiarize yourself with how a software program or database works before you start your research proper because, once you begin, you have little time to spend on unravelling the intricacies of a new system. That's the theory, and it's good sense, but not many of us live in an ideal world. Once your research starts, you will inevitably be short of time for the numerous things you have to do so. If you're working on a small project with relatively few references (say 20 or fewer), you should perhaps ask yourself whether the time and effort involved in becoming familiar with a new electronic system warrants such a commitment.

Organizations operate in very different ways, impose different conditions, regularly change their rules and, I'm afraid, it's up to you to find out which conditions apply in your own case. I do not wish in any way to imply that investing in and becoming competent in the use of a database or software package is a waste of time, money and effort – quite the reverse. Online referencing is a powerful tool, saving both time and effort but you should be clear about what is involved.

If you decide to go ahead, work at it and never suffer in silence. If you're baffled, search out people who aren't, particularly if they are frequent users of the database or software you have selected. Search online for other researchers on social networks and share experiences. Ask for their advice – and don't be embarrassed at asking what you're afraid may seem like stupid questions. Every database has its own idiosyncrasies and regular users may know some handy tips or shortcuts that may help you to search more effectively.

Backing-up: better safe than sorry

Never rely totally on your hard drive to save references or anything else for that matter. However reliable your PC, laptop, tablet, or mobile, keep back-ups of some kind. It's immaterial how, but something. Even the most sophisticated system or software can let you down sometimes – usually when you least expect it and when it will cause you the most inconvenience.

I still have memories of one terrible time when, somehow or another, almost 50 pages of a file disappeared without trace from my computer. So now I do my best to cover all eventualities. After all, what if a power cut loses all your work or, more likely, what if you forget to save and send ten chapters into oblivion? Back-up your work on an external drive or on a USB device or, even better, in the Cloud. Dropbox and Google Drive provide limited free storage that should be sufficient for most research studies. If you invest in a subscription Cloud storage provider, you can schedule back-ups to take place automatically every day or, in some cases, every few hours, which gets round the problem of remembering to do it. If only I had created a back-up copy, I wouldn't have lost 50 pages, would I? It's immaterial which method you choose – decide which suits you best and then keep to it.

Laptops, tablets, mobiles and PCs can be stolen, lost or suffer an unexpected, and perhaps fatal, crash. Don't be tempted to leave backing up your documents until later or until you 'get round to it', however busy you are. Ensure you save the latest version of your work on a memory stick or external drive or in the Cloud. Investing in a provider who stores all your documents in the Cloud automatically is worth every penny.

Making a note of references

As at every other stage in your research journey, it is important to make a note of all your references, whether you write them down or save them on your PC or laptop. Use whatever system your institution specifies. Most will require you to use the Harvard system. As advised earlier, ensure that you make a note of all the details of the reference, including page numbers where you have found quotes, especially if you have used them in your project. Also make a note of where you found the reference in case you need to return to it. If you found it online, include the URL. Make a copy of information you save on your hard drive or within the database itself, if it allows you to do so. You may wish to use the note-taking app on your smartphone or tablet to make 'on the spot' records of your references or even take a photo of it on your smartphone. If you use a separate note for each reference, you can use EverNote as a kind of index. Or, if you prefer to organize your references visually, you can get a digital version of Post-It® notes and create a virtual pinboard on your desktop, using colour coding for different types of references. You could even take pictures of title pages and use the pinboard style photo-sharing website Pinterest to 'pin' up your images. Whatever works for you. This advice may seem to be little obsessive but it is worth repeating that it is very difficult to remember the information necessary to trace a source that you have used in the past without writing down the detailed information required to do so.

The management of information

Even with a small project you will need to establish a cross-referencing and indexing system because there's no point in doing a large amount of reading if, at a later date, you can never find what you are looking for. This is especially important when you find information online. One of the methods I have used when searching online is to copy and paste the URL of a source into a separate references document, which I maximize when needed from my toolbar. I also bookmark the page as a back-up. I do this for every document I draw information from and later decide whether the information is relevant. If not, I keep the reference but use 'strikethrough' to cross it out and make a note with a date to explain to myself why I decided that it was irrelevant. Also, get into the habit of examining how authors classify their findings, how they explore relationships between facts and how key issues emerge. Methods used by other researchers may give you ideas about how you might organize and categorize your own data.

Those of you who have created and stored references on your PC and laptop will have had the opportunity to identify key words at the same time as you record your sources. This can be helpful, but whatever method of cross-referencing and indexing you select, the approach is fundamentally the same. Somehow or other, even in the very early stages of your research, you should be thinking about ways in which you will be able to find who wrote what about different topics. The last thing you need is to spend days or even weeks looking for something you know you read somewhere. You need to be able to go straight to it. Easy? Well not really. Orna and Stevens remind us:

> "By the very fact of bringing items together in one way (by author, by main subject, by date of addition to the store for example), it separates items that have other things in common. The same author may have written articles on a number of quite different subjects, so while that arrangement makes it easy to find everything by a given author, it makes it hard to find items on a given subject."
>
> (Orna 1995: 49)

Well, life was never meant to be easy and we just have to do the best we can to ensure we have some sort of system which is simple to maintain and which is likely to give reasonable access to most of the source material and topics in your store. I start a *cross-indexing system* almost from the start of reading. The main reference will include all the necessary detail using the Harvard system, but if that particular article or book raises interesting issues relating to 'grounded theory', 'research methods', 'women in leadership' or whatever, then I will create sub-headings underneath the main reference indicating where I came across those topics and where I can find notes or other books and journal articles relating to them. I start with general headings and only move to more detailed headings as the reading develops. For example, if I discover items relating to women chief executives in hospitals, I can add a subgroup to the 'women in leadership' sub-heading.

If you are saving your references in a file, devise a strategy that may well defy logic for everyone else, but which works for you. The one thing you can't do is to do nothing.

Your system should enable you to group and sort your findings under headings, allow you to refer to notes, quotations and comments about items in books or articles which you might have read months earlier and in all probability would have forgotten without it. Moreover, the small effort involved in producing a system will be providing you with the bones of a future literature review – and that will resolve many problems when the time comes to write it. There are also a number of online tools you can use to help you to manage your references. Two of the best are Delicious and Mendeley.

Delicious

Delicious (www.delicious.com) describes itself as:

> "a free service designed with care to be the best place to save what you love on the web. We keep your stuff safe so it's there when you need it – always. Delicious remembers so you don't have to.
>
> It's easy to build up a collection of links, essentially creating your own personal search engine. It's quick to organize your links so that when you're looking for something, you can find it within seconds.
>
> Our smart search makes that process even faster so you never waste any time trying to hunt down that one article you read that one time . . ."

In a nutshell, that is what Delicious is all about – a free resource where you can store URLs – website addresses. You can save online academic articles, journals, key words, links to resources online, in fact anything you would like to find later. Some websites include a Delicious icon at the foot of the page; clicking on it enables you to tag or save the link. Think of Delicious as another personal research secretary, helping you to find those all-important references whenever you need them.

Dropbox

Dropbox (www.dropbox.com) is a Cloud-based storage site where, instead of storing your documents on your laptop or PC, you save them to your Dropbox account, which you can organize into folders for different purposes. Dropbox gives you a generous amount of free storage and increases it each time someone you know accepts your invitation to sign up for their own Dropbox account. The two main advantages of Dropbox are: (1) you can access your document from any computer that is connected to the Internet; and (2) you can invite anyone to share your document and, if appropriate, give them editing rights. You could, for example, share the document with your tutor who could download it to their computer, add comments and then save it again to your Dropbox account, enabling you to access it again to make further changes which your tutor could read – and so on. If you have a Gmail address, Google has a similar service called Google Drive.

EndNote

EndNote (www.endnote.com) is a commercial reference management software package, used to manage bibliographies and references when writing essays and articles. It is not only a powerful research tool, capable of finding pdf documents saved on its site as well as published articles, but enables you to collaborate with other users by sharing and exchanging references. Your library may have access to EndNote or you can purchase it at a student rate with proof of enrolment at your university or college.

RefWorks

RefWorks (www.refworks.com) is very similar to EndNote. Both EndNote and RefWorks have a thirty-day trial period so you can try before deciding to buy, if your library doesn't have a subscription. However, as we have seen, university libraries have different ways of organizing their databases and providing access to them so, as always, be guided by the library staff and don't be afraid to ask for help. They won't think you are being foolish for asking and they are the experts; they could save you hours of searching by showing you the best way to find what you are looking for.

Google

The power of Google (www.google.com) as a search engine has been acknowledged earlier and it hardly needs any introduction here – in March 2014 around 67 per cent of all searches were carried out on Google, some 13 billion each month. I look at using Google Scholar in literature searches in Chapter 5 but Google also has a number of free apps that are well worth considering. I was so impressed with these apps that I signed up for Gmail, Google's email service, and uploaded Chrome as my browser so that I could build a package of products around Google. As mentioned earlier, there is Google Drive, which, like Dropbox, enables you to save and share files in the Cloud. Google Docs within Google Drive provides you with a basic editing tool so that you can share the editing of a document with another contributor or group of contributors. Google Hangouts are Google's version of conference calls where several people can have an online meeting or discussion or where you can interview a participant in your research. Then there is Google Calendar, which will help you to organize your research and remind you of important meetings. Google even has its own book search app called Google Books. Finally, Google has its own networking platform – Google+. Google+ enables users to create 'circles' of contacts (compare the term 'social circles'). Each circle can be given an identity such as friends, family, researchers, participants and so on. You can send messages exclusively to one circle, a number of circles or to all your circles – so you can share details of that good night out with your friends and send another message to your research participants to let them know you will be sending them a questionnaire later in the month.

No system is absolutely guaranteed to be perfect, and you may still occasionally find yourself in the position of looking through bits of paper or searching your hard drive or trying to dredge your memory about something you once read somewhere, but your system will ensure that searching and dredging are reduced to a minimum. We don't have time to spend on wild-goose chases, so get going with your cross-referencing.

It is vital that you keep detailed information on all books or articles that you consult, using the Harvard system or the system your institution requires you to use. You also need to cross-reference topics or themes with other sources so that you can find information about the same topic in other books or articles. Although this will seem laborious, it will save you hours of searching later for that all-important quotation. When you come to writing the literature review, it will also make the process so much easier.

A lot of fuss about nothing?

Well, no. Just acquiring the tools of the trade. Referencing can be irritatingly exacting and time-consuming, but once you've established a routine, recording information becomes (or should become) automatic. If you assimilate the information in this chapter and if you record your sources accurately and consistently, you will have begun to establish good research habits and to lay the foundations of your own research. You will be rewarded for your hard work if not in heaven, then certainly when you come to write your report. You will be able to locate information easily, to regroup and reclassify evidence, and to produce referenced quotations to support your arguments.

Incidentally, if you were thinking of asking whether I always get references exactly right every time, I would have to admit that I can't make such a bold claim. All I can say is that I do my best to check that I've noted and included everything because I know the grief errors and omissions will cause me if I'm careless. I doubt whether any researchers, even the most experienced and the best, would be bold enough to claim they never made a mistake. The Open University in the UK employs experienced course team writers and researchers to produce their course materials and readers. They are supported by expert, specialist course team librarians and have full access to the university library's print and online resources. Writing is their job, and yet one of the specialist librarians told me:

> "Unfortunately, from the number of whey-faced academics and researchers about to submit papers or theses who are found panicking in libraries as they desperately search for missing sources, page numbers, authors' initials and so on, it is apparent that even an occasional lapse in recording bibliographic details can result in hours of wasted time at the point when time is particularly short."

Trying to be kind, she continued:

> "It is inevitable that you will from time to time lack a similar detail from a reference – sometimes as a result of others' incorrect referencing – but if you adopt a disciplined approach to information management you will be able to minimize the number of occasions when this occurs."

She's right. So do your utmost to record every single detail at the time you read and that will go a long way to keep stress and frustration to a minimum. This issue is so important that I return to it again in Chapter 5 when covering the literature search.

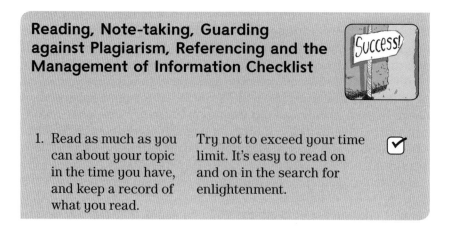

Reading, Note-taking, Guarding against Plagiarism, Referencing and the Management of Information Checklist

1. Read as much as you can about your topic in the time you have, and keep a record of what you read.	Try not to exceed your time limit. It's easy to read on and on in the search for enlightenment.	

2. Be on the lookout for recurring themes, categories and keywords.	These will become increasingly important in your search for a structure or framework for your own research.	☑
3. Remember that all your sources have to be acknowledged, including paraphrases of other people's work and ideas.	Plagiarism is using other people's words as your own. It could be just a few or thousands of other people's words.	☑
4. Decide on a system of referencing and stick to it.	The Harvard method is probably the easiest to deal with and the most prevalent, but check whether your institution has its own rules.	☑
5. When you record sources, make sure you always note the author's name, forename or initials, date of publication, title, place of publication and publisher. Remember to keep more than one copy.	There are variations for books, articles in collections and journal articles. Decide on ways of recording each one – and once you've decided, never change. It might be a good idea to keep a template of each as a reminder. Stick them on the wall or in some other readily available place. You will need to remind yourself many times during the course of your research.	☑
6. Make notes of what seem to you to be important issues. Look for and keep a 'first thoughts' list of categories and keywords in your research diary.	Make it clear in your notes which are the authors' words and which are your paraphrases, though paraphrases also need to be cited.	☑

7. Ask yourself whether you can trust what you read. Any signs of bias? Is referencing accurate?	What evidence do the authors provide to support their claims? Check Chapter 7 for information about sources, evidence and the analysis of documentary evidence.	☑
8. Electronic referencing can be the answer to all our prayers. You may have access to online databases at your own institution, so ask and, if familiarization courses are offered, make sure you attend.	But if you plan to work from home, consider the time it will take to familiarize yourself with the various techniques, the cost, whether you have sufficient space on your hard drive or an appropriate cloud-based storage plan for your needs.	☑
9. Take particular care when you cite online references.	If you have any doubts, check your institution's guidelines and/or consult some of the items in the further reading list.	☑
10. Establish a system of indexing and cross-referencing.	There's no point doing a large amount of reading if, at a later date, you can never find what you are looking for.	☑
11. If you record your sources accurately and consistently you will have begun to establish good research habits and to lay the foundations for your own research.	You will be rewarded if not in heaven, then certainly when you come to write your report.	☑

12. A lot of fuss about nothing?	Certainly not! Just getting to grips with the tools of the trade. If you decide you can't be bothered to deal with the detail or 'will sort it out later', then referencing will give you real grief later on in your research, so be warned. Keep those templates to hand and check each reference to make sure everything is included. Well, all right. I suppose that even the most conscientious among us isn't perfect, so if you know you have an incomplete reference, at least flag it or highlight it or do something to indicate that you need to get the detail sorted as soon as you can.	☑

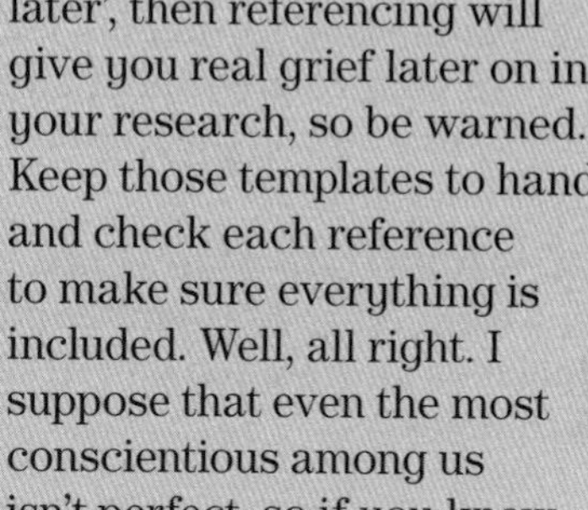

Further reading

Neville, C. (2010) *The Complete Guide to Referencing and Avoiding Plagiarism* (2nd edn). Maidenhead: Open University Press.
Colin Neville provides guidance for project, undergraduate and postgraduate students on the main referencing styles used in the UK. He also provides comprehensive guidelines on what plagiarism is and how to avoid it in assignments.

Orna, E. with Stevens, G. (2009) *Managing Information for Research: Practical Help in Researching, Writing and Designing Dissertations* (2nd edn). Maidenhead: Open University Press.
I particularly like the introductory 'First things first' page, which reminds us of the importance of recording information about our

references in an organized, methodical manner so that we can find them again easily. And then in the subsequent chapters, the authors set about advising us how to do it!

Pears, R. and Shields, G. (2013) *Cite Them Right: The Essential Referencing Guide* (9th edn). Basingstoke: Palgrave Macmillan.
In only 100 pages, these two librarians cover pretty well everything there is to know about referencing and citations, including sections on how to avoid plagiarism, setting out citations and quotations, setting out references in your reference list and bibliography, and how to cite any reference sources using the Harvard (author–date) style, as well as referencing online sources.

Rumsey, S. (2008) *How to Find Information: A Guide for Researchers* (2nd edn). Maidenhead: Open University Press.
This book includes information on virtual learning, electronic research and 'webliographies'.

Other books and journals relating to plagiarism

Google Scholar and other search engines list many other books and online journals which relate to plagiarism. However, you are unlikely to have time to read them all, so rely on your supervisor to highlight which items are considered worth consulting.

Any publications about plagiarism provided by your institution and/or department should be priority reading. Take careful note of everything that is said – and of the penalties for breaking the rules. At one time, some students might have got away with lifting whole paragraphs from the Internet, but now institutions are vigilant. Detection software has been widely adopted and that will certainly identify some defaulters, but you will also do well to remember that it is likely your tutors and supervisors will also have referred to and recognized the same online literature as you – so be careful.

5 Literature Searching

INTRODUCTION

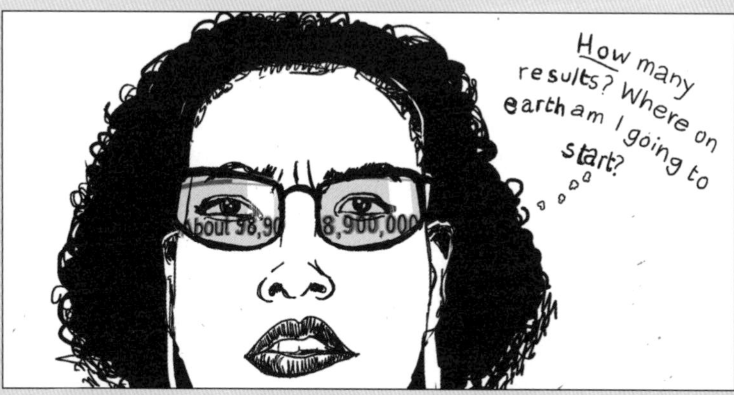

This chapter takes you through the process of literature searching, assuming you are a first-time researcher. It helps you to focus on what you are looking for, refine your search terms and appreciate the range of sources at your disposal. In this chapter, you will find help:

- Identifying search terms, refining and grouping keywords to optimize your search, both online and offline.
- Making Google work for you as a search tool, including using Google Scholar and Google Books.
- Using the library and how to conduct library database searches.
- Citing from the Internet and evaluating the academic credibility of online sources.

Key terms

In Chapter 4, I emphasized the importance of accurate referencing. Now, if your references are in good shape and if you have begun to establish an easy-to-manage system of cross-referencing, your hard work will be rewarded. If you are also familiar with some of the online search facilities such as Web of Knowledge and **COPAC** (two large databases of peer-reviewed research literature) and online bibliographic and referencing packages such as EndNote, Mendeley or Reference Manager, you are likely to have a head start in the literature-searching trail. However, even with these advantages, you will still need to develop a *search strategy* and to acquire search skills so that, as far as possible, you are able to identify only those items that relate directly to your topic and eliminate the many thousands that do not.

Take advantage of whatever guidance your supervisor, department, friends or library staff provide about searching. Find out whose job it is to help inexperienced searchers and always ask for help if you are stuck. Don't suffer in silence and never believe you are the only one who appears to be incapable of solving all search problems. You won't be. Many libraries provide courses on literature searching where you will be able to try out approaches and ask any questions. No matter how pressed for time you are, make sure you attend.

Libraries often have 'How to ...' or 'Easy Searching Guides', which will take you step-by-step through the requirements of some of the search tools and databases to which your institution subscribes. Study the instructions, keep them to hand for further reference and bookmark them so that you can find them in future rather than having to type the URLs every time. Or you could save the instructions to a folder called 'Research Project: How to Search', or whatever title will enable you to find your documents easily.

Literature searching involves special techniques and know-how but before you can begin to think about starting your search, you have some work to do. For most of you, the Internet will be your first and sometimes only line of inquiry. However, the basic principles involved in literature searching are the same, irrespective of whether your search is online or offline – namely, *defining the* ***parameters*** *of the study and refining and focusing* ***keywords*** that will allow you to identify relevant sources and, if possible, to eliminate sources that are irrelevant to your research topic.

Defining the parameters of your search (search limiters) and keywords

Ask yourself the following questions:

1 *Are you only interested in materials in English?* Do you want worldwide or only UK sources? What do you mean by 'English'?

Take care. If you are not sufficiently precise about your requirements, you are likely to generate vast amounts of online American material. Is that what you want? If you ask for too much at the start of your search, you may be overwhelmed by the amount of material you identify.

2 *Do you want information about literature from 1800 to the present day?* You don't have unlimited time on a 100-hour study, or on a much larger investigation, so start small. Limit yourself to what has been published in the past five or ten years and only look earlier when you need more information or when your supervisor says you should expand your search. Not all supervisors agree with the 'five-to-ten years' suggestion. Two experienced supervisors of scientific research who read drafts of this chapter made it clear that even in a short project, they would expect researchers to cover a much wider range of literature. They pointed out that if researchers ignored earlier quality research and what they described as 'standard texts', they would not be in a position to present a balanced picture of the development of knowledge in their topic area over a period of time. They're right of course. In a large investigation such as a PhD, researchers will almost always be required to produce a full literature review and to draw on quality research findings from 10 or 100 and, in historical research, for example, 1000 years or more. However, the amount of time a 100-hour researcher has to spend on searching is necessarily very limited, so ask your supervisor for guidance about literature search and review requirements. Try not to close the literature search door too soon, but keep a check on the amount of time you allow for searching, and do your best not to exceed it.

3 *Where do you plan to concentrate your study?* Hospitals, schools, start-up businesses, universities, colleges, prisons, adult education centres – somewhere else? Try including your location in your keywords and see what is produced.

4 *Are you only interested in one discipline area?* Nursing, Materials Science, Education, Engineering, Horticulture? What?

5 *Do you wish to identify only research carried out in England, Yorkshire, Durham, Stockport? Hong Kong, Scotland, Singapore, Australia, the USA, Worldwide? Where?*

6 *Does it matter whether members of your sample are in higher education or not?* If it's of no concern where they are, leave 'higher education' out of your keywords.

Focusing, refining and grouping your keywords

In the early stages of your search, you can't afford to spend too much time sifting through large numbers of references, so focus your requirements more sharply to eliminate more of the irrelevant items. Look back at the 'Defining the parameters' section and check whether you are clear about your answers to each item. Sometimes, if you are not finding useful results, you may need to try alternative keywords. Your *keywords* are 'mature students', 'barriers' (to learning) and 'higher education'. What about 'hurdles' instead of 'barriers to learning'? You might also have decided that 'higher education' wasn't precise enough but 'postgraduate' might be. Think of synonyms, consult a dictionary and a thesaurus such as *Roget's Thesaurus of English Words and Phrases*. Some databases provide a thesaurus that enables you to adopt the keywords used in the database. If so, use it and make a note of the accepted keywords for future use.

Let's return to the original purpose of your 'mature students' study. You have identified individual keywords that are likely to be important, but what you really want to discover is whether mature students (or older students) in higher education (or universities or colleges) experience any barriers (or hurdles) that impede their learning (or success) – and it is the grouping of these keywords that is important. If you are only interested in postgraduate engineering students, for example, then the grouped keywords could be 'students + hurdles + postgraduate + engineering'.

Digital or print?

In this chapter and throughout this book, the importance of libraries and librarians is emphasized because, despite widespread Wi-Fi, we still need access to what libraries provide and to the expertise of librarians. And we also need books and hard copies. If you are reading this book in print format, ask yourself what advantages there are in doing so. For the foreseeable future, digital and print will co-exist in libraries and researchers will make use of both. Academics will continue to inhabit a hybrid world of digital and print materials for some time to come and even when print has been largely supplanted, the need for continued access (local or remotely) will be crucial.

Libraries, librarians – and books

Bruce and Mertens (2013) describe a survey conducted in 2013 by JISC and RLUK in the UK of how academics carry out research, which revealed, among many other things, that the first resort of most researchers is a search engine and that academics spend much less time in the library than online. The survey concluded that, 'the role of the library has shifted from being the primary gateway to content to being a "buyer" and "owner" of content'. They go on to say that libraries have recognized the importance of making their content 'discoverable' online.

Most universities have well-equipped libraries that are more like centres of learning, with workstations, fast Wi-Fi connection and cafes nearby. Researchers are also discovering that some library staff provide courses and seminars on search techniques, learning styles and how to judge the quality of online sources. If you haven't been into your library for some time, take a look. Yours may have reinvented itself while you weren't looking.

Google search

There are a number of search engines that you could use to find academic research relevant to your own study. We focus here on Google because it is the most frequently used, giving birth to the verb, 'to google', to define online searching. In the month of January 2014, there were 12.9 billion searches on Google compared with the total of all Microsoft search sites, including Bing, which had 3.2 billion, and Yahoo! Sites, which attracted 2.2 billion visits.

Using Google to find relevant research studies will be second nature if you are a 'digital native', as you will probably google products ranging from books to holidays. So, there is probably little I will be able to tell you about what happens when you search on Google that you don't already know. However, I thought it might be helpful to give you some tips on how to make your search more effective. Although Google is a highly advanced technological tool for finding information, it is not sufficiently intelligent to interpret what you ask it to find if your search terms are vague or misleading – it bases its results on searching or 'crawling' through websites and indexing them according to the words or combinations of words you put into its search box. Let's see what happens when you are not specific. Let's say that you are researching the use of questioning by teachers in secondary classrooms. You enter

'Questioning' into the search box. Try it now ... What happened? Did you find what you were looking for? You may know what you mean by the topic 'Questioning' but Google doesn't. Obvious? Well, yes, in this example it is, but it's not always as clear as this. The general rule is that the more precise you are, the more relevant the search results will be.

I have found through trial and error that my Google searches are usually more effective and I get better results if I type a question into the search box, so my question about questioning (!) might be: 'How do teachers use questioning in the secondary school classroom?' Try it now and compare it with the search results for the word 'Questioning'. Although the most relevant result is still at the foot of the first page, this gives you a starting point and, once opened, the website will have content that will give you suggestions for further searches.

Apart from asking a question in the Google search box, if you type a keyword or group of words within quotation marks (e.g. 'teacher questioning'), Google will search for this phrase only. So, it won't search for the words 'teacher' or 'questioning' on their own, only in this precise combination.

There may be one or two search results at the top of the first page listed within a pale rectangular background. This does not mean that they are necessarily the most relevant search results. They are in this position and highlighted by their background because they are paid adverts from Google's 'Adwords' service. They may well be the most relevant but not always. Every time someone clicks on these adverts, the company sponsoring them pays Google. This is called pay-per-click (PPC) advertising. Some searches also produce small adverts on the right-hand side – they are sponsored adverts too but cheaper than the larger advert at the top of the page. So, paid adverts may not necessarily give you the most relevant website results. You will need to decide that for yourself.

You might also consider carrying out a similar search on Google Scholar. Google Scholar provides a simple way to find relevant work within the world of scholarly research. You can search across many disciplines and sources for articles, theses, books, abstracts and court opinions, academic publishers, professional societies, online stores, universities and other websites. Google Scholar also provides citation tracking for authors. This means that you can search for who has quoted ('cited') a particular author or researcher, perhaps in order to gain academic credibility for their own methodology or research findings.

Google Books

In addition to Google Scholar we now have Google Books, the aim being to make offline content searchable online. Although this is a very useful service, it has its limitations. If a book is out of copyright or the writer has given permission, books are available in 'full view' and free to download in pdf format. Other books are limited to a 'preview' or, where permission for a preview has not been given or when the owner of a book cannot be identified, 'snippets' of two to three lines of text are shown but the full text of the book is searchable. For other books that have neither a 'full view' nor 'preview', Google Books provides the book title. Each book includes an 'About this book' page with basic bibliographic data such as title, author, publication date, length and subject. For some books, you may also see additional information like key terms and phrases, references to the book from scholarly publications or other books, chapter titles and a list of related books. For every book, you'll see links directing you to bookstores where you can buy the book and libraries where you can borrow it.

A Google Book search for a specifically worded piece of text can be unsuccessful in identifying relevant sources, particularly if that text appears in a footnote, a figure caption, a boxed insert, or inside some quotation from a consulted source. Google Books searches cannot be regarded as an authoritative source of the frequency or extent of specific usages or terms because many books fall into the unsearchable category.

While it is important to recognize the limitations to Google Books, you may find it perfectly adequate when used in conjunction with databases available in your university library. At some point in the future, there may come a time when all books are available online. That will be wonderful. The digital production of books will give us outstanding research tools, particularly for books long out of copyright but, as far as I am concerned, it will certainly not mean that books are redundant. So, those of you who thought you never needed to enter a library or bookshop ever again, sorry, you're out of luck. Back to the shelves.

Check with your library catalogue to see what stock is held. Check what is on the shelves in and around your topic or return to your online references. If you see anything that might be of interest, get to work. Examine the contents lists. Titles can be misleading, but the contents lists will give you a good idea of what the book, article or journal is really about. Take a quick look at any chapters or sections that might be relevant to your topic, examine the index and the list of references, and note chapters or paragraphs that may be of particular interest. Highlight any items that you think might need to be followed up at a later stage, and always record the source.

As I advised in Chapter 4, if you use your smartphone, tablet or laptop to record sources on the spot, *you still need a back-up copy.* Establish your own almost foolproof approach to recording sources. I say 'almost' because it is unlikely any approach will be 100 per cent foolproof, but you can try to get as close to it as you can.

List possible *keywords* and add a note to remind you where you found the book (library classification number, floor and shelf number, main library or annexe, in another library, online, another country – anything that will help you to find it again). All is not lost if your library does not hold the items you need because if you familiarize yourself with your *library websites or databases*, I am sure they will tell you how to obtain access to information in other libraries. Then, it might be possible for you to borrow the book, make a photocopy, access a scanned copy of a journal article on the inter-library loan scheme or gain access to a digital copy.

Richard Pears, co-author of *Cite Them Right: The Essential Referencing Guide* (2013) and an experienced librarian at Durham University, points out that 'many library catalogues and bibliographic databases enable you to save search results and email them to your account or export results to reference management software such as Endnote'. He adds that it's a good idea to ask your subject librarian about this because he or she may be able to save you time when you produce your bibliography/list of references. Read on.

SCONUL (Society of College, National and University Libraries) provides access to the catalogues of more than 170 libraries in the UK and Ireland. This is particularly useful for those of you who do most of your searching away from your main campus, and who hope to be given access to a library nearer home. It gives useful information about what specialist stock is held and provides details about opening and closing times in term time and during vacations.

Many public libraries have their own *Public Library Catalogues* online and, as mentioned in Chapter 4, the **Consortium of University Research Libraries Online Public Access Catalogue (COPAC)** is particularly helpful in giving free access to the online catalogues of some of the largest research libraries in the UK and Ireland, including the British Library, Oxford and Cambridge University libraries, Trinity College Dublin library, National Libraries of Scotland and of Wales, and specialist libraries such as those of the Victoria and Albert Museum and Kew Gardens.

The British Library's public catalogue is now free online for the material that is held in the major Reference and Document Supply collections. You can also browse the British Library through COPAC.

Harvard's Open Collections Program (OCP) works in collaboration with the university's faculties, librarians and curators to develop highly specialized 'open collections', which are available to Internet users. In developing these collections, OCP produces digital objects and catalogue records that are open to anyone online.

Increasing numbers of universities now have their own digital repositories and are willing to give free (or subscription) access to their latest research. Try OAISTER (www.oaister.org), which provides another interdisciplinary source of research. If you want to keep up-to-date about what is available, always go first to the experts. In other words, it's best to ask your librarian what the latest software or database is.

Journals

Books date fairly quickly and so you will almost certainly need to consult journals, particularly journals in your specialist area, many (probably most) of which are now available in digital format. Your library catalogue will include a list of journals to which your institution subscribes but if you have specialist librarians, *always* make use of their expertise. They can point you in the right direction, help you to refine your research strategy, find appropriate sources, tell you where to find print copies of journals, appropriate web pages, indexes and abstracts – *and* they can help you to avoid many hours of unproductive searching. Journals are expensive, regardless of whether they are on library shelves or available digitally. Either way, the library has to pay and, as the cost of books and subscriptions to online materials increases, many institutions have to make decisions about what they can afford. If your library does not have what you are looking for, ask about an inter-library loan.

There are hundreds of journals, and it can be difficult to know which are likely to produce the most useful information, but all disciplines have a core of 'quality' journals that include nationally or even internationally *refereed* articles. A word about the importance of refereeing. All researchers hope their work will be published in good quality journals and they know that if they submit an article to one of the journals in this elite group, the editor will in all probability send it to other researchers in the same or similar field for their consideration. When their comments have been considered, the article may be accepted, rejected or suggestions made for adjustments. Accepting articles for publication is a serious business and all journal editors will spend time ensuring, as far as they possibly can, that the articles they accept will be of sufficient quality to merit publication.

Not all journals will have such demanding requirements. There are many others that might be equally useful, so ask your supervisor and specialist librarians about likely sources which are available digitally or in print and which, if any, are available on your library shelves. Consult subject indexes, abstracts, the list of contents at the front (or sometimes at the back) of the journals, read abstracts at the start of articles and make a note of any interesting items, possible keywords, any articles which are likely to be of use and which are related to your topic and, as with books, add a note to indicate where the journal was located. And remember that **you can't lift material either offline or online without acknowledgement**. Sorry to go on about this, but if you plan to draw on any material online, either by paraphrasing or by direct quotation, you must acknowledge it in a way that will enable readers to know where the information came from. Fail to do so and you will be plagiarizing. As noted earlier, the use of plagiarism detection software by universities and awarding bodies is widespread and you are likely to be in serious trouble when you are found out.

This is so important that I think it is worth revisiting how to cite online sources. Adopt the following citation order when dealing with web pages with individual authors:

- Author
- Year that the site was published/last updated (in parentheses)
- Title of Internet site (in *italics*)
- [Online]
- Available at: URL
- [Accessed: date]

For example:

> "Pennink (2013) *The UK Survey of Academics: how academics (re)search* [Online]. Available at http://networkcultures.org/wpmu/query/2013/06/25/the-uk-survey-of-academics-how-academics-research/ [Accessed 14 March 2014]."

Pears and Shields (2013) are quite right to remind us that we should evaluate all online information for accuracy, authority, currency, cover and objectivity, but that is easier said than done. I trust tutors and supervisors will provide guidance about ways of evaluating sources, but I would urge you also to contact library staff to find out whether courses are provided. If they are, make sure you attend.

Evaluating sources

As far as possible, it is your job as a researcher to consider the worth of the research you have identified in your searches. You can make a start by asking yourself a few questions, perhaps along the following lines:

- Have you only drawn on source material that supports your point of view, without making efforts to consult a range of sources?
- Have you really made an effort to carry out a critical examination of the evidence?
- Is the research well designed and are the data collection instruments suitable for the purpose?
- Do you see any terms that suggest *partisanship* or *bias*?

In Chapter 7, Brendan Duffy reminds us that 'writers will rarely declare their assumptions so it is the task of the researcher to expose them if possible'. He then asks: 'Does the evidence supplied convincingly support the author's arguments?' He was writing about the analysis of documentary evidence, but his advice is equally valid in considering the worth of all research reports.

Of course, it's not always easy to answer these questions. We may have few problems about identifying obvious signs of bias in another researcher but we need to be equally watchful about our own. For example, we may agree so strongly with an author's conclusions that we fail to question whether those conclusions are fully justified. Then there is the problem about insufficient information on which to make a judgement. If you are carrying out all your searches on the web, you may find that information about research design is not always provided in sufficient detail. All you can hope to do is to examine reports of research as thoroughly and objectively as time and your impartiality allow. However, if you know that articles have been 'refereed', you have a better chance of making judgements about them because, if the refereeing 'control system' works well, you will know that they have been read by at least one other experienced researcher, usually an academic, who will have commented and given an informed opinion on the quality of the report.

If you are struggling to find out which articles are refereed and which are not, ask your library staff and/or your supervisor for help, *but also* take note of the advice given by **Internet Detective**, the free Internet tutorial designed to help you 'discern the good, the bad and the ugly for your online research'. It gives some of the best advice on Internet searching I have seen. It is all good sense, well presented, in plain English and at times, quite funny. It all helps! If you've read and I hope noted what they say, read it all again and make a point of going back to it from time to time at www.vtstutorials.ac.uk/detective/ – or just insert Internet Detective in Google's search box, then bookmark the site so that you can easily find it in future.

Apart from bookmarking sites, you can also save URL references online by using Instapaper (www.instapaper.com) and, as described in Chapter 4, Delicious (www.delicious.com). Instapaper describes itself as 'A simple tool for saving web pages to read later on your iPhone, iPad, Android, computer or Kindle.' I often get sidetracked by opening a promising looking website and then moving from that website to follow up a reference within it. Before I realize, half-an-hour has passed and I've still got another twenty references on Google to search. Instapaper enables you to save references until you have time to search them properly. If you have a Smartphone or iPad, you can follow up the references 'on the go' wherever you have a Wi-Fi connection.

Copyright and licensing restrictions when downloading items from the web

It's always helpful to skim through complete articles and reports to see if they are as useful as they appear to be but if you want to download web pages to a file and to use extracts from them at a later date, you have to be really careful about copyright and licensing restrictions. I know you know that, but I'm reminding you again! Database helplines should inform you what you can download, print and use, and what you can't. If they don't, and if you have any doubts, ask for help from your supervisor and/or specialist librarian. Some institutions' web pages provide fairly full statements about what in legal terms is 'fair dealing' and what is not, so it's worthwhile seeing if yours is one of them. We all cut and paste from web pages but if you are careless and fail to give full details of where items come from (including paraphrases of items), when they were retrieved and whose words you are pasting into your own records, you could be in real trouble because, once again, you could find yourself involved in a plagiarism case. Sorry to repeat myself, but this issue is important. In the past, I think some researchers were caught in this particular spider's web because of genuine ignorance rather than deliberate attempts at deceit, but now so many verbal and printed warnings are given to students that institutions have little patience with the 'Well, I didn't know that was wrong' excuse. *So take care.*

The Top Ten Guide to Searching the Internet Checklist

1. Give yourself plenty of time.	It isn't called the World Wide Web for nothing! There are massive quantities of information and huge numbers of blind alleys and it is important to allocate enough time for the search within the project plan. But it is also important to set yourself a limit. Web searching can be addictive and it is difficult to know where to draw the line. Although there may be some sites you wish to return to throughout the project to check for updates, it is important that you keep web searching in proportion with the other aspects of your literature review.	☑
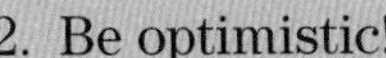 2. Be optimistic!	Start by typing in exactly what you are looking for, for example, 'barriers to learning for mature students in higher education'. You might get lucky, and if not, it can often be interesting to see what the search engine thinks is relevant. I have found that typing the full question that I would like answering reduces the ambiguity of the search and produces the information I am looking for.	

3. Be prepared with search limiters.	Before you start, think about how you are going to frame your search just as you would with a journal search. What other search terms, for example, could be used for 'adult participation in learning'? Think through whether you want to limit your search to UK sites only (most search engines will let you specify this). It is also worth setting yourself parameters in terms of the age of articles referenced or the sector.	☑
4. Know your search engines.	Apart from the ubiquitous Google, there are also specialist sites such as Google Scholar, so it is worth spending some time to see which of these sites is bringing up the most relevant hits for your search.	☑
5. When you find something, don't lose it!	It is worth writing down, copying and pasting into a document or bookmarking the exact URL of the page you have found, as sometimes a lot of time can be wasted trying to retrace your steps. Making a note of the site may not always be enough, as sometimes websites are so complicated it can be difficult to relocate the exact page you were looking for. You can also bookmark web pages, which is also a handy way of making the information available offline. The ranking of a site on Google can change over time, depending on the effectiveness of its Search Engine Optimisation (SEO), compared with other sites. It may not be on the same page the next time you look for it, so noting the URL or bookmarking it will save you time having to search for it again. You might also want to take a screenshot and save it as an image. If you are using a smartphone or a tablet, you could even take a photo of your laptop	☑

	or PC screen and email it to yourself or save it to a cloud-based storage system such as Google Drive or Dropbox, where it can be accessed from any browser on any device.	
6. Don't underestimate the news.	Sites such as The Guardian, the BBC and Sky have dedicated education and other specialist departments. Not only can these sites provide current stories that can help to bring your research right up-to-date, they might also contain links to any reports referenced or to relevant organizations.	☑
7. Avoid spam.	Many sites will ask you to register before you can access information, in many cases just to help them by monitoring who is using their site. Registering will often mean entering your email address and unfortunately this can mean your name gets onto email lists and you will start receiving spam emails. One way to get round this is to set up a dedicated email address for your research. This way you can monitor the address for useful emails and then close the account once you have finished so you don't receive unwanted emails to your main address.	☑
8. Networking – online and offline.	Your best route to finding the most relevant sites and search engines is to talk to your contacts. See if they have stumbled over any relevant websites. With so many routes to accessing information, word of mouth can save a lot of time but don't just limit yourself to other people on your course. It is worth contacting anyone who is researching your area. Look for research networks in your field and join them.	☑

9. Referencing.	It can be difficult to keep track of where quotes have come from, so whenever you paste a quote, paste the web link too. As pointed out earlier, you will also need to reference the exact date you accessed the site because of the evolving nature of content on the web. Take particular care when using online collaborative environments such as wikis where users are able to edit content without the changes going through a process of peer review. While these open resources can provide valuable research information, it needs to be verified and so try to trace the original source and then apply your usual process of critiquing who wrote the document and why.	
10. Patience and persistence!	The web is an invaluable tool for researchers because of the vast amount of information available. It also easy to become distracted when online and it is tempting to check your emails, texts or your social networks. Switch your mobile off or put it on silent and focus on the task in hand – become unavailable while you are searching. Online searches can be very frustrating and often feel like searching for a needle in a haystack but once you find that needle, everything becomes worthwhile.	

Don't forget to obtain a copy of your library, institution *and* departmental guides on searching for references. Quite often, departments will have their own rules and regulations that must be followed.

Further reading

Hart, C. (2001) *Doing a Literature Search: A Comprehensive Guide for the Social Sciences*. London: Sage.
This useful book considers aspects of the literature search in the social sciences and includes references to relevant books and articles. Although it has not been updated to include online searches, the principles of offline literature searches remain much the same.

Keeble, H. and Kirk, R. (2007) Exploring the existing body of research, in A.R.J. Briggs and M. Coleman (eds) *Research Methods in Educational Leadership and Management* (2nd edn). London: Sage.
This chapter includes guidance on constructing a search category, searching library catalogues and electronic databases, citations searching, using search engines – and much more.

Pears, R. and Shields, G. (2013) *Cite Them Right: The Essential Referencing Guide* (9th edn). Basingstoke: Palgrave Macmillan (online search tool at http://www.citethemright.co.uk).
This excellent book is the definitive work on referencing.

6 The Review of the Literature

INTRODUCTION

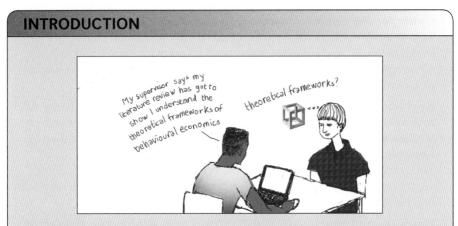

This chapter explains what a literature review is, and why it is included in a research project. It aims to take you through some key terms and illuminate the distinction between a list of references and a critical literature review. The chapter uses extracts of case studies to help you understand what kind of review is needed to show that findings have been identified in similar research studies, and what the similarities and differences are to your own study. The chapter provides:

- A definition of 'literature review', and how to create an insightful and critical review rather than just a list of literature that you have read.
- Key definitions of important terms, such as 'theory' and 'framework'.
- Extracts of case studies of different types of literature reviews to illustrate how they may differ according to the requirements and scope of the research.

Key terms

Writing about health and social care, Aveyard defines a **literature review** as:

> "a comprehensive study and interpretation of literature that relates to a particular topic. When you undertake a literature review you identify a **research question,** then seek to answer this question by searching for and **analyzing** relevant literature using a systematic approach. This review then leads you to the development of new insights that are only possible when each piece of relevant information is seen in the context of other information. If you think of one piece of information as part of a jigsaw, then you can see how a review of the literature is like the whole completed jigsaw."
>
> (Aveyard 2010: 5-6: emphasis in original)

Hart agrees that a literature review is important because:

> "without it you will not acquire an understanding of your topic, of what has already been done on it, how it has been researched, and what the key issues are. In your written project you will be expected to show that you understand previous research on your topic. This amounts to showing that you have understood the main theories in the subject area and how they have been applied and developed, as well as the main criticisms that have been made of work on the topic."
>
> (Hart 2001: 1)

In Hart's view, 'the review is therefore a part of your academic development – of becoming an expert in the field'. A critical review of the literature will be required in most cases for a PhD, but a project lasting two or three months will not require anything so ambitious. If your supervisor agrees, you may decide to omit an initial review altogether. However, evidence of reading will still be required and the procedures involved in producing that evidence will be much the same, regardless of the size of the task or discipline.

The 'critical review' of the literature

The main point to bear in mind is that a review should provide the reader with a picture, albeit limited in a short project, of the state of knowledge and of major questions on the subject. In principle, that sounds easy enough but in practice it can prove to be anything but easy. Haywood and Wragg wryly comment that critical reviews are more often than not uncritical reviews – what they describe as:

> "The furniture sale catalogue, in which everything merits a one-paragraph entry no matter how skilfully it has been conducted: Bloggs

> (1975) found this, Smith (1976) found that, Jones (1977) found the other, Bloggs, Smith and Jones (1978) found happiness in heaven."
>
> (Haywood and Wragg 1982: 2)

They remind us that it requires discipline to produce a review which demonstrates 'that the writer has studied the work in the field with insight'. It is easy to produce a furniture sale catalogue, to collect facts and to describe what is, but not so easy to produce this 'critical' review. It involves questioning assumptions, querying claims made for which no evidence has been provided, considering the findings of one researcher versus those of others and evaluating. All researchers collect many facts, but then must select, organize and classify findings into a coherent pattern. Verma and Beard agree that literature reviews must identify and explain relevant relationships between facts, but they also consider that:

> "the researcher must produce a concept or build a theoretical structure that can explain facts and the relationships between them ... The importance of theory is to help the investigator summarise previous information and guide his future course of action. Sometimes the formulation of a theory may indicate missing ideas or links and the kinds of additional data required. Thus, a theory is an essential tool of research in stimulating the advancement of knowledge still further."
>
> (Verma and Beard 1981: 10)

This raises a number of issues relating to the meaning of 'theory' and of 'theoretical structure' and thus, before we look at extracts from some successful literature reviews, perhaps I should make sure we all mean the same thing when we speak about 'theory'. And that presents a few problems because different people have slightly different views about meaning.

Theory and theoretical (or conceptual) frameworks

Theory has been described as being 'a set of interrelated abstract propositions about human affairs and the social world that explain their regularities and relationships' (Brewer 2000: 192), or 'theory at the lowest level can be an ad hoc classification system, consisting of categories which organise and summarise empirical observations' (Bowling 2002: 139). Bowling continues:

> "It can be a taxonomy which is a descriptive categorical system constructed to fit the empirical observations in order to describe the

> relationships between categories (e.g. in a health care budget: spending on acute services, non-acute services, health promotion activities and so on)."
>
> (Bowling 2002: 140)

However, it can be, and often is, merely taken to refer to the current state of knowledge in a subject derived from the published literature – what Wolcott (1992: 3–52) described as 'theory first' rather than 'theory after'. Punch clarifies the difference between the two as follows:

> "In theory-first research, we start with a theory, deduce hypotheses from it, and design a study to test these hypotheses. This is theory verification. In theory-after research, we do not start with a theory. Instead, the aim is to end up with a theory, developed systematically from the data we have collected. This is theory generation."
>
> (Punch 2005: 16)

Care has to be taken before embarking on a 'theory after' approach, mainly because it requires the collection of a great deal of data that is inevitably well beyond the timescale and scope of most small (or smallish) studies. Not impossible for a PhD, but still difficult.

Cohen *et al.* point out that **'model'** is sometimes used instead of or interchangeably with 'theory':

> "Both may be seen as explanatory devices . . . though models are often characterized by the use of analogies to give a more graphic or visual representation of a particular phenomenon. Providing they are accurate and do not misrepresent the facts, models can be of great help in achieving clarity and focusing on key issues."
>
> (Cohen *et al.* 2000: 12–13)

I particularly like Miles and Huberman's admirably clear statement about what they see as theory building and conceptual **frameworks**. They write that:

> "Theory building relies on a few general constructs that subsume a mountain of particulars. Terms such as 'stress' or 'role conflict' are typically labels we put on bins containing a lot of discrete events and behaviours. When we assign a label to a bin, we may or may not know how all the contents of the bin fit together, or how this bin relates to another. But any researcher, no matter how inductive in approach, knows which bins to start with and what their general contents are likely to be. Bins come from theory and experience and (often) from the general objectives of the study envisioned. Laying out those bins,

> giving each a descriptive or inferential name, and getting some clarity about their interrelationships is what a conceptual framework is all about."
>
> (Miles and Huberman 1994: 18)

The label is not important, but the process of establishing a map or framework of how the research will be conducted and analysed is. As Polit and Hungler point out:

> "**A framework** is the conceptual underpinnings of a study . . . In a study based on a theory, the framework is referred to as the **theoretical framework**; in a study that has its roots in a specified conceptual model, the framework is often called the **conceptual framework** (although the terms conceptual framework and theoretical framework are often used interchangeably)."
>
> (Polit and Hungler: 1999: 110; emphasis in original)

So, a theoretical framework is an explanatory device 'which explains either graphically or in narrative form, the main things to be studied – the key factors, constructs or variables – and the presumed relationships among them' (Miles and Huberman 1994: 18).

Polit and Hungler comment on how helpful frameworks can be to the researcher:

> "Frameworks are efficient mechanisms for drawing together and summarizing accumulated facts . . . The linkage of findings into a coherent structure makes the body of accumulated knowledge more accessible and, thus, more useful both to practitioners who seek to implement findings and to researchers who seek to extend the knowledge base."
>
> (Polit and Hungler 1999: 111)

I find that 'theory' and 'theoretical frameworks' can on some occasions be used in variable ways, depending on the interpretation and understanding of individual researchers. I do sometimes become concerned at the view that research cannot proceed unless it has a sound 'theoretical base', mainly because I am not always sure what that means in the context of some of the research being considered. These issues need to be discussed or else, 'what might become an opportunity for an informed dialogue about theory, and a concomitant review of the roles it can play, is represented instead as an obstacle' (Wolcott 2001: 80). I hope you will always be able to engage in 'informed dialogue' with your supervisor and to ask for clarification if terminology, principles, meaning and ideas are new or unclear to you.

The 'critical review' in practice

All the work you have already done in identifying keywords, major issues and categories will now help in establishing a framework for your analysis and review of the literature. Even when all the necessary groundwork has been done, difficulties may still remain, not least because any research involving human beings has to take account of the inevitably large number of variables involved, which makes it difficult to establish any common patterns of behaviour or experience. And then there is the difficulty of researchers starting from different bases so that comparing like with like becomes problematic. However, in spite of the difficulties inherent in the production of any review, it is still perfectly possible to succeed, as did Gilbert Fan, a first-time researcher, and John Richardson and Alan Woodley, two very experienced academics and researchers. Let's look now at short extracts from their successful reviews.

The Gilbert Fan review

When he carried out his research, Fan was a member of staff in a School of Health Sciences in Singapore and was involved in his institution's Diploma in Nursing programme. He knew that certain concerns were being expressed nationally and internationally about nurse education, including a decline in student enrolment in nursing programmes, the apparent low status of nursing, which was believed to have contributed to poor recruitment, and high attrition rates leading to a shortage of nurses. He decided that a study of students' perceptions of their diploma programme in particular and of the nursing profession in general would be useful to him and would contribute to the school's understanding of the programme from a student perspective.

He had read widely and his literature review was extensive. He knew he could not include all his sources and so he had to decide on specific topics which were of particular interest to him and under which he could group his findings. Though there were relatively few Singaporean studies on which to draw, he found there was plenty to choose from other countries, mainly the USA, the UK and Australia. He grouped his findings under the headings of:

- the decline in student enrolment in nursing education;
- curricula, types of nursing education and nursing competencies;
- teaching and clinical supervision in nursing education programmes;

- the relationship between nursing education and the profession; and
- nursing as a career choice.

Each of the above topics was thoroughly explored and documented and the review ran to 32 pages – more than was required for a Master's thesis, but Fan was nothing if not thorough. This small extract, which covered only half a page, is part of the section on the decline in student enrolment, but I hope it gives you an idea of how he approached his task.

> "Pillitteri (1994: 132) sees the decline in student enrolment in nursing education programmes to be a serious concern for the profession and Naylor (1990: 123) projected that the total number of new graduates from all the nursing programmes in the USA would drop from 82,700 in 1985 to 68,700 in 1995. Among the reasons for such a decline was that students did not find nursing attractive as a lifelong career. Such perceptions were perpetuated by unrealistic portrayals of nursing in the mass media and the alternative careers that women could enter today (Brooks 1989: 121; Fagin et al. 1988: 367; Kelsey 1990 cited in Pillitteri 1994: 132)."
>
> (Fan 1998: 31)

Subsequent paragraphs deal further with research findings from all four countries (the USA, the UK, Australia and Singapore), which, in spite of the fact that each has a different system of nurse education, identified similar reasons for the decline in student recruitment and high turnover; namely, the traditional structure of nurse education, poor career advancement, job dissatisfaction, inflexible work schedules, staff shortage, low pay, family commitments, relocation of family, unsupportive supervisors and lack of opportunities for career advancement. He supports each of the items with the name, date and page number of the sources and, of course, the full details of each are provided in the full list of references at the end of the thesis.

Fan made a good job of categorizing his findings under the five main headings, each of which had sub-headings. Even with the ongoing work of recording, categorizing and re-categorizing, the production of this review must have been complex. However, he succeeded and not only produced a good review, but also a good thesis.

The Richardson and Woodley review

On to the second example, which is a small extract taken from a journal article produced by John Richardson and Alan Woodley and entitled 'Another look at the role of age, gender and subject as predictors of academic attainment in higher education' (Richardson and Woodley 2003). Both are experienced researchers, and over the years have produced a number of research papers concerned with this topic (Woodley and McIntosh 1980; Woodley 1981, 1984, 1985, 1998; Richardson and King 1998).

In 2003, they published the results of their updated and extended investigation into the academic attainment of mature students in higher education. Consider the first paragraph of the introduction to this study, which makes clear what they intend to do. They write:

> "In this article, we examine the role of a student's age, gender and subject of study as predictors of their academic attainment in higher education, and in particular as predictors of the classes of first degrees awarded by institutions of higher education in the UK. There has been a good deal of interest in this topic over the last 30 years, and our analysis builds on the findings of several previous investigations that examined the performance of graduates in the UK."
>
> (Richardson and Woodley 2003: 475)

Readers are then referred to a table listing previous analyses of predictors of academic attainment in UK higher education from 1964 to 2001.

They continue by analysing their own findings under the headings of: age and academic attainment; gender and academic attainment; subject of study and academic attainment. These are followed by variations and groupings relating to age, gender and subject of study. The following extract is taken from their section on age and academic attainment:

> "Interest in the role of age as a predictor of academic attainment is often motivated by a stereotype of older people as being deficient in intellectual skills (Richardson and King 1998). Cross-sectional studies comparing groups of different ages have indicated that there is a slight decline in intellectual function between the ages of 18 and 60, with a more pronounced decline thereafter (e.g. Nyberg et al. 1996; Verhaeghen and Salthouse 1997). Such results are, however, contaminated by cohort differences in life experience, and longitudinal studies comparing the same groups at different ages often find no statistically significant decline before the age of 60 (Schaie 1996: 107–36). When any age-related changes in performance are observed, they typically amount to a reduction in information processing, whereas access to stored information is usually unaffected (Klatzky 1988; Nyberg et al. 1996). There is thus no reason to expect a reduction in attainment with advancing age in situations that demand the retrieval of knowledge

(Baltes et al. 1984), except when they involve time pressure (Verhaeghen and Salthouse 1997). Of course, one situation that fits the latter description is the traditional unseen examination."

(Richardson and Woodley 2003: 477–8)

Read this again, but perhaps more slowly this time. Take note of the language Richardson and Woodley use, the care they take in drawing conclusions from the research findings and the way some of the findings are qualified. If you have time, consult the full article and examine the ways in which findings are categorized.

Reviewing the reviews

Look back at the two extracts in this chapter. Richardson and Woodley already had extensive knowledge of their topic before they undertook the work involved in their 2003 article and they were able to produce an exhaustive review of previous studies relating to the influence of age, gender and subject of study on academic attainment. Gilbert Fan was a first-time researcher, and although he knew a great deal about issues relating to his work and had identified an area of interest very early in his studies, he did not have the advantage of a firm knowledge base about previous research. He was not required to produce an exhaustive review of the research findings relating to his topic: it was sufficient for him to produce a relatively brief account of the selected literature and to draw some conclusions where possible, bearing in mind the care needed in making claims. His early ideas about likely headings, groups and categories were based mainly on his personal and professional experience, and were gradually added to, adapted or completely changed during the course of his reading.

A literature review should be more than just a list of references that are relevant to your research topic. A critical review involves questioning assumptions, querying claims made for which no evidence has been provided, considering the findings of one researcher versus those of others and evaluating the conclusions drawn.

Remember!

We can all learn a great deal by reading what other researchers have done. Look critically at all reviews that come your way. Ask yourself whether they are furniture sale catalogues or well-organized accounts that are relevant to the topic. Research findings can be dangerous if they are used in an undisciplined way and I feel a certain anxiety when I am told that 'research proves x or y' when I see no corroborating evidence to warrant such an assertion. Inferences may possibly be drawn, results 'might indicate', but remember that in any dealings with human beings, 'proof' is hard to come by.

Review of the Literature Checklist

1. Evidence of reading will always be required in any research.	Although in a small study, it may not be necessary to produce a full literature review.	☑
2. Researchers may collect many facts but then must select, organize and classify findings into a coherent pattern.	The aim is to produce a critical review, not a list of everything you have read.	☑
3. Your framework will not only provide a map of how the research will be conducted and analysed, it will also give you ideas about a structure for your review.	It will help you to draw together and summarize facts and findings.	☑
4. Literature reviews should be succinct and, as far as is possible in a small study, should give a picture of the state of knowledge and of major questions in your topic area.	If you have been able to classify your reading into groups, categories or under headings, writing your review will be relatively straightforward.	☑

5. Ensure that all references are complete. Note the page numbers of any quotations and paraphrases of good ideas. **You cannot use them without acknowledging the source**. If you do, you may become involved in a plagiarism challenge.	It should be possible for any readers to locate your sources.	☑
6. Watch your language. Perhaps inferences may be drawn, but 'proof' is hard to come by when dealing with human beings.	Make no claims that cannot be justified from the evidence you have presented. Consider again the wording Richardson and Woodley use in the extract from their article.	☑
7. Examine your sources critically before you decide to use them.	Any sign of bias, inappropriate language or false claims? Are you able to trust the authors' judgements?	☑
8. Remember that unless you are comparing like with like, you can make no claims for comparability.	Researchers often start their research from different bases and make use of different methods of data collection. You may still wish to use their findings, but be careful about how you discuss them.	☑
9. Do not be tempted to leave out any reports of research merely because they differ from your own findings.	It can be helpful to include differing results. Discuss whether they undermine your own case – or not.	☑

10. Start the first draft of your review early in your reading. Many more drafts will be required before you have a coherent and 'critical' account but better to start small and then build on your first attempt than to have to make sense of everything you have read at one attempt. As you continue, entries will be deleted and others added, but you will have made a start. Better to be faced with a badly written, inadequate review as a starting point, than a blank page.

Further reading

Aveyard, H. (2010) *Doing a Literature Review in Health and Social Care: A Practical Guide* (2nd edn). Maidenhead: Open University Press.
This is a small book but it is full of useful information and guidance about developing research questions, literature searching and literature reviews.

Bell, J. and Opie, C. (2002) *Learning from Research: Getting More from Your Data*. Buckingham: Open University Press.
Chapter 4.3, pp. 137–43 (and elsewhere in this book) considers reviews produced by five experienced and successful postgraduate students in very different higher educational institutions in Australia, England and Singapore.

Hart, C. (1998) *Doing a Literature Review: Releasing the Social Science Research Imagination*. London: Sage, in association with the Open University.
Even if a full review is not required, the appendices on 'The proposal', 'How to cite references', 'Presentation of a dissertation', 'Managing information and keeping records' and 'A checklist of do's and don'ts for reviewing' will still be useful.

Laws, S. with Harper, C. and Marcus, R. (2013) *Research for Development: A Practical Guide* (2nd edn). London: Sage.

Chapter 5, pp. 101–19 provides excellent checklists about planning, carrying out and writing up the literature, together with guidance about using a library and how to research online.

Murray, R. (2011) *How to Write a Thesis* (3rd edn). Maidenhead: Open University Press.
Pages 122–35 discuss definitions and purposes of literature reviews and justification for the inclusion and omission of literature, while pages 135–44 provide detailed advice on how to avoid plagiarism.

O'Dochartaigh, N. (2007) *How to Do Your Literature Search and Find Research Information Online* (2nd edn). London: Sage.

Richardson, J.T.E. and Woodley, A. (2003) Another look at the role of age, gender and subject as predictors of academic attainment in higher education, *Studies in Higher Education*, 28 (4): 476–93.

Ridley, D. (2012) *The Literature Review: A Step-by-Step Guide for Students* (2nd edn). London: Sage.
This book goes through the various stages of reading, organizing information, literature searching and writing up the review.

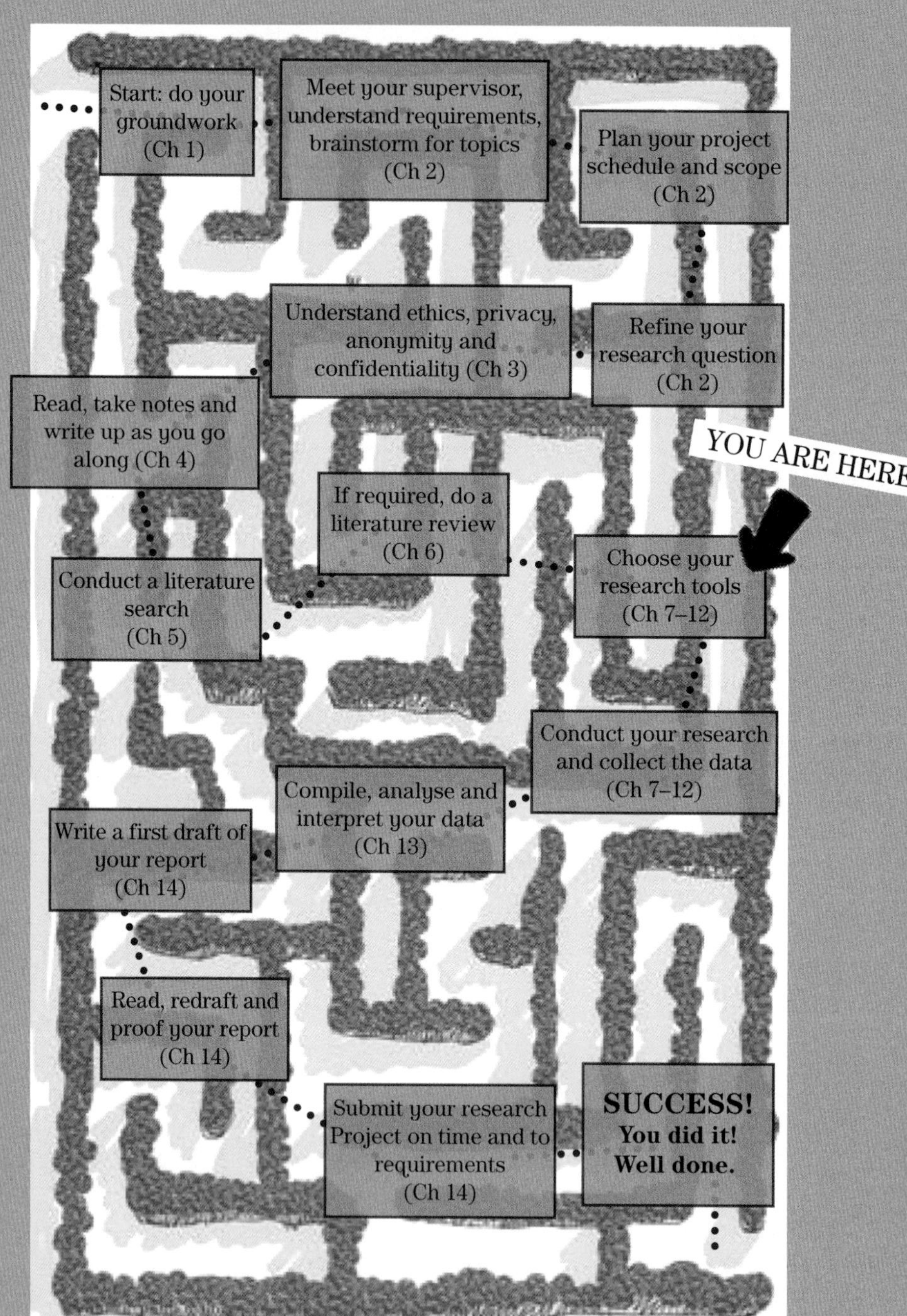
Start: do your groundwork (Ch 1)
Meet your supervisor, understand requirements, brainstorm for topics (Ch 2)
Plan your project schedule and scope (Ch 2)
Refine your research question (Ch 2)
Understand ethics, privacy, anonymity and confidentiality (Ch 3)
Read, take notes and write up as you go along (Ch 4)
Conduct a literature search (Ch 5)
If required, do a literature review (Ch 6)
YOU ARE HERE
Choose your research tools (Ch 7–12)
Conduct your research and collect the data (Ch 7–12)
Compile, analyse and interpret your data (Ch 13)
Write a first draft of your report (Ch 14)
Read, redraft and proof your report (Ch 14)
Submit your research Project on time and to requirements (Ch 14)
SUCCESS! You did it! Well done.

PART II

Selecting Methods of Data Collection

Introduction

Key terms

When you have decided on a topic, refined it and specified objectives, you will be in a position to consider how to collect the evidence you require. The initial question is not 'which methodology?' but 'what do I need to know and why?' Only then do you ask 'what is the best way to collect information?' and 'when I have this information, what shall I do with it?'

No approach depends solely on one method any more than it would exclude a method merely because it is labelled 'quantitative', 'qualitative', 'case study', 'action research' or whatever. As I indicated in Chapter 1, some approaches depend heavily on one type of data collection method – but not exclusively. You may consider that a study making use of a questionnaire will inevitably be quantitative, but it may also have qualitative features. Case studies, which are generally considered to be qualitative studies, can combine a wide range of methods, including quantitative techniques. Methods are selected because they will provide the data you require to produce a complete piece of research. Decisions have to be made about which methods are best for particular purposes and then data collection instruments must be designed to do the job.

Constraints

The extent of your data collection will be influenced by the amount of time you have. This may seem a rather negative approach, but there is no point in producing a grandiose scheme that requires a year and a team of researchers if you are on your own, have no funds and in any case have to hand in the project report in three months. Even so, if possible, efforts should be made to cross-check findings, and in a more extensive study, to use more than one method of data collection. This multi-method approach is known as *triangulation*.

Laws (2013: 143) points out that 'the key to triangulation is to see the same thing from different perspectives and thus to be able to confirm or challenge the findings of one method with those of another'. She warns:

> "accounts collected from different perspectives may not match tidily at all. There may be mismatch and even conflict between them. A mismatch does not necessarily mean that the data collection process is flawed – it could be that people just have very different accounts of similar phenomena. You need to critically examine the meaning of any mismatches to make sense of them."
>
> (Laws 2013: 144)

One problem for short-term researchers is that examining the meaning and making sense of any mismatches takes time and so most 100-hour projects are likely to be limited to single-method studies. You just do the best you can in the available time. There are likely to be other constraints. For example, if you wish to observe meetings, you will be limited by the number and timing of meetings that are scheduled to take place in the period of your study. The willingness of people to be interviewed, or observed, to complete the questionnaire or diaries will inevitably affect your decisions as to which instruments to use.

Reliability and validity

Whatever procedure for collecting data is selected, it should always be examined critically to assess to what extent it is likely to be reliable and valid. *Reliability* is the extent to which a test or procedure produces similar results under constant conditions on all occasions. A clock that runs 10 minutes slow some days and fast on other days is unreliable. A factual question that may produce one type of answer on one occasion but a different answer on another is equally unreliable. Questions that ask for opinions may produce different answers for a whole range of reasons. The respondent may just have watched a TV programme that affected their opinion, or may have had some experience that angered or pleased and so affected their response. Writing about interviews, Wragg (1980: 17) asks: 'Would two interviewers using the same schedule or procedure get a similar result? Would an interviewer obtain a similar picture using the procedures on different occasions?' These are reasonable questions to put to yourself when you check items on a questionnaire or interview schedule.

There are a number of devices for checking reliability in scales and tests, such as *test–retest* (administering the same test some time after the first), the *alternate forms method* (where equivalent versions of the same items are given and results correlated) and the *split-half method* (where the items in the test are split into two matched halves and scores then correlated). These methods are not always feasible or necessary, and there are disadvantages and problems associated with all three. Generally, unless your supervisor advises otherwise, such checking mechanisms will not be necessary unless you are attempting to produce a test or scale. The check for reliability will come at the stage of question wording and piloting of the instrument.

Validity is an altogether more complex concept. Most definitions state that validity tells us whether an item or instrument measures or describes what it is supposed to measure or describe, but this is rather vague and leaves many questions unanswered. Sapsford and Jupp (2006: 1) offer a more precise definition. They take validity to mean 'the design of research to provide credible conclusions; whether the evidence . . . can bear the weight of the interpretation that is put on it'. They argue that what has to be established is whether data '*do* measure or characterize what the authors claim, and that the interpretations *do* follow from them. The structure of a piece of research determines the conclusions that can be drawn from it (and, more importantly, the conclusions that *should not* be drawn from it)' (Sapsford and Jupp 2006: 1).

If an item is unreliable, then it must also lack validity, but a reliable item is not necessarily also valid. It could produce the same or similar responses on all occasions, but not be measuring what it is supposed to measure. Measuring the *extent of validity* can become extremely involved, and there are many variations and subdivisions. For the purpose of 100-hour projects that are not concerned with complex testing and measurement, it is rarely necessary to delve deeply into the measurement of validity, though efforts should be made to examine items critically.

Ask yourself whether another researcher using your research instrument and asking factual questions would be likely to get the same or similar responses. Tell other people (colleagues, pilot respondents, fellow students) what you are trying to find out or to measure, and ask them whether the questions or items you have devised are likely to do the job. This rough-and-ready method will at least remind you of the need to achieve some degree of reliability and validity in question wording even though it is unlikely to satisfy researchers involved with administering scales and tests with large numbers of participants. If you are involved in the validity of scaled measures, you might wish to consult the items included in the further reading below.

Thinking about computerized data analysis?

If you think you might wish to make use of a software package to analyse your returns, take care over the design of all your data collection instruments because the way you word questions may result in responses that are difficult to analyse. Data has to be filtered to get to the *meaning* of all those figures and to understand what can be claimed from them and what can't. If possible, decide which software package you will use in advance so that your results closely match how the data needs to be entered into the software. It is more difficult to enter data into analysis software if you decide to do it after your data has been collected.

Perhaps the most widely known and most often used software package for statistical analysis is IBM's SPSS Statistics. The package, originally known as the Statistical Package for the Social Sciences, became Statistical Product and Service Solutions to indicate its application beyond the social sciences before being renamed IBM SPSS Statistics. The SPSS software is expensive and beyond the limited budget of the individual researcher but many university departments have multi-user licences that may provide you access or at least enable you to submit your data to an IT technician to enter on your behalf. Data that has been analysed can be presented in a number of ways, including charts and graphs, so you will need to decide which is the most appropriate for your project before your data is entered. There are two excellent books which are recommended by many universities to students intending to use IBM SPSS Statistics Software: Andy Field's *Discovering Statistics Using IBM SPSS Statistics* and Julie Pallant's *SPSS Survival Manual* (see further reading below). As well as being invaluable during data analysis, either of these publications will enable you to understand how data needs to be entered into the software so that you can decide how best to conduct your data collection.

Many departments have a research and data analysis adviser or data expert, so make sure you know who that is. The way you word your questions may influence the type of analysis you are able to carry out, so always make sure the wording is checked by your supervisor/research adviser/data analysis adviser before you finalize all data collection instruments and regardless of whether your research will be mainly quantitative or qualitative.

Not thinking about computerized data analysis?

No problem. And particularly in small or relatively small, time-limited studies, it may be better to keep to manual methods of data analysis and interpretation of the results. As I've said throughout this book, it is about careful selection of a topic, being sure about the purpose of your study, negotiating access to institutions, materials and people, devising suitable methods of data collection, observing the ethics of research, collecting, analysing and interpreting results, and producing a well-written report *on time*. So, time to move on.

A reminder!

First-time researchers often worry about how many questionnaires should be distributed or interviews conducted. There are no set rules, and you should ask for guidance from your supervisor before you commit yourself to a grand plan that will be far in excess of what is required. Your aim is to obtain as representative a range of responses as possible to enable you to fulfil the objectives of your study and to provide answers to key questions.

Research instruments are selected and devised to enable you to obtain these answers. The instrument is merely the tool to enable you to gather data, and it is important to select the best tool for the job. The following chapters take you through the processes involved in the analysis of documentary evidence, how to use social media in your research, designing and administering questionnaires, planning and conducting interviews, diaries and observation studies. Little attention is given to the analysis of data in this part, but all data has to be analysed and interpreted to be of any use, and so Chapters 13 and 14 in Part III should be studied in association with the chapters in Part II.

Further reading

Field, A. (2013) ***Discovering Statistics Using IBM SPSS Statistics*** **(5th edn.). London: Sage.**

Pallant, J. (2013) ***SPSS Survival Manual: A Step by Step Guide to Data Analysis Using IBM SPSS*** **(5th edn.). Maidenhead: Open University Press.**

7 The Analysis of Documentary Evidence

INTRODUCTION

This chapter aims to provide you with a framework for selecting and evaluating documentary evidence. This evidence may be used to supplement other research findings or may form the basis of your research; in both respects, it is important to evaluate the evidence and avoid bias in your findings. Here is what you will find in this chapter:

- A look at the nature of documentary evidence and how to find it.
- Definitions of deliberate and inadvertent primary and secondary sources and witting and unwitting evidence.
- A guide to selecting documents relevant to your research.
- Advice on analysing the content of documentary evidence, including external and internal criticism.
- Understanding the importance of determining fact or bias in documentary evidence.

Key terms

Most educational projects will require the analysis of documentary evidence. The aim of this chapter is to help you to locate, categorize, select and analyse documents. Its approach is derived from historical methods, which are essentially concerned with the problems of selection and evaluation of evidence. Such methods were first developed by von Ranke and have influenced the form of all academic report writing (Evans 2000: 18; Barzun and Graff 2003: 5). In some projects, documentary analysis will be used to supplement information obtained by other methods; for instance to check the reliability of evidence gathered from interviews or questionnaires. In others, it will be the central or even exclusive method of research. It will be particularly useful when access to the subjects of research is difficult or impossible, as in the case where a longitudinal study is undertaken and staff members no longer belong to the organization being investigated. The lack of access to research subjects may be frustrating, but documentary analysis of educational files and records can prove to be an extremely valuable alternative source of data (Johnson 1984: 23).

The nature of documentary evidence

During the **document** search, it is helpful to clarify exactly what kinds of documents exist. 'Document' is a general term for an impression left on a physical object by a human being. Research can involve the analysis of images, films, videos or other non-written sources, all of which can be classed as documents, but the most common kinds of documents in educational and medical research are printed or manuscript sources, so this chapter concentrates on these. Increasingly, records are kept in electronic form but the scholarly approach to both online and offline documents is the same. Sources can also be quantitative or statistical in nature but it would be mistaken, of course, to regard these so-called 'hard' sources of evidence as being more reliable than other kinds of material. It is vitally important to employ the recommended critical method of analysis to check how the figures have been produced. What has been counted, how correctly, by whom, when, where and why? (Stanford 1994)

Approaches to documents

When embarking on a study using documents, it is possible to have two different approaches. The first is called the **source-oriented approach** in which you let the nature of the sources determine your project and help you generate questions for your research. The feasibility of the project is determined by the nature of extant (existing) sources so that a particularly full collection of material, for example on the restructuring of a college or hospital, would lead to an investigation of that area. Rather than bringing predetermined questions to the sources, you would be led by the material they contain. The second and much more common way of proceeding employs the **problem-oriented approach**, which involves formulating questions by using other research methods and then by reading secondary sources. This method investigates what has already been discovered about the subject before establishing the focus of the study and then researching the relevant primary sources (these terms are defined below). As your research progresses, a much clearer idea of what sources are relevant will emerge and more questions will occur to you as your knowledge of the subject deepens (Tosh 2010).

The location of documents

Document searches need to be carried out in exactly the same way as literature searches in order to assess whether your proposed project is feasible and to inform you about the background to, and the nature of, the subject. The document search may have to cover both local and national sources of evidence.

National records have proliferated since the advent of a national educational system and the introduction of the National Health Service (NHS), and it is important to decide what official sources are needed for a particular local project. Such sources may be published or unpublished. A project on curriculum development in a school or local authority or one on the role of district nurses in an area may require a trawl of government green papers, white papers, guidance papers, government statistics, Office for Standards in Education (Ofsted) reports, statutes, policy papers and sources in the National Archives, as well as scrutiny of the local sources. The Internet is an invaluable aid to locating official documents but as a researcher you must also be prepared to hunt down other sources of information, particularly in the local context (McCulloch and Richardson 2000: 86). **It can never be assumed, of course, that because documents exist they will be available for research. Some sources may be regarded as too confidential to be released, so enquiries would have to be made about access and availability.**

At the local level, the nature of the project will lead you to particular sources. In the NHS and medicine generally, there is a great emphasis on evidence-based research and the importance of documents, along with individual responsibility of staff for any records they create or use in the course of their duties. The NHS has developed a code of practice for the management of records that stipulates that each NHS organization is required to have an overall policy statement on how records are managed, and this will be helpful to researchers. Organizations are encouraged to establish a records inventory that will help the researcher to find out what health and non-health records exist in an institution. A project on the role of a ward manager, for example, would need to ascertain what administrative and personnel records as well as health records exist to provide information. Minutes of meetings, memos, policy statements and diaries, as well as clinical and caseload records would be fruitful sources if they were available. Other ideas for projects are offered by Walsh and Wigens (2003).

The NHS provides detailed guidance on the retention of records and specifies minimum retention periods for different types of documents. It also provides guidance on dealing with records which have ongoing research or historical value and which should be preserved in the National Archives. Records from different hospitals that have been archived have been used to study, for example, the 1918 influenza epidemic.

Different projects will require different searches. A project on the relationship between a college and its funding body, for example, would require a document search of the records of both institutions, and account would have to be taken of their special characteristics. If the college had an academic board or equivalent, its minutes would be one source; if the funding authority's departments dealt with different aspects of the college's administration, their records would be significant. It is important to ask what archives or collections of records exist in an organization. What records are preserved by the school office, the governing body, the bursar or financial officer or the library, and what records are stored by individuals or departments in the institution? Does the local authority hold records for particular schools? How long do organizations hold on to records before they dispose of them? Schools have a legal duty to preserve attendance registers for ten years after the register was closed. The safeguarding of 'school annals' to record events deserving of permanent record in the history of a school is at the discretion of the school. Researchers can be frustrated by the official and unofficial weeding policy of institutions and of government departments that may have resulted in the destruction of sources later discovered to be significant (Duffy 1998: 29–30).

Primary and secondary sources

Documents can be divided into primary and secondary sources. **Primary sources** are those that came into existence in the period under research (for example, the minutes of a hospital's governing body). **Secondary sources** are interpretations of events of that period based on primary sources (for example, a history of that hospital which obtained evidence from the board's minutes). The distinction is complicated by the fact that some documents are primary from one point of view and secondary from another. If the author of the hospital history was the subject of research, for example, his book would become a primary source for the researcher. The term 'secondary analysis' used in a narrow sense by some social scientists to mean the re-analysis of data such as survey material or primary documents gathered by other researchers in collections is not to be confused with the use of secondary sources (Hakim 2000).

Deliberate and inadvertent sources

Primary sources can in turn be divided into:

1 **Deliberate sources**, which are produced for the attention of future researchers. These would include autobiographies, memoirs of politicians, medical practitioners or educationalists, diaries or letters intended for later publication, and documents of self-justification (Elton 2002). They involve a deliberate attempt to preserve evidence for the future, possibly for purposes of self-vindication or reputation enhancement.
2 **Inadvertent sources** are used by researchers for some purpose other than that for which they were originally intended. For example, they are produced by the processes of local and central government and from the everyday working of the health and education systems.

Examples of such primary evidence from the education system include:

- the records of legislative bodies, government departments, agencies and local authorities;
- evidence from national databases, such as RAISEonline (Reporting and Analysis for Improvement through School Self-Evaluation: www.raiseonline.org) and the FFT (Fischer Family Trust: www.fischertrust.org), both of which include performance data on individual schools;

- inspection reports;
- national surveys;
- newspapers and journals;
- the publications of professional associations, subject teaching associations and trades unions;
- the records of agencies like the Specialist Schools and Academies Trust (SSAT);
- the minutes of academic boards, local consortia, senior management groups, middle management meetings, subject departments, working groups, staff meetings and parents' associations;
- letters and correspondence of educational institutions, including email;
- annual governors' reports;
- handbooks and prospectuses;
- examination papers;
- school timetables;
- attendance registers;
- personal files;
- staffing returns;
- option-choice documents;
- records of continuing professional development;
- bulletins;
- budget statements;
- school or college websites and other Internet material.

Examples of documents from different bodies in the NHS include:

- the summary care records of primary care trusts;
- patient health records, including GP medical records;
- hospital ward books;
- diaries of health workers;
- personnel records;
- budgetary records;
- research project records;
- hybrid records of health bodies, which are a mixture of electronic and paper records;
- policy statements;
- financial and accounting records;

- notes associated with complaints;
- pamphlets and leaflets produced by health authorities that are classed as 'grey literature' (Gerrish and Lacey 2010: 67).

Such inadvertent documents are the more common and usually the more valuable kind of primary sources. They were produced for a contemporary practical purpose and would therefore seem to be more straightforward than deliberate sources. This may be the case but great care still needs to be taken with them because it cannot be discounted that inadvertent documents were intended to deceive someone other than the researcher, or that what first appear to be inadvertent sources (some government records, for example) are actually attempts to justify actions to future generations (Elton 2002: 71). Some of the documents generated by a school for an inspection, for example, may have the aim of giving the best possible impression to the inspectors; without the imminent inspection, the school might not be so prolific in its production of policy statements and schemes of work or be so up to date in its staff handbook.

Witting and unwitting evidence

A final point about the nature of documents concerns their 'witting' and 'unwitting' evidence. **Witting evidence** is the information that the original author of the document wanted to impart. **Unwitting evidence** is everything else that can be learned from the document (Marwick 2001: 172–9). If, for example, a government minister made a speech announcing a proposed educational reform, the 'witting' evidence would be everything that was stated in the speech about the proposed change. The 'unwitting' evidence, on the other hand, might come from any underlying assumptions unintentionally revealed by the minister in the language he or she used, and from the fact that a particular method had been chosen by the government to announce the reform. If a junior minister is given the job of announcing a reduction in educational expenditure that may well indicate that more senior colleagues anticipate that the government will be criticized. All documents provide 'unwitting' evidence, but it is the task of the researcher to try to assess its precise significance.

The selection of documents

The quantity of documentary material you can study will inevitably be influenced by the amount of time that is available for this stage of your research. It is not usually possible to analyse everything and so you must decide what to select. Familiarity with the different categories of evidence will help you to make decisions about what is fundamental to the project, and 'controlled selection' is then needed to ensure that no significant category is left out (Elton 2002). Try not to include too many deliberate sources and take care not to select documents merely on the basis of how well they support your own views or hypotheses. Your aim is to make as balanced a selection as possible, bearing in mind the constraints of time. Periodically check with your schedule, and if you find that you are encroaching on time allocated for the next stage of your research, take steps to reduce your selection. Your perception of what is valuable will grow as the project develops.

Content analysis

The proper selection of documents is particularly important in what is termed **content analysis**, which has been defined as 'a systematic, replicable technique for compressing many words of text into fewer content categories based on explicit rules of coding' (Stemler 2001), and as 'any technique for making inferences by objectively and systematically identifying specified characteristics of messages' (Holsti 1969: 14). Krippendorff (2012: 24) defines it as 'a research technique for making replicable and valid inferences from texts (or other meaningful matter) to the contexts of their use'. Essentially, it is a research tool with which to analyse the frequency and use of words or terms or concepts in a document, with the aim of assessing the meaning and significance of a source. Content analysis can be used for television, film and websites as well as written documents (Brett Davies 2007: 181–2). It can be used for different purposes, including, for example, analysing the sentence length in school textbooks or health pamphlets, the ethnicity of names in reading books, or the positive and negative language in performance management assessments (Burton *et al.* 2008: 120). It is useful for analysing the significance of speeches and articles by political leaders. For example, *The Times* (2009) analysed a speech in which David Cameron, who went on to become Prime Minister, used the term 'people' ten times and the term 'power' 50 times.

It has been suggested that the best approach in content analysis is that which starts with a research question and then decides on a sampling strategy after the 'coding' or 'recording units' have been defined. There are different ways of defining such units but essentially they are sampling units like health policy statements or leaflets in GP surgeries, which will then be analysed in sentences or paragraphs, using categories such as the purpose of the policies or the advice given to patients. As in the approaches to documents explained above, content analysis could develop 'emergent coding', with the categories being formulated as the sources are explored, or there can be *a priori* coding based upon previous reading and the generation of theoretical ideas. Although the most common recording unit is a word, it might also be possible to use a joint term, repetition of phrases, themes, or whole paragraphs on a subject. The approach usually involves counting the number of times particular terms or recording units occur in a sample of sources, but it could also involve such methods as counting the number of column inches devoted to a subject in a newspaper or the number of photographs in a publication. Stemler (2001) warns about assuming that the words mentioned most often are the ones reflecting greatest concerns because synonyms may be used and words like 'state' or 'power' have multiple meanings. If your source can be converted into a Word document, you can use the 'Search in Document' feature to highlight keywords for you.

The chosen sampling method is very important and needs to be justified and replicable. It might be possible to study all the documents in a particular category such as school newsletters or prospectuses, but in other cases a sampling technique is needed, for instance if a daily newspaper is selected in a research project investigating tabloid newspapers' attitudes to comprehensive schools or the health effects of alcohol consumption (Walsh and Wigens 2003: 18). You could examine all the editions of a newspaper over a three-month period or you could take the first week in each month over a one-year period. You must be able to justify the sample and it must be sufficiently large to allow valid conclusions. If you are interested in the media presentation of teachers' or nurses' associations, the sampling of newspapers from the first week of each month would be inappropriate because significant references to specific associations are unlikely to be confined to this time-frame. Having established the frequency of your chosen terms, you must then be able to place them in context before interpreting and explaining them.

After analysing word frequency, it is valuable to assess the context of the key words to test for consistency. Stemler (2001) gives advice about valuable software used for content analysis, much of which allows the researcher to see how the word was used in context. Content analysis of documents using simple word counts can be arid in its approach if the nature of the documents is not analysed in the way suggested below and this may not be appropriate for many small-scale studies.

The critical analysis of documents

External criticism

The analysis of documents can be divided into *external* and *internal criticism*, even though these may overlap to a large extent. **External criticism** aims to discover whether a document is both genuine (that is, not forged) and authentic (that is, it is what it purports to be and truthfully reports on its subject: Barzun and Graff 2003: 69n). For example, an observer could write a report of a meeting he had never attended. His report would be genuine because he actually wrote it, but it would not be authentic because he was not present at the meeting.

With external criticism, it is necessary to know for certain that the author produced the document, so certain questions need to be asked. In the case of a letter, they would include the following:

- Was the author of the letter known to be in the place from which it came at the time it was supposed to have been written?
- Do other sources corroborate that the person wrote the letter? Is the letter consistent with all other facts known about the author?
- Does it use the same structure and have the same form as similar documents?
- Is it typical of other letters or documents written by the author?

You may not always be able to identify forgeries or hoaxes but an attempt should be made to decide whether a person did actually compose the speech delivered or write or sign the letter.

Internal criticism

The analytical method more likely to be used in small-scale educational research is **internal criticism**, in which the contents of a document are subjected to rigorous analysis, which first seeks answers to the following questions:

- What kind of document is it – a circular, a statute, a policy paper, a set of minutes, a letter from a long correspondence? How many copies are there?
- What does it actually say? Are the terms used employed in the same way that you would use them? Documents such as statutes or legal papers may use a specialized language which must be mastered, and private correspondence may contain terms in an idiosyncratic way that also need to be understood.

- Who produced it? What is known about the author?
- What was its purpose? Did the author aim to inform, command, remind (as in a memorandum) or to have some other effect on the reader? A document is always written for a particular readership and shaped according to the writer's expectations of how intended readers will interpret it. In the same way, the reader should try to be aware of the purposes and intentions of the writer during the act of reading.
- When and in what circumstances was it produced? How did it come into existence?
- Is it typical or exceptional of its type?
- Is it complete? Has it been altered or edited? It may be that there is more chance of completeness if it is published a long time after the events it describes.

You will also need to assess the assiduousness of the producers of documents. Staff will complete documents very carefully if they are to be used in appeals procedures or public meetings, and their approach to reporting on a pupil may be influenced if they know the pupil's parents. After asking these basic questions, you will need to ask further questions about the author:

- What is known about the author's social background, political views, aims and past experience?
- Did the author experience or observe what is being described? If so, was he or she an expert on what was being witnessed and a trained observer of the events described?
- Did the author habitually tell the truth or exaggerate, distort or omit?
- How long after the event did the author produce the document? Is it possible that their memory played tricks?

All these questions may not be relevant to all documents, but in aiming at critical analysis it is important not to accept sources at face value. Examine them carefully. Gaps in the evidence can sometimes be very significant, as they may indicate a prejudice or a determination to ignore a proposed change. Decide whether a particular political affiliation might possibly influence the tone or emphasis of a paper and try to come to a conclusion based on all the available evidence. An assessment of the document's reliability must involve the question: 'Reliable for what?' Is it a reliable explanation of the author's views on an issue? In other words, is it representative of those views? It might not be truthful in a more general sense; for instance, a supporter of streaming in schools may not necessarily convey the truth about the effects of using this method of organizing classes but it would nevertheless be a truthful and therefore reliable expression of this individual's views on the subject. Alternatively, the source might be a reliable example of its type, as in the case of a document from a long series.

Fact or bias?

One important aim of critical scholarship is to assess whether fact or **bias** is the main characteristic of a document (Barzun and Graff 2003: 154–7). Writers will rarely declare their assumptions, so it is the task of the researcher to expose them if possible. Watch particularly for any terms that suggest partisanship. Ask yourself whether the evidence supplied in the document convincingly supports the author's arguments. Was the author a supporter of a particular course of action in which he had a stake? If the document goes against the author's own interest, it may increase the likelihood that it tells the truth. Was the author affected by pressure, fear or even vanity when writing the document? (Best 1970: 105). Look for clues.

If you detect bias, it does not necessarily mean that the document should be dismissed as worthless. In some cases, the most useful evidence can be derived from biased sources that reveal accurately the true views of an individual or group. Inferences can still be drawn from the 'unwitting' testimony, even if the 'witting' evidence is thought to be unsound. A prejudiced account of curriculum development, for example, could provide valuable insights into the political processes involved in innovation. The biased document will certainly need to be analysed cautiously and compared with evidence from other sources, but it can still be valuable.

Try to put yourself in the position of the author of the document and to see through his or her eyes. Instead of jumping to early conclusions, deliberately seek contrary evidence to test the truthfulness of a document as rigorously as possible – and watch out for your own bias. It may be easier to recognize bias in others than in oneself, and it is tempting to reject evidence that does not support your case, but try to resist the temptation. Sources can be interpreted in different ways (even though some sources can reasonably be understood in only one way) but the postmodernist view that documents can be subjected to an infinity of meaning has been brilliantly demolished by Evans (2000). The guiding principle in document analysis is nevertheless that everything should be questioned. Qualities of scepticism as well as empathy need to be developed.

Scrutinize documents for bias – what may appear to be a presentation of the 'facts' may be a careful selection of data to present a particular point of view. Don't assume that because a document is 'official' (such as a government paper) that it is unbiased.

It could be argued that the techniques of document analysis suggested here are merely the application of common sense. This is partly true but, as you study the sources, you will gradually gain insights and detailed knowledge that will give you a 'higher common sense', which will in turn permit a fuller appreciation of the worth of the evidence (Barzun and Graff 2003: 122–4). Eventually, the critical method becomes a habit, which will allow you, in Marwick's phrase, to 'squeeze the last drop' from each document (Marwick 2001: 233).

The Analysis of Documentary Evidence Checklist

1. Decide how you want to use documentary evidence.	Will it be used to supplement other sources of evidence or will you use it as the exclusive method of gathering data?	☑
2. Decide on your approach to the documents.	You could let the source material determine your research questions or, more commonly, formulate your research questions after reading the literature on the subject and take these questions to the sources.	☑

3. Undertake a document search to ascertain the existence of different sources of information.	These may be found in different places in an organization, so it is important to be persistent. **Always negotiate access to the documents and do not assume that you can consult them; some information may be confidential.**	☑
4. Analyse the nature of the sources used.	Some sources will be deliberately produced for the attention of future researchers. More usually, however, sources are inadvertently produced by the everyday working of, for example, the health or education system.	☑
5. If the documents are bulky, it may be necessary to decide on a sampling strategy.	Try to read a balanced selection of documents in the time you have available. The strategy must be appropriate to the purposes of your search and be capable of being justified in the report.	☑
6. Be aware that there may be different kinds of evidence in each document.	Look for 'witting' and 'unwitting' evidence.	☑
7. Subject each document to the 'what does it say?' critical method and ask a range of questions.	Who wrote it? Why? How did it come into existence? Is it typical of its kind? Is it complete?	☑
8. Compare the document with other sources to see if it is accurate or representative.		☑

9. Then ask further questions about the authors of documents.	What is their background? What are their social and political views?	☑
10. Look for bias in the document.	Remember that biased evidence can still be very valuable.	☑
11. Decide whether the document is reliable for a particular purpose.	Check it against other sources to ascertain its truthfulness but remember that, although it may not be an accurate account of an event or development, it will be a reliable expression of the author's views.	☑
12. Strive to gain a full appreciation of the value of a source.	Use your accumulating knowledge to gain insights and try to make the critical method a habit in your research methods.	☑

Further reading

Atkinson, P. and Coffey, A. (2011) Analysing documentary realities, in D. Silverman (ed.) *Qualitative Research* (3rd edn). London: Sage.

As Silverman explains in his introduction, 'Paul Atkinson and Amanda Coffey draw upon ethnomethodology's study of "the documentary method of interpretation" and literary accounts of narrative and genre. They apply these contemporary concepts to the documents through which organisations represent themselves and the records and documentary data they accumulate.'

Bowen, G.A. (2009) Document analysis as a qualitative research method, *Qualitative Research Journal*, 9 (2): pp. 27–40.

This article is aimed at research beginners and examines the function of documents as a data source and discusses document analysis in the context of actual research experiences.

Noakes, L. and Wincup, E. (2004) Using documentary evidence in qualitative research, in *Criminological Research: Understanding Qualitative Methods* (pp. 106–20). London: Sage.
Chapter 7 explores the value of the written word and other forms of documentary evidence to the qualitative researcher in the context of criminological research.

8 Using Social Media in Research

INTRODUCTION

This chapter looks at the influence of social media and specifically how it can be harnessed for academic research. You probably use social media to keep in touch with your friends and to share experiences and post content, but have you considered how it could be a source of data or information for your research and enable you to network with other researchers? In this chapter, you will find:

- How to use social media as a research tool.
- How to choose the right social media tools based on the goals and aims of your research project.
- An introduction to using blogs, open community research sites, crowdsourcing, LinkedIn, Twitter, Facebook, YouTube and more.
- How the Social Media 3 Cs – Community, Content and Conversation – can feed into your research.
- How to achieve a balance between social and work – avoiding common pitfalls when on social media.

Key terms

> "Socia Media is the term commonly given to Internet and mobile-based channels and tools that allow users to interact with each other and share opinions and content. As the name implies, social media involves the building of communities or networks and encouraging participation and engagement."
>
> (Chartered Institute of Public Relations 2011: 4)

Since Facebook was launched in 2003, the number of people connecting through social media has grown at an astonishing rate. According to visual.ly, which specializes in presenting data through images, it took television 13 years to reach 50 million people. Facebook reached that number in 3½ years. In 2012, the addictive game puzzle video game 'Angry Birds' achieved 50 million users in 35 days after it launched its mobile phone version.

In 2013, the online encyclopedia Wikipedia identified that there were over 200 social networking sites. If the use of Facebook expands at its present rate of 40 per cent each year, there will be over 2 billion active Facebook users by the time this book is published. Twitter, the microblogging tool with a character limit for 'tweets' (messages), has over 600 million users worldwide, with an average of 500 million tweets sent each day and a total of over 800 billion tweets sent since Twitter was formed in 2006. LinkedIn, the professional networking site, has over 225 million members in over 200 countries and territories. It seems that we have an unlimited need online to play games, have conversations, to make friends and belong to groups.

You may be asking yourself: 'Interesting though these statistics are, how can I use Facebook, Twitter, LinkedIn and other social media tools in my research?' If so, you will be joining a small but steadily growing number of academics exploring how the use of social media can contribute to the research process. The publication of information about how to use social media for research by universities and online conversations about how to apply social networking to the research process are relatively recent phenomena.

In her blog on the London School of Economics website, Sarah-Louise Quinnell (2011) is in no doubt of the value of social networking:

> "Social media isn't the future of research, it is the present and we need to embrace it. I was the first person in my department to actively engage with social media and digital research methods to conduct my PhD research ... It also enabled me to increase the impact of my research

> through the different audiences I could reach through blogging and tweeting.″

Social media and the research process

Academic recognition that social media can play a significant role in research is growing. Alampi (2012) believes that 'Social Media platforms can inform every step of the research process'. Cann *et al.* assert that, whereas searching for information via search engines such as Google 'can provide you with answers only to the questions you ask ... social media can also provide you with intelligently-filtered information that helps to stimulate new questions, in the same way that a conversation with a colleague might' (Cann *et al.* 2011: 9). They advise that 'the process of building, curating and filtering useful networks is a skill which needs to be practised' (2011: 9), and that being an active member of relevant communities is very important in social media, as it is in academic discourse. The National Centre for Social Research (2013) points out in its blog that researchers were not 'predicting the demise of traditional methods such as the social survey. They were trying to work out what social media research can add to ... existing ... methodological tools and what research problems may be better tackled by social media methods.' Minocha and Petros suggest that researchers should focus on both a social and a digital strategy:

> ″Developing a **social strategy** implies deciding with whom, what, how and when you would communicate to share, learn and create and enhance relationships with others. A **digital strategy** implies the technologies to achieve the social strategy.″
>
> (Minocha and Petros 2012: 14; emphasis added)

When I use the terms 'social media' and 'social digital' in this chapter, by 'social' I mean the creation and maintenance of relationships with others; by 'media' I refer to the ways in which messages and information are stored and sent to other people; and by 'digital' I mean the technologies – the tools – that enable us to communicate in this way with others. An example would be a message to other researchers inviting them to exchange ideas ('social') via a LinkedIn group that we had set up ('media') and sent via a LinkedIn app on a mobile phone ('digital'). Of course, there are times when the terminology will overlap, and distinguishing between the three functions is not always this clear-cut.

Social media tools

As with any research methodology, it is important to ask yourself the following questions when you are considering using social media in research:

- What are your goals?
- Who do you want to reach?
- Why do you want to reach them?
- Which digital tool or platform will be most effective in enabling you to reach your goals?
- If you already spend time each day using social media for personal reasons, how much time are you able to set aside each day to use social media for research?
- At what time of day will you engage on social media? (Take into account time differences if you are communicating globally.)

As you know, it is easy to lose track of time online. Plan your online research activity as you would any other aspect of research. You need to be in control of it rather than allowing it to control you.

You will need to consider two key factors when you use social media for research:

1. Your profile and how you appear to other people who may be interested in engaging with you. This can be a relatively brief profile such as a Facebook identity or a very detailed profile as in LinkedIn.
2. The groups or communities to which you belong.

If you are going to use social media to contact other researchers or academics, it is very important that you update your profile so that, whatever social media platforms you use to share your research, you present a professional view. This can be welcoming and friendly but needs to convey that you are serious about your academic work and want to connect with others in a similar position. Consider your profile photo too. It should be engaging but professional. You should be smiling, looking directly into the camera and the image should be either a headshot or head and shoulder photo, with your shoulders turned slightly sideways. You should also be wearing clothes you would wear to go to an interview or smart–casual dress. So I'm afraid that 'selfie' you took of yourself at your birthday party just won't do. It may cost you, but a professionally taken headshot is worth every penny. If you don't believe me, have a look through the profile photos and profile descriptions of your followers and contacts and ask yourself, 'If I didn't know this person, would I be encouraged to discuss my research with them?' If the answer is no, what are the reasons for this? Have a look at my LinkedIn profile at www.linkedin.com/in/stevewaters1 – after many attempts, my photo was taken professionally and I received advice from a social media consultant on how to structure my profile. I am sure that I could make further improvements but I think it does the job.

In addition to the creation of personal profiles, sites like Facebook and LinkedIn also allow members to create business or professional pages. You may be able to find pages with members who share your interest in research or, if you are fortunate, who are researching the same topic or field. You could even start a page of your own, although the job of gaining members and ensuring that the page remains active would be your responsibility, at least in the early stages. LinkedIn enables similar networking through its groups. You may find groups to join which are relevant to your research interests or you can start one of your own and invite your contacts.

The value of engaging online can be summarized in the three Cs: Community, Content and Conversations. In your everyday, offline life you may be a member of a number of different communities, such as your family and friends; if you are a parent, your children's school; and, of course, your fellow research students. When you talk to someone online it will be because you believe that you have something to say, the equivalent of having a conversation in the physical world. And, whether you are online or offline, you will either initiate conversation or join in with conversations that other people have started. The value of belonging to a social network lies in what you are prepared to contribute as well as what you gain by 'listening' to other people's conversations. If you are a lone researcher, you can feel isolated; having online relationships and belonging to online communities can help to overcome this.

In the next section, I look in detail at the various ways social media can help you in your research. Regrettably, it is outside the scope of this chapter to explain how to set up accounts on the various platforms and sites. You will find detailed instructions on each site, usually by clicking on the 'Help' button or by googling 'How to …' information that has been posted on the Internet by users, social media experts and social digital companies.

Using social media in research

Blogs

The word 'blog' is a shortening of 'web logs'; a **blog** therefore is a log – a kind of diary, record or journal – published on the web. It consists of entries ('posts'), usually of up to 1000 words, published in date order with the most recent posts appearing at the top of the page. Blogs can be set up free on sites like www.blogger.com or www.tumblr.com or on Wordpress, which is also a free website construction site. Tumblr is a microblogging platform and social networking website that enables you to post multimedia and other content, such as details of your research, to a short-form blog. Users can follow other users' blogs, as well as make their blogs private. Most of the Tumblr website's features can be accessed from the 'dashboard' interface, where you have the option to post your own content and read posts by people who are following blogs on the site.

Alternatively, some websites invite you to submit your own blog and give you a link to do so. Some blog writers or 'bloggers' update their blogs regularly, sometimes daily. Unlike a personal diary, a blog usually includes a discussion around a topic and can also provide readers with content or information. Blogs are easily found by Google, so they are a good way of getting your name and content recognized. There is a very good description of how to start a blog and what to include in it at http://www.startbloggingonline.com/ (StartBloggingOnline.com 2013). Blogs have a range of functions. They can be a source of data, such as in a research study of how online communities use blogs to exchange political ideas, and this function is described further in Chapter 11, or they can be used as a kind of public diary, as described below, to let people in your community know what you are doing, to share ideas or to offer and gain support from other people in your research community.

Research blogs can be used to inform your readers about the progress of your research project and to invite comments and ideas. They can also be used for publishing project updates and for linking to similar content in blogs written by other researchers. Unlike publishing conventional academic research findings, which include references to other researchers by citing their name and the date of publication, blogs include hyperlinks to other relevant websites/blogs. Clicking on the hyperlink takes you out of the blog you are reading to another relevant blog or website. Social media sites such as Facebook, Twitter and, as you will see later, Google+ can provide readers with links to blogs, connecting personal networking with research.

Cameron Neylon, a biophysicist, explains how he became involved in writing a blog:

> "I got interested in the more general ideas of effective communication on the web and found there was a community already out there. I wanted to be able to record my own ideas in this space in a way that was 'native' to it and to engage with that community, so blogging was a natural course to take."
>
> (quoted in Cann *et al.* 2011: 10)

A good example of a site that is devoted to blogs about academic research can be found at http://blogs.lse.ac.uk/impactofsocialsciences/ (LSE 2013), a London School of Economics site that is called 'Impact of Social Sciences: Maximizing the Impact of Academic Research'.

One researcher summarized her blog in the following way:

> "a place that I can keep it [*sic*] updated with the research and events in my specialized area ... it is like having a web presence for my research that I can myself edit ... I have kept it very simple ... a blog for me is a platform to show that the work is in progress ... WordPress is easy to use; once you have set up the parameters, you are ready to go."
>
> (quoted in Minocha and Petros 2012: 18)

www.academia.edu

This is an open and free **academic research community website**. Members upload their research to share their findings and to ask fellow academics to comment on their drafts, to offer advice or to review research studies that they have completed. The site allows you to search for relevant research papers that have been uploaded. The site also enables you to ask questions of those who follow you on the site, to seek their advice or to make suggestions about your research. This is very useful if you are researching alone. The site has a higher character limit than Twitter and therefore you have more room to ask specific questions.

www.figshare.com

This is also an open community research site, mainly targeted at scientists, although other research disciplines are represented. Like academia.edu, Figshare enables individual researchers to upload research papers or smaller-scale findings and to make them available online and searchable. A useful feature of this site is that it presents the full citation or reference in a box from which you can open or download the research article.

Crowdsourcing

> "Crowdsourcing is the practice of obtaining needed services, ideas, or content by soliciting contributions from a large group of people, and especially from an online community, rather than from traditional employees or suppliers. This process is often used to subdivide tedious work or to fund-raise start-up companies and charities, and can also occur offline. It combines the efforts of numerous self-identified volunteers or part-time workers, where each contributor of their own initiative adds a small portion to the greater result. Crowdsourcing is distinguished from outsourcing in that the work comes from an undefined public rather than being commissioned from a specific, named group."
>
> http://en.wikipedia.org/wiki/Crowdsourcing

Wikipedia explains that the *Oxford English Dictionary* may provide one of the earliest examples of **crowdsourcing**. Seventy years ago, an open request was made for contributions by volunteers to identify words in the English language and provide example quotations of their usage. Over 6 million submissions were received, by post prior to the advent of the Internet, and then online. Wikipedia, launched in 2001, is the most prolific recent example of crowdsourcing. Formed from a combination of the Hawaiian word 'wiki' meaning 'quick' and the 'pedia' from 'encyclopedia', Wikipedia describes itself as:

> "a collaboratively edited, multilingual, free Internet encyclopedia supported by the non-profit Wikimedia Foundation. Wikipedia's 30 million articles in 287 languages, including over 4.3 million in the English language, are written collaboratively by volunteers around the world. Almost all of its articles can be edited by anyone having access to the site. It is the largest and most popular general reference work on the Internet … having an estimated 365 million readers worldwide."
>
> http://en.wikipedia.org/wiki/W%C4%B0K%C4%B0PED%C4%B0A

So, how can crowdsourcing help you as a researcher? At the outset, it's important to say that if you are not active on social media networks, crowdsourcing is not for you. But then, I'm guessing that if you were not interested in developing your use of social media for research, you wouldn't be reading this chapter. Crowdsourcing only works when you have already built up a wide audience, for example by taking part in Twitter conversations or retweeting other people's tweets to show that you agree or like their comment, or by clicking 'Like' on Facebook updates or to show your appreciation for a Facebook page, or by inviting and accepting friend requests. If you intend to crowdsource for professional reasons associated with your research, it is also important that you have a LinkedIn profile so that fellow researchers and interested academics can check your credentials.

Let us suppose that you want to find out how other students use social media in their research. If the idea of crowdsourcing on the web to seek the views of researchers seems to be overwhelming because you just don't know who to target, focus on the research community that you are already a member of – your university. Find out if online research communities already exist and post your request to them. If your tutor has a Facebook or Linkedin account, become their friend on Facebook or connect with them on LinkedIn before you send your request to your followers or connections. Ask your tutor to look out for your post and forward it on to his or her followers and contacts. Remember that every individual within a research community, or any other community for that matter, has their own contacts, who in turn have their contacts, and so on. So, if your request also asks members of a community to forward your message to anyone else who might be able to help, the potential number of people who may contact you increases exponentially.

Linkedin (www.linkedin.com)

As we have seen, LinkedIn is a **social networking** site for professionals. One of its main features is the creation of a detailed LinkedIn profile, which is a kind of online CV but with a more personal touch. Some employers ask for résumés that follow the same structure as LinkedIn profiles. Unlike Facebook, which is mainly about your social persona, LinkedIn focuses on your academic and professional life. Members of LinkedIn invite other members to connect with them and, once the contact is accepted, users can send each other messages within the LinkedIn network. You can also join groups or set up a group of your own; for example, you could form a research interest group around your research topic. LinkedIn's user demographic has been estimated at people aged 30–40; this may be an advantage, as it could enable you to connect with more experienced researchers.

Here are some tips to ensure that you use LinkedIn effectively:

- Ensure your profile is as near 100 per cent complete as possible.
- Upload a good quality photo – as advised earlier in this chapter, it is worth getting a professional headshot or using a head and shoulders image.

- Start your own research group if a relevant group doesn't exist.
- Recommend people for their research skills (but only if you really know their work).
- Link your email contacts to your LinkedIn profile – this will enable you to see which of your contacts are also on LinkedIn so that you can connect with them.

Twitter

If you have a Twitter account, you will probably have used it to initiate, retweet or join in with conversations or to share views on current issues. The use of the hashtag (#) to identify conversation topics makes it possible to find other academics that are 'talking' about similar research areas to your own. Alternatively, you can start a conversation or ask a question by creating a new hashtag. As Twitter is used by researchers to build relationships with the research community, the University of Exeter (2013) offers timely advice: 'Remember that your Twitter account is an ambassador for your research and the University so avoid getting involved in sensitive subjects that could damage your reputation' (http://www.exeter.ac.uk/staff/web/socialmedia/).

Salma Patel (2011) suggests several ways in which researchers can use Twitter. The first – join the research community – can be done by following the conversation #phdchat. As the name suggests, the hashtag is used mostly by doctoral researchers. Her other suggestions include:

- Share links to publications and research.
- Keep in touch with the 'outside world' – other researchers, colleagues, conferences.
- Ask your community for help.
- Network – follow other researchers, recruit participants for your research studies. Ask followers to retweet your messages to their network of followers to increase the number of people you are able to reach.
- Share your experiences – other people will do the same.
- Keep in touch with what is going on in your field or research area.
- Collaborate with other researchers to ask for their advice on research methodology you are intending to use.

Gulliver (2012) suggests looking for hashtags that may relate to your area of research. You can also create one of your own or learn which hashtags are regularly used for your research field or topic and use them to create or join a network. As Gulliver advises, 'Build an audience first, and the audience will follow if they like you and will then listen once you have something to pitch.' She makes the point that it is important to convey your personality as well as to post what you are doing academically. Engagement and building a relationship is vital:

> "Thanks to Twitter, I have been sent copies of obscure articles much faster than I would have received them from an interlibrary loan. I just need to tweet 'Does anyone have access to the Journal of X, 1972?' and within an hour someone will have e-mailed me the PDF. It's tremendously useful."
>
> (Gulliver 2012)

Facebook (www.facebook.com)

Facebook was the global social network of choice for young people, but is now used by people of all ages who want to interact with friends and family online. In fact, young people are migrating from Facebook to WhatsApp (bought by Facebook in 2014) and SnapChat because their parents are on Facebook! The power of Facebook prompted interest in its use for professional networking. Facebook members will get friend requests from their work colleagues and managers as well as from their personal friends or friends of friends. So, how can you use Facebook in your research? The simple answer is to build relationships with fellow researchers and academics who are researching the same topic or the same field so that you can share ideas and support and help one another. Sundberg (2013), on the site 'The Undercover Recruiter' (www.theundercoverrecruiter.com), addresses Facebook members who would like to use it for professional purposes. The following points have been informed by his thoughtful advice:

- Check your privacy settings. If your Facebook profile is set so that everyone can see everything, personal messages and images that you post to your friends can be seen by academic contacts. Build different lists of contacts so you can target relevant and appropriate comments to each list (compare the use of circles on Google+). Amusing though it may be, it is unlikely that you will create a good impression if a potential academic contact sees messages to your friends about you making a fool of yourself at a stag or hen do during the weekend!
- As for your LinkedIn and Twitter accounts, make sure that your profile picture looks professional but friendly. A headshot or a

head and shoulders shot is best. A 'selfie' taken by you holding your mobile at arm's length as you look in the mirror is definitely not going to create the professional image you are seeking to convey!

- Complete your personal profile by adding the name of your university or organization. Make sure you state what you do, rather than who you are – for example, 'I am a PhD student, researching the use of social media in qualitative research'.
- When you update your status (i.e. post/write a comment), try to share something informative and of interest to your research network (e.g. a new book that has recently been published or a link to an article or business or a pertinent quotation).
- Consider using Facebook groups to bring people together who have similar research interests to you by creating a network.
- Think about setting up a Facebook page to promote yourself as a researcher. Give yourself a professional profile and image.

The University of Exeter (2013) gives sound advice via its blog on the language you should adopt on your professional Facebook page, which applies equally to all the social networks you use:

> "The content that you post should be professional in tone and grammatically correct, but should avoid overly formal language. Talk to your followers as you would talk to them face-to-face in a professional setting."
>
> http://www.exeter.ac.uk/staff/web/socialmedia/linkedin/

Make sure your profile on social media sites presents a welcoming but professional image. Have your headshot taken by a photographer. Describe yourself as a researcher and, in a few words, describe what you are researching.

YouTube

YouTube is often visited to access humorous, embarrassing or innovative videos (see Blendtec (2010), for example, at http://www.youtube.com/watch?v=lAl28d6tbko, if you would like a short break from your research!). However, there are also a huge number of videos on

YouTube that are aimed at the professional researcher. For example, the video at http://www.youtube.com/watch?v=SfxrrMVzXK0 (Arguadiola 2012) identifies the most important considerations when writing a literature review. When you find a video that is useful, you can 'subscribe' to that video, which makes it easy to find again. You will also be notified of new YouTube videos from that creator who is likely to produce videos on similar topics.

Summary

I hope this chapter has given you an overview of how you might use social media to let other researchers know who you are and what you are doing, to build contacts with fellow researchers and to help you to organize and structure your research. Social media is hugely powerful and you can harness some of that power to make you a more effective researcher and to save you time and expense, especially during data collection. Although the potential of social media is unarguable, as with all of your research activities you need to manage your time effectively – social media activity can be addictive and hours can slip by almost unnoticed. If you get it right, you will be able to counteract the isolation that many lone researchers face and be able to receive and give advice to other researchers.

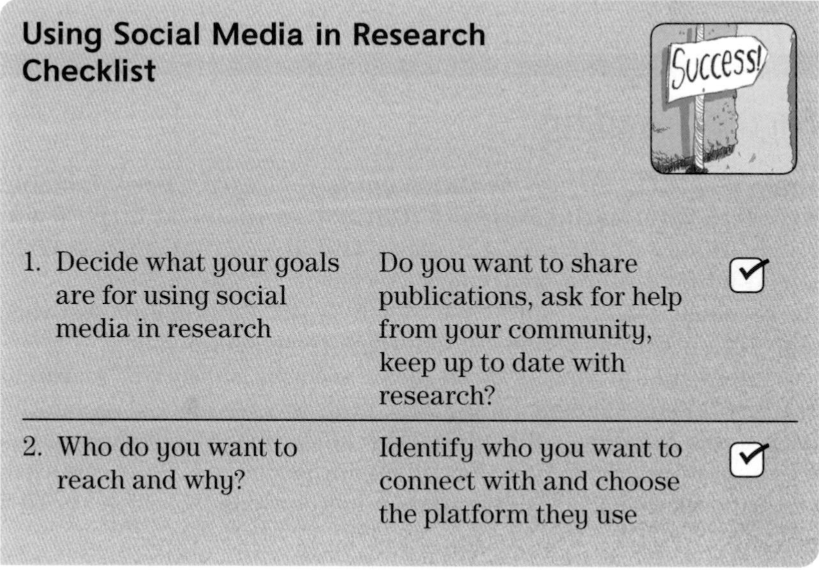

Using Social Media in Research Checklist

1. Decide what your goals are for using social media in research	Do you want to share publications, ask for help from your community, keep up to date with research?	☑
2. Who do you want to reach and why?	Identify who you want to connect with and choose the platform they use	☑

3. Which tool or platform is appropriate?	Different platforms offer different functionality – explore your options	☑
4. How much time do you want to spend on social media for research?	Balance the time you want to spend on social media for personal reasons with the time you spend on social media for research purposes	☑
5. Social media is about 3 Cs: Community, Content and Conversations	Consider how the 3 Cs can contribute to your research	☑
6. Make sure that you have a professional profile as a researcher on LinkedIn	Consider whether your profile on social media gives a professional impression	☑

Further reading

Gray, C. (2011) *Social media: a guide for researchers*. London: Research Information Network [Online]. Available at http://www.rin.ac.uk/our-work/communicating-and-disseminating-research/social-media-guide-researchers [Accessed 10 March 2014].

As its name suggests, the UK-based Research Information Network (RIN) is a research community that supports the development of effective information strategies. It is targeted at a wide audience of 'researchers, institutions, funders, information professionals and everyone who plays a role in the research information landscape'. The guide explains the range of social media tools and platforms that are at the researcher's disposal and includes case studies. It is downloadable from the RIN website.

Poynter, R. (2010) *The Handbook of Online and Social Media Research*. Chichester: Wiley.
Although the focus of Poynter's book is market research, there is a great deal of information about online research methodology that is generic or can be adapted to other research disciplines. The book also challenges conventional notions of academic research, which has been slow to adapt to the online world and social media.

Thomas, M. (2012) *Social Media Made Simple: How to Avoid Social Media Suicide*. Berkshire: AppleTree Publishing.
Mary Thomas's title summarizes the content of her book perfectly. This is a jargon-free and clear explanation of social media and the range of platforms you might use. It also includes templates that you can adapt to help you to plan your research.

9 Designing and Administering Questionnaires

INTRODUCTION

Designing a questionnaire is a skilled task requiring careful planning and thought. This chapter aims to equip you with a basic but thorough introduction to designing a questionnaire, including compilation of the questions through piloting, distribution and analysis of the completed questionnaires either in print on online. This chapter contains:

- An introduction to the use of the questionnaire to gather research data, looking at how online tools such as Survey Monkey can help you to design and structure it.
- Guidance on identifying what information you need to find out and the range of question types to consider.
- Advice on avoiding pitfalls such as ambiguity, imprecision, double questions and making assumptions.
- Ideas for the visual presentation of your questionnaire.
- Instructions for drawing up a representative sample, piloting and distributing questionnaires, including your responsibility for informing respondents how the data you acquire will be stored and used.

Key terms

Operationalizable	161	Likert scale	163

You will only reach the stage of designing a questionnaire after you have done all the preliminary work on planning, consulting and deciding exactly what you need to find out. Only then will you know whether a questionnaire is suitable for the purpose and is likely to be a better way of collecting information than interviews or observation, for example, or whether it will be more effective if used in addition to other data collection methods. Whatever its purpose, you will need to ensure you produce a well-designed questionnaire that will give you the information you need, that will be acceptable to your respondents and that will give you no problems at the analysis and interpretation stage.

Whether you are designing a Word document or an online survey by using dedicated software such as Survey Monkey, it is harder to produce really good questionnaires than might be imagined. They are fiendishly difficult to design and should never be considered by anyone who believes that 'anyone who can write plain English and has a modicum of common sense can produce a good questionnaire' (Oppenheim 1992: 1). Of course, as Oppenheim says, common sense and the ability to write plain English are always a plus in any walk of life, but designing a questionnaire requires rather more. It requires discipline in the selection of questions, in question writing, in the design, piloting, distribution and return of the questionnaires. What is more, thought has to be given to how responses will be analysed at the design stage, not after questionnaires have been submitted or returned. (The same point was made in Chapter 6, where you were advised that before using IBM's SPSS Statistics software to analyse data, you must plan in advance the nature of the data that you wish to acquire from respondents.) If you send out questionnaires and just hope for the best, you may find the returns impossible to deal with.

Survey Monkey (www.surveymonkey.com) is the most popular and versatile online questionnaire and survey tool, with over 1½ million surveys completed online each day in 2014 and over 16 million users worldwide. The free version is more than adequate for 100-hour projects and, unless the research is heavily dependent on quantitative data, for most PhD dissertations too. Survey Monkey helps you to design the questionnaire, taking you through the process step-by-step and gives you more than 20 different templates to choose from. With the free plan, you get up to 10 questions per survey, 15 available question types, up to 100 responses, and the facility to collect responses by weblink, email and Facebook. Questionnaires are integrated with a mailing facility, so you only have to add the email addresses of your respondents to the Survey Monkey template and click 'send'. You can track responses and display results graphically, which enables you to present your results professionally in your research report.

A piece of advice – consider planning and writing or typing your questionnaire before designing it in Survey Monkey. It is possible to structure the questions and produce the design simultaneously within Survey Monkey, but you need to be able to juggle both while also being able to keep the overall framework of the questionnaire in your mind. You may be able to do all of this, but I struggle to balance all these factors at the same time. It is also important to trial the questionnaire to find out if participants will have difficulty understanding the questions or in following its structure. Enlist the help of family and friends by sending them the pilot questionnaire and asking them to respond via email.

If you do not intend your questionnaire to be completed online, you can still design it in Survey Monkey and print a hard copy or reproduce it as a Word document.

Exactly what do you need to find out?

Your preliminary reading and your research plan will have identified important areas for investigation. Go back to your hypothesis or to the objectives and decide which questions you need to ask to achieve those objectives. You will need several attempts at wording in order to remove ambiguity, to achieve the degree of precision necessary to ensure that respondents understand exactly what you are asking, to check that your language is jargon-free, to decide which question types to use and to ensure that you will be able to classify and analyse responses. Guidance on analysis is provided in Chapter 13; before you complete your questionnaire design, you should read this chapter carefully. Time spent on preparation will save many hours of work later on.

Question types

It is as well to be aware of the advantages and limitations of different question types, to be as sure as you can be that each item in your questionnaire will produce the information you need, and that each will produce analysable responses. Different people give them different names, but most will include some or all of Youngman's (1982) list of seven question types:

Verbal/ Open	The expected response is a word, a phrase or an extended comment. Responses to verbal questions can produce useful information but analysis can present problems. Some form of content analysis may be required for verbal material unless the information obtained is to be used for special purposes (see Chapter 7). For example, you might believe it necessary to give respondents the opportunity to provide their own views on the topic being researched – or to raise a grievance. You might wish to use questions as an introduction to a follow-up interview, or in pilot interviews where it is important to know which aspects of the topic are of particular importance to the respondents. Well-structured questions will not present so many problems at the analysis stage.
List	A list of items is offered, any of which may be selected. For example, a question may ask about qualifications and the respondent may have several of the qualifications listed.
Category	The response is one only of a given set of categories. For example, if age categories are provided (20–29, 30–39, etc.), the respondent can only fit into one category. Take care not to use overlapping ages such as 20–29 and 29–39.
Ranking	In ranking questions, the respondent is asked to place something in rank order. For example, the respondent might be asked to place qualities or characteristics in order.
Quantity	The response is a number (exact or approximate), giving the quantity of some characteristic.
Grid	A table or grid is provided to record answers to two or more questions at the same time.
Scale	Various styles of scaling devices can be used in questionnaires, but they require careful handling (more about scales in Chapter 13).

Students have discovered that once they have tried out and become familiar with different ways of analysing and presenting questionnaire responses to list, category, ranking, scale, quantity or grid questions, they are able to select the most appropriate format when they come to the stage of designing and analysing data in their project.

Question wording

Ambiguity and imprecision

Words that have a common meaning to you may suggest something different to other people, so you need to consider what your questions might mean to different respondents. For example, suppose you wanted to find out how much time mature students spend studying. You ask: 'How much time, on average, do you spend studying?' You invite your respondent to tick the box for 'a great deal', 'a certain amount' or 'not much'. What will you do with the responses? What will they mean? 'A great deal' may mean something different to student A than to student B. In any case, students may spend 20 hours a week at some times of the year but probably not more than four at other times. What is 'average'? If you really wish to know how much time students spend studying, you will need to find different ways of putting the question. When you think about this topic, you may decide you have to ask students to keep a diary for a specific period of time. You may need to specify the time spent studying different subjects. It will all depend on exactly what it is you need to know. Once you are clear about that, you will be able to word your questions sufficiently precisely to ensure that they mean the same to all respondents.

Precision in wording is important. Remember that concepts such as 'satisfaction' and 'class' can't actually be observed. There are many 'satisfaction questions' in the questionnaires I receive from banks, credit card companies, hotels, shops, hospitals, financial advisers – and many others. 'How satisfied are you with . . .?', or even 'Are you satisfied with . . .?', with an instruction to tick the 'yes/no' box. Satisfaction is a concept and, as we can't actually observe concepts, we have to find different ways in which they might be observable, and therefore measurable. Rose and Sullivan provide a useful example of ways in which the concept of 'class' might be measurable. They write that:

> "If we wish to understand something about class (a concept and therefore . . . not observable), what can we observe in the world which

> manifests class? That is, what indicators can be used for class so that we can obtain data about class? This is the essence of the measurement problem and when we link an unobservable concept with an observable indicator we are producing operationalizations."
>
> (Rose and Sullivan 1996: 12–13)

They explain that **operationalizable** refers to 'the rules we use to link the language of theory (concepts) to the language of research (indicators)'. So, what indicators of 'class' or 'satisfaction' might there be? Think about it. Ask friends, colleagues, family members for measurable alternatives, and as always, go back to the beginning and ask yourself, what do you really need to know?

Assumptions

If respondents are confused, irritated or even offended, they may leave the item blank or even abandon the questionnaire. You want answers to all questions if at all possible, so try to avoid confusion and watch out for assumptions. Consider the following question:

> "Which type of school does your child attend?"

The respondent is asked to tick the appropriate box from a long list of types of school. The researcher has assumed the respondent has one child, but what if she has no children? Does she ignore this question? What if she has more than one child – one in an infant school, one in a high school, and so on – what does she do then? Does she put the number of children in the appropriate box? Are you prepared for a category response, or had you intended this to be a list? It may not matter, but if your analysis is planned on the basis of a category response, you will create for yourself extra trouble when list responses are given. Incidentally, your respondents might well ask why you want this information. Is the information essential for your study? If not, leave it out.

Memory

Memory plays tricks. If you were asked to say which television programmes you saw last week, could you remember everything? Could you be sure that one particular programme was last week – or was it the week before? Consider the following question, which appeared in a questionnaire concerned with parents' education:

> "What subjects did you study at school?"

If respondents left school recently, they may be able to remember quite clearly, but if they left school 20 or more years ago, they may find it difficult to remember. If they do not include English in the list of subjects, would that mean that no English was studied or did they just forget to include it? Consider what information you really need. If you want to know which of a list of subjects that respondents studied, you might decide it would be better to provide a list of subjects that can be ticked. That way, you would ensure that main subjects were covered – but the type of question will depend on the type of information needed.

Knowledge

Take care with questions that ask for information the students may not know or may not have readily to hand. For example, it may seem reasonable to ask mature students what the criteria are for allocating students to tutorial groups. But the likelihood is that they will not know; and if respondents have to search for information, they may put the questionnaire to one side until they have time – and forget all about it.

Double questions

It may seem obvious to remind you that double questions should never be asked, but it's easy to overlook the following type of question:

> "Do you attend research methods and statistics courses?"

Would the answer 'yes' mean that you attend both, or one? If you need to know, the question should be divided into:

> Do you attend research methods courses?
>
> *and*
>
> Do you attend statistics courses?

It is common to come across questionnaires with double questions, particularly in hotel feedback forms, such as:

> The management is always looking for ways of improving the service to guests. We should be grateful if you would circle the appropriate number below and return the completed form to reception.
>
> How would you rate the service and cleanliness of the hotel?

Excellent	Very good	Good	Satisfactory	Less than satisfactory
5	4	3	2	1

I found this in the bedroom of a large chain hotel and all the subsequent questions followed a similar format. Assuming any of the guests bothered to complete the questionnaire, I can imagine that responses to 2–5 would be grouped together and would therefore provide 'evidence' that 95 per cent of guests were very satisfied with the service and cleanliness of the hotel. The conclusion that would be drawn from the results would be misleading. The double question is obvious but there are other issues in this item. Perhaps you considered the service was good in parts. Helpful, pleasant and efficient receptionists, a maid who did a remarkably good job, but the porter was surly and the restaurant service appalling. As far as cleanliness was concerned . . . well, I won't go on.

Likert scales (originally devised by R. Likert in 1932) of the kind in this hotel questionnaire are devices used to discover strength of feeling or attitude towards a given statement or series of statements, and the implication here is that the higher the category chosen, the greater the strength of agreement, but care has to be taken not to read too much into these ranked scales. They are usually, though not always, ranked on a 3-, 5- or 7-point scale and ask respondents to indicate rank order of agreement or disagreement by circling the appropriate number. They certainly arrange individuals or objects from the highest to the lowest, but the intervals between each may not be the same. We cannot say that the highest rating (5 in the hotel example) is five times higher than the lowest (which is 1). All that can be said is that they indicate order. In spite of these limitations, Likert scales can be useful, as long as the wording is clear, there are no double questions, and no unjustified claims are made about the findings.

Leading questions

It is not always easy to spot a leading question, but the use of emotive language or the way a question is put can influence respondents to answer questions in one way. For example:

> "Do you not agree that mature students should have the right to express their views in tutorials?"

Well, it might be difficult for students to answer 'no' in response to that question.

Presuming questions

Presuming questions are often a source of error in questionnaires. When they are included, it is often because the researcher holds strong views about a subject and overlooks the fact that everyone may not feel the same way. For example:

> "Does the university/college/hospital make adequate provision for counselling?"

Is that for students, patients, staff – someone else? You may think all institutions should provide a counselling service. But what if your respondents do not? What if they do not really know what a counselling service does? In its present form, 'adequate' is meaningless. There is a presumption in the question that a counselling service is necessary, and that makes the question invalid.

Hypothetical questions

Look out for questions that will provide only useless responses. Most hypothetical questions come into this category. For example:

> "If you had no family responsibilities and plenty of money, would you travel around the world and live in 5-star hotels?"

But, a respondent might answer, 'I do have family responsibilities. I have no money and never shall have as far as I can see, so what's the point of thinking about it?'

Offensive questions and questions covering sensitive issues

It goes without saying that questions that may cause offence should be removed. If you really need information on what might be regarded by some respondents as sensitive issues, you will need to take extra care in the wording and positioning of questions. Some researchers think it is better to place such questions towards the end of the questionnaire, the theory being that if respondents abandon the questionnaire at that point, you at least have answers to all the earlier questions.

Age is often considered to be in the sensitive category and, rather than asking respondents to give their exact age, it may be better to ask them to tick a box to indicate age category (perhaps 21 or younger; 22–25; 26–30, and so on). Again, be careful not to have overlapping categories. It's quite common to see age categories listed as 21 or less, 21–25, 25–30, and so on.

If you are using numerical ranges in questionnaires to place the respondents in categories, take care not to overlap them, e.g. 'What is your age?' 21–30, 30–40, 40–50. This will make it impossible to allocate responses to a specific category.

Appearance and layout

A really well-prepared questionnaire will lose much of its impact if it looks untidy. Look at published surveys that used a questionnaire as one method of data collection and they will give you ideas about layout. Recipients need to be encouraged to read and to answer the questions, and they may be put off by a poorly structured document that has been hastily prepared. There are no hard-and-fast rules about layout, but there are a few common-sense guidelines that will help with appearance.

1. Instructions should be clear (in capitals, or in a different font).
2. Spacing between questions will help the reader and will also help you when you analyse responses.
3. If you want to keep the questionnaire to a limited number of sheets, it may be better to reduce the size of the document or photocopy.
4. Keep any response boxes in line towards the right of the sheet. This will make it easy for respondents and will help you to record responses.
5. Allow space on the right of the sheet for coding, if necessary. (Find out more about coding in Chapter 13.)
6. Look critically at your questionnaire and ask yourself what impression it would give if you were the recipient.
7. Take care over the order of the questions. Leave sensitive issues to later in the questionnaire. Start with straightforward, easy-to-complete questions and move on to the more complex topics.

8 Remember your promise to respect anonymity and confidentiality. Refer back to Chapter 3 if you've forgotten.

9 Keep names off questionnaires if at all possible.

Drawing a sample

The number of respondents in your investigation will necessarily depend on the amount of time you have. If you are working on a 100-hour project, you will not be able to include all mature students in the country. If you have decided to restrict your research to one institution, then you will need to find out how many mature students there are. If there are 100, it's unlikely you will have the time or the means to include them all. You will need to select a sample.

In very large surveys, like the census, techniques are employed to produce a sample that is, as far as possible, representative of the population as a whole. Generalizations can then be made from the findings. In small studies, we have to do the best we can.

All researchers are dependent on the goodwill and availability of respondents, and it will probably be difficult for an individual researcher working on a small-scale project to achieve a true random sample. If that proves to be the case, you may be forced to interview anyone from the total population who is available and willing at the time. Opportunity samples of this kind are generally acceptable, as long as the make-up of the sample is clearly stated and the limitations of the data are realized. However, even in a small study, efforts should be made to select as representative a sample as possible. Say you decide to include 50 per cent of your population. A random sample will give each of the individuals concerned an equal chance of being selected. You may decide to select alternate names on an alphabetical list, the first person being selected by sticking a pin in the paper. Everyone selected may not be willing to participate, and so it is wise to have reserve names available. For example, if the twentieth person refused or was not available, you might have decided beforehand, and as part of your research design, to approach the twenty-first.

There may be occasions when you wish to include representative sub-groups. You perhaps wish to select the appropriate proportion of men and women, of individuals in different age categories or some other sub-group of the target population. If so, you might have the following type of stratification:

Total target population: 100

Number of men: 60. Number of women: 40.

Instead of selecting alternate names, the sample population could be selected on the basis of every second man and every second woman, and so 30 men and 20 women would be selected. If a more scientific approach is required for your project, you will need to read more widely and to acquire a certain amount of statistical expertise.

There is helpful advice on creating an online survey in the Survey Monkey blog at http://blog.surveymonkey.com/blog/2012/04/13/10-online-survey-tips/. Even if you do not intend your questionnaire to be completed online, a great deal of the advice given also applies to offline surveys.

Piloting the questionnaire

All data-gathering instruments should be piloted to test how long it takes recipients to complete them, to check that all questions and instructions are clear, and to enable you to remove any items that do not yield usable data. There is a temptation in a small study to go straight to the distribution stage but, however pressed for time you are, do your best to give the questionnaire a trial run, even if you have to persuade members of your family or friends. Ideally, it should be tried out on a group similar to the one that will form the population of your study, but if that is not possible, make do with whoever you can get. Respondents will tell you how long it took to complete the questionnaire, and if they leave any questions unanswered, you will be able to find out why. The purpose of a pilot exercise is to get the bugs out of the instrument so that respondents in your main study will experience no difficulties in completing it. It also enables you to carry out a preliminary analysis to see whether the wording and format of questions will present any difficulties when the main data is analysed. If you intend to email the questionnaire or use Survey Monkey, use the same distribution method with your pilot volunteers. That way, you will know if there are any problems with the distribution and return method itself.

Ask your volunteers the following questions:

1 How long did it take you to complete?

2 Were the instructions clear?

3 Were any of the questions unclear or ambiguous? If so, would you say which and why?

4 Did you object to answering any of the questions?

5 In your opinion, has any major topic been omitted?

6 Was the layout of the questionnaire clear/attractive?

7 Any comments?

Their responses will enable you to review the questionnaire and amend it if necessary for the main distribution. It will take you some time to achieve a good standard of design and presentation, but if the preparation is sound, it will save you hours and even weeks of work at the analysis stage.

Distribution and return of questionnaires

Remember that under no circumstances can you distribute your questionnaires until you have obtained clearance to proceed from your supervisor, your institution's research committee, ethics committee and any other body that has responsibility for scrutinizing students' topics, project plans and proposed methods of collecting data. In my view, written approval should always be obtained, so never assume it will be 'all right' and that verbal agreement given over a coffee will suffice. It might, but it might not. You need to be sure of your own position. Once you have the necessary approval, you will need to decide how to distribute your questionnaire and what to do about non-response.

There are distinct advantages in being able to give questionnaires to respondents personally. You can explain the purpose of the study and, in some cases, questionnaires can be completed on the spot. You are likely to get better cooperation if you can establish personal contact but, if this is impossible, you will need to investigate other ways of distribution. Permission can sometimes be obtained to distribute through internal mailing systems but it is more likely that you will use the respondents' personal email addresses. If you use Survey Monkey, this is how it will distribute your questionnaires. If all else fails, you may have to mail copies, but postal surveys are expensive and response rates are generally low, so you would only wish to resort to distribution by post if you found it impossible to contact potential respondents by any other means.

Before you distribute your questionnaire, you must obtain permission from your supervisor and check whether you need clearance from any official body such as a research or ethics committee.

The rights of respondents and your rights and responsibilities

As mentioned in Chapter 3, even if you will be meeting respondents face-to-face, it is my view that they should be provided with a written statement about their rights and your responsibilities and the purpose of the research. Make it clear that official approval has been given and say what will be done with the completed questionnaires. Who will see them? Will they be deleted or shredded when you have finished with them or when your report has been examined? If you intend to store them, do you have a good reason for doing so? How long will it be for? And can you guarantee security of the data? Does the collection of data conform to the requirements of the Data Protection Act? If *confidentiality* and *anonymity* are guaranteed, make it clear what you mean by both. Look back at Chapter 3 if you have doubts. Promise what you know you can deliver and nothing more.

If you are not able to distribute your questionnaires face-to-face, a letter will be required, in addition to your statement. The letter can form the body of your email. Take care with the wording of your letter. A letter that is too brusque or too ingratiating can have an adverse effect on response, so show your draft letter to a few friends and ask their opinion. Remember to give the return date, either in the letter or in a prominent position on the questionnaire. Experience has shown that it is unwise to allow too long. If no date is specified or if too long is given, it becomes too easy for potential respondents to put the questionnaire to one side, which often means that it will never be seen again. Two weeks is a reasonable time for completion. Give the precise day and date rather than relying on a polite request for the questionnaire to be submitted or returned in two weeks' time. For some reason, it seems to help to jog memories if the day as well as the date is stated. Include a self-addressed envelope (stamped, if respondents have to return the questionnaire by post).

Non-response

Keep a record of the date questionnaires are distributed and the date they are submitted or returned. Generally, there is a good response at first and then returns slow down. Inevitably, they will not all be submitted or returned by the specified date but if you do not include any method of identification on the questionnaires in order to guarantee anonymity, for example, you will have no way of knowing who has replied and who has not and so there can be no follow-up. Non-response is a problem 'because of the likelihood – repeatedly confirmed in practice – that people who do not return questionnaires differ from those who do' (Moser and Kalton 1971: 267–8). So, if at all possible, some effort should be made to encourage more people to return completed questionnaires.

Opinions vary as to the best time to send out follow-up requests, assuming your guarantees of anonymity and confidentiality will allow follow-ups, but in a limited-time project you will need to write about a week after the original date if you are to complete data collection in the time allocated. In some large projects, a third and even a fourth reminder will be sent, but the number of returns obtained by this process is unlikely to warrant the time and trouble it will involve.

Analysis of data

In an ideal world, it would be best to wait for all questionnaires to be submitted or returned and to glance through all responses before beginning to code and record. In a limited-time project, it may be necessary to begin recording responses as soon as the first questionnaires are submitted or returned. The procedures for analysing and presenting results, described in Chapter 13, may influence the way you structure the questionnaire and word the questions, so before you decide finally on content and format, read Chapter 13 carefully and make sure you read the checklist to this chapter to be sure you have covered all essential tasks.

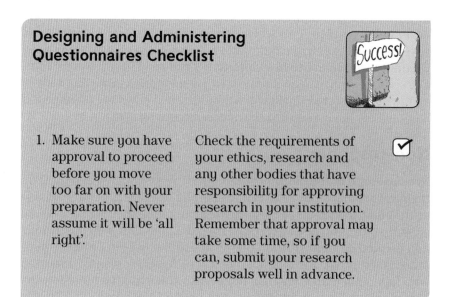

Designing and Administering Questionnaires Checklist

1. Make sure you have approval to proceed before you move too far on with your preparation. Never assume it will be 'all right'.	Check the requirements of your ethics, research and any other bodies that have responsibility for approving research in your institution. Remember that approval may take some time, so if you can, submit your research proposals well in advance.	

2. Decide what you need to know and list all items about which information is required. Ask yourself why you need this information.	Don't clog up your questionnaire with irrelevant items just in case they might come in handy. They won't.	☑
3. Is a questionnaire the best way of obtaining the information?	Consider what information you need. If another method of data collection is likely to be better, consider the alternatives.	☑
4. If you decide a questionnaire will be best, begin to word questions. Write them on separate cards or Post-It® notes, to enable you to order them easily later on.	Remember that concepts can't be measured, so if you really do need to know about respondents' satisfaction with x or y, think of indicators of satisfaction.	☑
5. Check the wording of each question. Is there any ambiguity, imprecision or assumption? Are you asking respondents to remember things? Will they be able to? Are you asking for knowledge respondents may not have? Any double, leading, presuming, hypothetical or offensive questions?	Keep language simple. Don't use words respondents may not understand (that includes technical language) unless you are dealing with a professional group, all of whom understand your linguistic shortcuts.	☑

6. Decide on question type.	Verbal, list, category, ranking, scale, quantity or grid. Each type requires a different analysis (see Chapter 13 for further information about analysis).	☑
7. When you are satisfied that all questions are worded well and of the right type, order them.	It is often better to leave sensitive questions to the end.	☑
8. Write out instructions to be included on the questionnaire.	Respondents must be clear about how they are to answer questions (ticks in boxes, circling items, yes/no?).	☑
9. Instructions must be clearly presented (perhaps in a different font and displayed in a prominent position?). Decide whether you need a right-hand margin for coding.	Consult Chapter 13 about coding and possible ways of analysing responses before you finally decide on the wording, content and structure of your questionnaire.	☑
10. Consider layout and appearance. A scrappy appearance will not encourage respondents to take it seriously.	If using Survey Monkey or a similar online survey tool, use the design tools to make sure it looks attractive on the screen. If designing a questionnaire in Word, take time to format the questionnaire attractively and check that it prints neatly.	☑

11. Decide on your sample.	Try to select a sample that is as close to your final population as possible. If you have to make do with an opportunity sample, say why in your report.	☑
12. Always pilot your questionnaire, no matter how pushed for time you are.	Ideally, it should be sent to people who are similar to your selected sample. However, if that is not possible, ask friends, family or colleagues to help.	☑
13. Try out your methods of analysis. Again, read Chapter 13 before you decide finally on your format.	Even with only five or six completed pilot questionnaires, you will be able to see whether any problems are likely to arise when you analyse the main returns.	☑
14. Make any adjustments to the questionnaire in the light of pilot respondents' comments and your preliminary analysis.	Consider timing. If it took your volunteers too long to complete, decide whether any items might be removed or reworded. Eliminate any items that are not directly related to your topic. Check again that nothing is included merely because it might come in handy at some future stage.	☑
15. Decide how the questionnaire is to be distributed. But before you distribute, check (yet again) that you know what you mean by anonymity	By internal mail? To respondents' personal email addresses? Directing respondents to a URL in an online survey by email? By post? By personally delivering questionnaires to respondents? Also	☑

	and confidentiality – *and* that you make your definitions clear to respondents.	include a letter and a statement of conditions and guarantees explaining respondents' rights and your responsibilities.	
16.	Don't forget to say when you would like questionnaires to be submitted or returned, if possible. Give the preferred day and date.	Keep a record of when questionnaires were distributed and when submitted or returned.	☑
17.	Decide what you are going to do about non-respondents and 'bounce backs', where your email is returned because the address is incorrect, before you distribute the questionnaires.	Remember that you will not be able to send out reminders if all responses are guaranteed to be anonymous. A returned unread email is not the same as a non-response and therefore these categories have to be coded separately for data analysis.	☑
18.	Begin to record responses as soon as completed questionnaires are received. In online questionnaires, such as Survey Monkey, the software compiles the results for you.	You do not have time to wait for stragglers before you begin your analysis of the data. Do this as you go along.	☑
19.	Do not get involved with complicated statistics unless you know what you are doing. Use the	It is perfectly possible to produce a good report without extensive statistical knowledge, as long as the structure of the	☑

tools in your online survey platform or IBM SPSS Statistics to create graphs or tables but ensure that you understand how to present the data you have gathered accurately.

questionnaire is well thought out.

Further reading

Most books dealing with research methods will have a chapter on the design of questionnaires and so the only items listed here are standard texts, most of which should be available in libraries. All provide good advice and will provide a sound foundation if you plan to design a questionnaire as part of your investigation.

Bell, J. and Woolner, P. (2012) Developing and using questionnaires', in A.R.J. Briggs, M. Coleman and M. Morrison (eds) *Research Methods in Educational Leadership and Management* (3rd edn). London: Sage.

Blaxter, L., Hughes, C. and Tight, M. (2010) *How to Research* (4th edn). Maidenhead: Open University Press.
Pages 170–2 provide useful advice about sampling.

Bowling, A. (2009) *Research Methods in Health: Investigating Health and Health Services* (3rd edn). Maidenhead: Open University Press.
Chapter 7 concentrates on methods of sampling. Chapters 11 and 12 consider aspects of questionnaire design such as planning, piloting, questionnaire layout, the covering letter, order of wording and checking the accuracy of responses. Chapter 14 introduces issues relating to the preparation of quantitative data for coding and analysis, all of which is useful.

Cohen, L., Manion, L. and Morrison, K. (2011) Case studies, in *Research Methods in Education* (7th edn). Abingdon: Routledge.

Chapter 8 (Sampling) and Chapter 10 (Validity and reliability) are well worth consulting.

Denscombe, M. (2010) *The Good Research Guide for Small-scale Social Research Projects* (4th edn). Maidenhead: Open University Press.
Chapter 9 (Questionnaires) provides almost 20 pages of useful information, including Internet questionnaires and a checklist for the production of a questionnaire. Denscombe writes well and is invariably worth consulting.

Fogelman, K. and Comber, C. (2007) Surveys and sampling, in A.R.J. Briggs and M. Coleman (eds) *Research Methods in Educational Leadership and Management* (2nd edn). London: Sage.
The authors discuss methods of sampling, including probability, random, systematic, stratified, dimensional and snowball sampling.

Oppenheim, A.N. (1992) *Questionnaire Design, Interviewing and Attitude Measurement*. London: Continuum.
Chapters 1, 2 and 3 provide guidance about survey design and Chapters 7, 8 and 9 cover questionnaire planning, question wording, basic measurement theory – and much more.

Youngman, M.B. (1994) Designing and analysing interviews, in N. Bennett, R. Glatter and R. Levaćič (eds) *Improving Educational Management through Research and Consultancy*. London: Paul Chapman.
The author covers the importance of planning, question specification, questionnaire design, distribution and return. This is an excellent chapter and worth keeping as a permanent record and checklist.

10 Planning and Conducting Interviews

INTRODUCTION

This chapter examines the important tool of the research interview in detail, equipping you with an understanding of how to plan, conduct and record interviews for a research project. This chapter covers:

- The important ethical considerations you need to be aware of before interviewing.
- Assessment of whether the interview is the right tool for your research by understanding its advantages and disadvantages.
- How to word questions and how to use the different styles of interview, including structured and unstructured interviews, group interviews and focus groups.
- How to record interviews so that the information you obtain is relevant and significant to your research.
- Using technologies such as Skype and Google Hangouts to conduct interviews online.
- Being aware of bias and other ethical and practical considerations.

Key terms

Structured interview	179	Focus group	182
Unstructured interview	181		

Advantages and disadvantages of the interview

One major advantage of the interview is its adaptability. A skilful interviewer can follow up ideas, probe responses and investigate motives and feelings, which the questionnaire can never do. The way in which a response is made (the tone of voice, facial expression, hesitation, and so on) can provide information that a written response would conceal. Questionnaire responses have to be taken at face value, but a response in an interview can be developed and clarified.

There are problems, of course. Interviews are time-consuming, and so in a 100-hour project you will be able to interview only a relatively small number of people. It is a highly subjective technique and therefore there is always the danger of *bias*. Analysing responses can present problems, and wording the questions is almost as demanding for interviews as it is for questionnaires. Even so, the interview can yield rich material and can often put flesh on the bones of questionnaire responses.

Moser and Kalton (1971: 271) describe the survey interview as 'a conversation between interviewer and respondent with the purpose of eliciting certain information from the respondent'. This, they continue, might appear a straightforward matter, but the attainment of a successful interview is much more complex than this statement might suggest.

Preparation for interviews follows much the same procedures as for questionnaires. Topics need to be selected, questions devised, methods of analysis considered and a schedule prepared and piloted.

The ethics of conducting interviews

In Chapter 3, I spoke about codes of practice, contracts and protocols, which require researchers to ensure that participants are fully aware of the purpose of the research and that they understand their rights. It will be helpful if you refer to the 'ethical guidelines and protocols' section in Chapter 3 before you get too far in planning your interviews, because you should not proceed without respondents' consent to participate. If you are researching in a hospital or in fact in any health-related area, for example, I should be very surprised if you were not required to produce a written protocol. Conditions vary and so it's essential that you find out what the requirements are at an early stage.

Obtaining *informed consent* may not be as easy as it sounds, and if you are working on a 100-hour project, you will have little time to prepare and trial the sort of protocol required in a major study. However, whatever the size of the project, you will still have a responsibility to explain to respondents as fully as possible what the research is about, why you wish to interview them, what will be involved and what you will do with the information you obtain. I personally feel that this should not be presented verbally at the start of an interview, but sent beforehand so that respondents have an opportunity to query the meaning and implications of any statements – and even to withdraw at that stage. Better for participants to withdraw at the start rather than halfway through or after the interview.

In case you are coming to the conclusion that this is just one more bureaucratic and unnecessary procedure, I would ask you to remember that it not only ensures that your respondents know about their rights and your responsibilities but it is also protects your own position from accusations that interviewees were coerced into participating.

Question wording

Although question wording is important, it is not quite as important to be precise about the use of certain terms as for questionnaires, though of course the language you use must be understandable to the respondents. In the chapter on questionnaire design, I gave the example of students having been asked how much time they spent studying, and suggested that 'a great deal', 'a certain amount' and 'not much' would mean different things to different people. In an interview, it would be possible to ask 'How much time do you spend studying?' and then to follow with a prompt along the lines of 'For example . . .'.

Follow the rules laid down for questionnaire design (no leading, presumptive or offensive questions, etc.). Consider the issues you wish to cover and the order in which you might put your questions. The order may be important in establishing an easy relationship with the interviewee. The manner in which you ask questions certainly will be.

Try out question wording and, when you are as satisfied as you can be, write the questions and/or prompts on cards or on separate pieces of paper or in a document on a tablet so you can scroll up to the next question.

The interview schedule

Structured and semi-structured interviews

If you decide to use a **structured or semi-structured format**, which allows you to tick or circle responses on your previously prepared schedule, you should be able to leave the interview with a set of responses that can be fairly easily recorded, summarized and analysed. It's not quite so easy if you have decided on an unstructured format but you will still need to prepare a list of items you wish to discuss and a few prompts or probes to remind you about the particular issues you wish to cover. Say you are carrying out a survey of staff participation in a company's in-house French language programme. Company headquarters are in Paris and it was felt that the language programme would be a good idea. However, take-up was disappointing, possibly because although half an hour of work time was allowed, participants had to give a further half-hour of their own time.

You think it might be useful to know whether there was any difference between male and female participants; the length of time staff had worked for the company; whether they had spent time at the Paris headquarters; their seniority in the firm and (an issue which had unexpectedly cropped up during the pilot interviews) whether attendance brought any increase in salary or even promotion; and, of course, the extent of employees' participation in the French language programme.

It's fairly easy to circle numbers on your checklist, but not so easy to write down what people say. The last thing you want to do is to write furiously throughout the interview, so the more items you can surreptitiously circle, the better. You need to record whether your respondent is male or female but you don't need to ask. You can see, so circle the M or F at the start of your schedule. Recording the interview makes writing notes during it less urgent but remember to ask permission to do so and inform participants of what will happen to the recordings afterwards. Recording equipment can fail, so carry out a test before you start by asking a question, recording an answer and then replaying it.

You might prepare the draft schedule along the following lines. Try it out with your pilot study volunteers and if it does not work, then redraft until you are satisfied it serves your purpose.

Title: Survey of staff participation in the French language programme

Date of interview: Venue:
Name/number of interviewee: M or F

Q1: To what extent have you participated in the French language programme?

Prompt: 6-week basic programme	1	2	3
12-week improvers' programme	1	2	3
1-year advanced programme	1	2	3
2-year bilingual oral programme	1	2	3

1 = not at all (any particular reasons?)
2 = to a certain extent (ask for examples)
3 = a great deal (ask for examples).

You might then wish to probe further.

After the interview, all the circled numbers can be entered into your summary sheet and the process of analysing responses has begun. Some people add a summary column on the right-hand side of the schedule; others prefer to work on a separate sheet.

Questions and coding can be developed during the course of pilot interviews. There may be changes as you go on. What seemed to be a good idea at the start may not be appropriate as you proceed. Code numbers do not need to be indicated on the schedule. Unless you plan to key your numbers into a spreadsheet or software package, there is no reason why you should work with numbers. You could use letters, which will immediately give you the key to the question item. If the majority of your data collection is to be via interviews, you are unlikely to accumulate very large numbers and, if you are coding by hand, the letters have considerable advantages over numbers. So, on your summary sheet, you would have headings of M and F and the numbers of participants who were male or female would be listed under the appropriate heading. Easy.

Unstructured interviews

Unstructured interviews centred round a topic may, and in skilled hands do, produce a wealth of valuable data but such interviews require a great deal of expertise to control and a great deal of time to analyse. Conversation about a topic may be interesting and may produce useful insights into a problem, but it has to be remembered that an interview is more than just an interesting conversation. It is a conversation with a purpose; you are seeking information that will enable you to gather data to address your research question or topic.

Preliminary interviews can probably be placed at the 'completely unstructured' end of the continuum of formality. This is the stage when you are trying to find out which areas or topics are important and when people directly concerned with the topic are encouraged to talk about what is of central significance to them. You are looking for clues as to which areas should be explored and which left out. Interviews of this kind require only the minimum of note-taking, and as long as your notes are clear enough to enable you to extract points of interest, and topics for inclusion in the study, they will suffice.

Most interviews carried out in the main data collection stage of the research will come somewhere between the completely structured and the completely unstructured point on the continuum. Freedom to allow the respondents to talk about what is of central significance to them rather than to the interviewer is clearly important, but some flexible structure to ensure all topics considered crucial to the study are covered does eliminate some of the problems of entirely unstructured interviews. The **guided or focused interview** fulfils these requirements. No questionnaire or checklist is used, but a framework is established by selecting topics on which the interview is guided. The respondent is allowed a considerable degree of latitude within the framework. Certain questions are asked, but respondents are allowed the freedom to talk about the topic and give their views in their own time. The interviewer needs to have the skill to ask questions and, if necessary, to probe at the right time, but if the interviewee moves freely from one topic to another, the conversation can flow without interruption.

The advantage of a focused interview is that a framework is established beforehand and so recording and analysis are greatly simplified. This is important for any research, but particularly so for limited-time studies.

Group interviews and focus groups

One-to-one interviewing is not the only way of meeting respondents and in some cases you might feel it would be more useful to consider group interviewing. There is nothing new about group interviewing, although focus groups in particular are popular, especially in social science and health research. As their name indicates, the purpose of **focus groups** is to focus discussion on a particular issue. They can be structured, where there are pre-prepared questions and checklists, or completely unstructured, where the intervention of the researcher is minimal. It all depends on the purpose of the interview. They can be formal or informal gatherings of a varied group of people who may not know each other, but who might be thought to have a shared interest, concern or experience in issues like treatment in hospital or vandalism in their area. They may all have had similar experiences, or are known to have a professional concern about, and knowledge of, the issues involved. The intention is that participants will interact with each other, will be willing to listen to all views, perhaps to reach consensus about some aspects of the topic or to disagree about others, and to give a good airing to the issues which seem to be interesting or important to them. The researcher becomes less of an interviewer, more of a moderator or facilitator.

Focus groups are undoubtedly valuable when in-depth information is needed 'about how people think about an issue – their reasoning about why things are as they are, why they hold the views they do' (Laws 2013: 205). However, there can sometimes be problems. Hayes warns us that:

> "Groups have to be carefully balanced in relation to the age, sex and ethnic status of respondents: for example, if young people, women, or people in ethnic minority groups are in disproportionately fewer numbers in the group they may feel socially constrained and not contribute freely to the discussion. It may sometimes be necessary to have single sex groups in similar age ranges in order for the atmosphere to be permissive and relaxed."
>
> (Hayes 2000: 395)

With experience, researchers will devise their own techniques of keeping the strong personalities in line and of drawing the silent members into the group. Laws (2013: 207) suggests that one way might be to make a periodic check in order to discover whether all group members are in agreement with statements being made, along the lines of 'Is that what everyone thinks?' or 'Does everyone agree with xyz?' and that seems to be a reasonable approach.

There appear to be many views about the 'right' and the 'wrong' way to manage group – particularly focus group – interviews. Some people consider a checklist, topic guide and prepared questions are essential; others disagree and feel that such a structure would be too directive to achieve the required exploration of respondents' beliefs, interpretations and understanding of issues. All I can say, as I always do, is that we all have our own ways of doing things, so suit yourself, select the approach that is right for your purpose and call it what you will. As long as you remember that the ethics of research always have to be adhered to, that consent has to be given, full information provided about the purpose of the research and guarantees given about your definition of anonymity and confidentiality, all will be well.

Recording interviews

It is always difficult to decipher who said what in group interviews, but in one-to-one interviews, audio- or video-recording can be useful to check the wording of any statement you might wish to quote, to allow you keep eye contact with your interviewee, to help you look interested – and to make sure that what you write is accurate. Recording can be especially helpful if you are undertaking any form of *content analysis*, in that you can listen several times to identify categories, but perhaps it is most useful because it allows you to code, summarize and to note comments that are of particular interest without having to try to write them down during the course of the interview (see Chapter 7 for Brendan Duffy's discussion of content analysis).

However, you cannot assume that all your respondents will be willing for their comments to be recorded. Audio- and video-recording can sometimes inhibit honest responses. Interviewees will, rightly, wish to know what you propose to do with the recording, who is to have access to it and how long it will be kept. You also need to be prepared for a refusal. Even if respondents had agreed previously to be recorded, they may change their mind when the time comes and so you have to do all the necessary preliminary preparation of questions, prompts and probes in order to ensure, or try to ensure, that all the main issues you wish to explore have been covered – and you will need a checklist or schedule and a summary sheet.

Your difficulties are not at an end even if respondents do agree to be recorded. Many experienced researchers and supervisors feel strongly (and in fact state categorically) that all recordings must be transcribed. They make the point that if a transcription is not made and made available for scrutiny if required, then interviewers can say what they like, even going so far as to suggest that they might even make up 'quotations' that suit their purpose. However, if you have to do the transcribing yourself, you can count on at least 4–5 hours' work for every hour of interview even if you are skilful and quick on the keyboard, but significantly more if you are not. In a short project, it is questionable whether you have the time for transcription, but in case anybody wishes to check any particular point, make sure you keep the recording until after the report has been examined – and until you are sure that no corrections or rewriting are required.

If respondents do not agree for the interview to be recorded, all is certainly not lost. We all learn to devise our own shorthand system for noting responses, but as soon as the interview is over, do your utmost to write up as much as you can remember. If your interview guide or schedule has been well-planned and piloted, your questions, items and headings will help you not only to record responses but also to remind you of what was said under each heading. Prompts listed on the schedule may never need to be used as prompts, but they will still serve as sub-headings and will provide the beginnings of a structure for your report. Whenever possible, statements that will be quoted in the report should be verified with the respondent. The last thing you want is for a statement to be challenged at the report stage.

One other thing. Sometimes, and particularly if they enjoyed the interview, respondents may ask if you will let them know how the research goes. There can be time and money costs here, so take care not to promise too much. (Remember the problems Stephen Waters faced in Chapter 3!) However, your interviewees will have given you their time for free, so if you can manage it, it would be a courtesy to agree to let them have a very brief summary of findings – as long as such findings are not confidential. Once the summary is produced, it can be presented, if required, at meetings of research committees, ethics committees, departmental meetings, governing bodies, and to those who were involved in piloting your data collection instruments.

Remember to ask permission from your interviewees to make a recording well in advance. Offer them a copy of the recording, and the transcript if you make one. They may decline but they will appreciate your offer.

Skype and Google Hangouts

When conducting empirical research on the use of social media by early career researchers, Minocha and Petros (2012) found that face-to-face interactions with supervisors, fellow researchers and participants are key in research dialogues. In the past, researchers who wished to interview participants had to limit their geographical location or brace themselves to pay for travel costs to reach their interviewees. With Skype and Google Hangouts, calls between account holders are free and both platforms can be used for conference calls. Skype is free to download and to speak with or video-call another Skype user via the Internet, wherever they are in the world. Skype uses your computer's in-built microphone or camera or, if your device doesn't have one, your webcam. It enables you to interview participants who it would be difficult or impossible to meet face-to-face and saves travelling time and costs, as well as being more convenient for the interviewee. Once you have set up a Skype account, you need to invite your interviewee to accept you as a contact by sending them a message from within Skype itself. Once they accept your invitation, either party can contact the other.

Ensure that you have secured agreement from your participant to be interviewed and that they are happy for you to send them an invitation on Skype to add you as a contact, otherwise your invitation will come out of the blue – not the ideal way to get your interviewee on your side. While some interviewees may be happy to use video calling, others may be self-conscious about doing so and may prefer you to interview them using audio only. If you are going to record the interview by using a separate recording device or, better still, by adding an application such as 'Call Recorder' to Skype, make sure that your interviewee is aware of this and has given their permission for you to do so. Call Recorder is very useful for professional discussions and interviews with research participants and enables you to give your full attention to the conversation and to replay it afterwards, rather than trying to concentrate on what the other person is saying while taking notes at the same time. Offer your interviewee a copy of the recording and the transcript if you make one – they may be able to use it for their own professional purposes and, even if they decline your offer, they will appreciate it being made.

Meetings with your supervisor can also be held over Skype and via Google Hangouts, saving both time and expense.

Bias – the old enemy

There is always the danger of bias creeping into interviews, largely because interviewers and the way they interact may have an impact on the interviewee. Where a team of interviewers is employed, serious bias may show up in data analysis, but if one researcher conducts a set of interviews, the bias may be consistent and therefore go unnoticed. Dictionary definitions of bias generally centre on the notion of distortion of judgement, prejudiced outlook and unfair influence. That sounds obvious enough but there can be problems over interpretation because one person's 'fair and unbiased point of view' may well be judged to be 'prejudice' by another (Bell and Opie 2002: 233).

Many factors can result in bias and there are always dangers in research carried out by individual researchers, particularly those who have strong views about the topic they are researching. It can occur in many ways, deliberately or unwittingly. It is very easy to fall into the bias trap, for example by selecting only those items in the literature review that support your point of view, using inappropriate language that might indicate strength of feeling in one direction, and permitting value judgements to influence the way research findings are interpreted. In her doctoral study of truancy in Western Australian schools, Jan Gray (2000) was very conscious of the fact that she was researching a topic in which she had a keen interest and about which she held strong views. She recalls that it was her constant questioning of practice and her critical attitude towards the interpretation of data that helped her to recognize signs of bias – and it is this kind of discipline that is required. Miles and Huberman remind us that:

> "We have moments of illumination. Things 'come together'. The problem is that we could be wrong. A near-library of research evidence shows that people (researchers included) habitually tend to *overweight* facts they believe in or depend on, to *ignore or forget* data not going in the direction of their reasoning and to *see confirming instances* far more easily than disconfirming instances (Nisbet and Ross 1980). We do this by differentially weighting information, and by looking at part of the data, not all of them."
>
> (Miles and Huberman 1994: 253–4)

Gray called her 'moments of illumination' when things came together as 'the process of enlightenment'. She still had to ask herself whether she had overweighted any facts because of her personal beliefs. Perhaps one of her main strengths was that she knew what the dangers were. She was constantly on the lookout for signs of bias and she placed great emphasis on reflection, on practice and on triangulation. (For a discussion of Gray's research, see Bell and Opie 2002: 129–70.)

So, we must be wise and vigilant, critical of our interpretation of the data, regularly question our practice and wherever possible triangulate. A supervisor who is familiar with the literature relating to your subject will quickly remind you if you have placed too much emphasis on x or y or have ignored a or b, and it's always wise to listen to what supervisors have to say. If you don't agree, that's up to you and as long as you make your own strong case, based on the available evidence and not merely on your opinions, you will be safe.

Remember!

People who agree to be interviewed deserve consideration and so you will need to fit in with their plans, however inconvenient that may be for you. Try to fix a venue at a time when you will not be disturbed. Trying to interview when your mobile is constantly ringing or people are knocking at the door will destroy any chance of continuity.

Before you make the appointment, make sure official channels, if any, have been cleared. A letter from your supervisor, head of department, principal or research officer, saying what you are doing and why, will always help. Of course, your statement about guarantees, anonymity and confidentiality issues should have been sent before the interview takes place.

It is difficult to lay down rules for the conduct of an interview. Common sense and normal good manners will, as always, take you a long way. You should always introduce yourself and ask if the respondent has any queries. When you make the appointment, say how long you anticipate the interview will take. Ask if that is acceptable and if the respondent says it is too long, you will have to try and discuss your main issues early on. You're not in charge: the respondents are and you need them more than they need you. Interviews are very time-consuming. If you allow one hour maximum for the actual interview, there is also travelling time and time lost through any one of numerous mishaps (respondent late home, sudden crisis with children which causes delay, unexpected visitor who interrupts the interview, and so on). Then there is the time needed to consider what has been said during the interview, to go through notes and to extend and clarify points that may have been hastily jotted down. If you are working full-time, you are unlikely to be able to carry out more than one interview in an evening and, even if you are able to devote yourself full-time to the task, it is difficult to cope with more than two or three interviews during the course of a day. Your original project plan should take account of the time required for planning and conducting interviews, for coping with cancelled arrangements, second visits and finding replacements for people who drop out.

Interviewing is not easy and many researchers have found it difficult to strike the balance between complete objectivity and trying to put the interviewee at ease. It is difficult to know how these difficulties can be overcome, although honesty about the purpose of the research and integrity in the conduct of the interview will help. Daphne Johnson, a very experienced researcher and skilful supervisor, makes the point that it is the responsibility of the interviewer, not the interviewee, to end an interview. She writes:

> "It may have been difficult to negotiate access and to get in in the first place, but the interviewer who, once in, stays until he is thrown out, is

> working in the style of investigative journalism rather than social research ... If an interview takes two or three times as long as the interviewer said it would, the respondent, whose other work or social activities have been accordingly delayed, will be irritated in retrospect, however enjoyable the experience may have been at the time. This sort of practice breaks one of the ethics of professional social research, which is that the field should not be left more difficult for subsequent investigators to explore by disenchanting respondents with the whole notion of research participation."
>
> (Johnson 1984: 14–15)

Apart from these specific guidelines, most of the advice and protocols detailed in this chapter about interviewing face-to-face also apply to interviewing over the Internet. If you are using audio only, don't cut corners simply because your interviewee can't see you! Ensure your preparation, documentation and methods of making a written record of the interview as you proceed, as well as afterwards, are as thorough as if you were meeting the participant face-to-face.

Planning and Conducting Interviews Checklist

1. Decide what you need to know.	List all the items about which information is required.	☑
2. Ask yourself why you need this information.	Examine your list and remove any item that is not directly associated with the task.	☑
3. Is an interview the best way of obtaining this information?	Consider alternatives.	☑
4. If it is, begin to devise questions in outline.	The final form of questions will depend on the type of interview.	☑

5. Decide on the type of interview.	A structured interview will produce structured responses. Is this what you want, or is a more open approach required?	☑
6. Refine the questions.	Write questions on cards or in a Word document on a tablet. Check wording (see questionnaire checklist).	☑
7. Consider how questions will be analysed.	Consult Chapter 13 before deciding finally about question type and question wording.	☑
8. Prepare an interview schedule or guide and draft a summary sheet.	Consider the order of questions. Prepare prompts in case the respondent does not provide essential information freely – but don't push your own point of view.	☑
9. Pilot your schedule and summary sheet.	Both need to be tested, and you need practice in asking questions and recording responses.	☑
10. Review the schedule, if necessary.	Take account of pilot respondents' comments.	☑
11. Watch for bias.	If you have strong views about some aspect of the topic, be particularly vigilant. If someone else asked the same question, would they get the same answer?	☑
12. Select who to interview.	Interviews take time. Try to select a representative sample. Decide what to do if selected people are not willing or able to give an interview. Be realistic about the number of interviews that can be conducted in the time available.	☑

13.	Try to fix a time and place where you will not be disturbed.	Switch mobiles off. If you are using Skype, turn off audible notifications of email, Twitter or Facebook messages. Ask your interviewee to do the same.	☑
14.	Make sure official channels have been cleared, and let interviewees see any protocol documents beforehand.	A letter from your supervisor, head or principal explaining the purpose of the research may be helpful.	☑
15.	Introduce yourself and give interviewees the opportunity to ask for any necessary clarification. You will, of course, have already contacted them to explain the purpose of the research.	Say what will happen to the information provided by the interviewee. Clarify the meaning of anonymity in the context of the study.	☑
16.	Agree with the interviewee how long the interview will last.	Do your utmost not to exceed the time limit.	☑
17.	Try to check the accuracy of your notes with interviewees.	But don't promise to check with respondents after the interview if this is likely to prove difficult.	☑
18.	If you wish to record the interview, you must obtain permission from the interviewee.	Remember that it takes a long time to transcribe a recorded interview, if this is what you intend to do. Write up as you go along. Don't wait until all interviews are completed.	☑

19. Honesty and integrity are important.	Make no promises that cannot be fulfilled. Respect respondents' views about anonymity. If you know a respondent has been indiscreet in revealing confidential information, never take advantage.	☑
20. Common sense and good manners will take you a long way.	People who agree to be interviewed are doing you a favour. They deserve consideration.	☑
21. Don't leave the research field more difficult for future researchers by disenchanting respondents with the whole notion of research participation.	There are many ways in which participants can become disenchanted: appointments not kept or the interviewer arriving late; taking longer than promised; promising a summary of findings but not delivering; conducting the interview in a hostile manner – and failing to thank the interviewee.	☑
22. Thank interviewees by email or via social networks or send them a card or letter.		☑

Further reading

Barbour, R. (2008) *Doing Focus Groups*. London: Sage.
The author discusses uses and abuses of focus groups, sampling, practicalities of planning and running groups, ethics, making sense of and

analysing group data, and the advantages and limitations of using focus group discussion.

Bowling, A. (2009) *Research Methods in Health: Investigating Health and Health Services* (3rd edn). Maidenhead: Open University Press.
Chapters 11 and 13 in Section IV discuss interviews and their response rates in quantitative research, including techniques of survey interviewing. Chapter 16 in Section V deals with unstructured interviews and focus groups in qualitative research.

Darlington, Y. and Scott, D. (2002) *Qualitative Research in Practice: Stories from the Field*. Buckingham: Open University Press.
Chapter 3 considers the various stages of in-depth interviewing. It is perhaps unlikely you will have the time to become involved in such interviews but time is not the only precondition. As Darlington and Scott make clear, considerable skill, experience and training are required. If you have these attributes and feel you would be interested in considering this approach, it would be advisable to consult your supervisor and to read this chapter before making up your mind.

Denscombe, M. (2010) *The Good Research Guide for Small-scale Social Research Projects* (4th edn). Maidenhead: Open University Press.
Chapter 10, 'Interviews', is an excellent read, covering the advantages and disadvantages of interviews, 'When is it appropriate to use interviews', 'Types of research interview', 'Internet interviews' and 'The validity of interview data: how do you know the informant is telling the truth?'

Gillham, B. (2005) *Research Interviewing: A Practical Guide*. Maidenhead: Open University Press.
Gillham addresses what research interviewing is, what techniques are used and how interview data is analysed and written up.

Hayes, N. (2000) *Doing Psychological Research: Gathering and Analysing Data*. Buckingham: Open University Press.
Chapter 7 deals with interviewer effects, conducting interviews, stages of interview research and ethical issues in interview research.

Keats, D. (2000) *Interviewing: A Practical Guide for Students and Professionals*. Buckingham: Open University Press.
Keats considers the use of interviews in research and, in particular, issues involved in interviewing young children, the elderly and people from ethnic communities.

Kvale, S. (2008) *Interviews: An Introduction to Qualitative Research Interviewing* (2nd edn). London: Sage.

This book addresses the seven stages of an interview investigation. Also includes a discussion of newer developments in qualitative interviewing, such as narrative, discursive and conversational analyses.

May, T. (2011) *Social Research: Issues, Methods and Process* (4th edn). Maidenhead: Open University Press.
This is a useful book, particularly Chapter 6, 'Interviewing: methods and process', which provides a review of different types of interview in social research, issues in interviewing and the analysis of interviews.

Oliver, P. (2003) *The Student's Guide to Research Ethics.* Maidenhead: Open University Press.
Pages 12–16 discuss informed consent and situations where engaging in research may be ethically undesirable. Chapter 3, 'Research and the respondent: ethical issues during the research', considers the ethics of tape-recording interviews and the right of respondents to end their involvement in the research.

11 Diaries, Logs, Critical Incidents and Blogs

INTRODUCTION

Another research method for collecting data is to ask respondents to complete diaries, logs or blogs of events over a period of time. These personal accounts can provide useful insights into aspects of their lives or behaviour, for example their day-to-day tasks or their practices in a particular environment such as a school, hospital, university or workplace setting. Similarly, blogs can provide useful, and sometimes more personal, sources of information. This chapter covers:

- The pros and cons of using blogs as part of a research project, including the ethical aspect of using blogs in research that were originally written for different, sometimes personal, purposes.
- A review of the diary method – what it can discover, how to set up a diary research task, how to write your instructions and other considerations.
- Five case studies of diaries in different settings, including a primary school, individual patient care and further education. These examples will provide ideas for how you might use diaries as a research tool for your own project.

Key terms

Although there is some overlap between them, it is helpful to define what we mean by the terms diary, log and critical incident. According to Isabel Santafe's excellent description:

> "A diary study involves asking . . . people to record their experiences related to a particular subject over a period of time. It is a useful tool to help learn about user behaviour as it provides a record of thoughts and actions in **context**."
>
> (Santafe 2013, emphasis in original)

Alaszewski (2006) defines a **diary** as 'a document created by an individual who has maintained a regular, personal and contemporaneous record', and which 'is organized around a sequence of regular and dated entries over a period of time during which the diarist keeps or maintains the diary' (p. 2). He includes 'logs' in his diary definition, the simplest form being 'the log that contains a record of activities or events without including personal comments on such events' (p. 2). Whereas diaries are usually personal reflections or private records, **logs** are often intended to be read more widely by a group of people requiring a permanent record of events. So, a diary might be kept by someone on a cruise to capture not only where the cruise liner went, but personal thoughts and emotions related to the journey. The ship's log, on the other hand, would document only facts such as the ship's speed, its course and wind direction.

As defined in Chapter 8, a **blog** (short for weblog) is one or more articles or personal reflections on a subject that are 'posted' on the web, either on the writer's website or on a site set up to host blogs, such as Blogger or WordPress. If the writer or blogger posts more than one blog, they will be arranged in reverse date order, with the most recent 'post' at the top of the page.

A **critical incident**, as described by Flanagan, who devised the Critical Incident Technique (CIT) of research, is:

> "any specifiable human activity that is sufficiently complete in itself to permit inferences and predictions to be made about the person performing the act. To be critical the incident must occur in a situation where the purpose or intent of the act seems fairly clear to the observer and where its consequences are sufficiently definite to leave little doubt concerning its effects."
>
> (Flanagan 1954: 327)

Oxtoby describes a critical incident as being a task or an incident event which makes the difference between success and failure in carrying out important parts of the job and which is:

> "an attempt to identify the most 'noteworthy' aspects of job behaviour [which are] based on the assumption that jobs are composed of critical and non-critical tasks ... The idea is to collect reports as to what people do that is particularly effective in contributing to good performance and then to scale the incidents in order of difficulty, frequency and importance to the job as a whole."
>
> (Oxtoby 1979: 230)

Despite its name, a critical incident does not have to be a dramatic or unusual event to be considered worthy of investigation. One example would be how nurses conduct the 'handover' from the night staff to the day staff – a routine daily procedure. A researcher might observe the process and report back the behaviour and actions of the two teams. The analysis of this critical incident might lead to changes in procedure to make the handover more efficient and to reduce the length of time it takes.

On the face of it, diaries, logs, critical incidents and blogs are attractive ways of gathering information about the way individuals spend their time, each of which is selected with a view to obtaining different types of information. Each approach might provide valuable information about work patterns and activities, provided that the researcher is clear about what information is needed and the participants are similarly clear about what they are being asked to do – and why.

All three approaches almost always cover an agreed time span – a day, a week, a month or, occasionally, longer – depending on what information is required. At certain specified times, 'on the spot' or retrospectively, respondents are asked to say what they did and, in some cases, why. Instructions need to be explicit. Do you really want to know that someone made a cup of tea, paid a bill or had a bath? Well, in some cases, perhaps you might, but only if you are interested specifically in activities of daily living.

Completing diary forms can be time-consuming and irritating for a busy person who has to keep stopping work to make an entry, and if respondents are not completely sympathetic with the task, or have been coerced into filling in diary forms, they will probably not complete them thoroughly, if at all. The task might be less onerous if they can make a recording, for example by using a Smartphone, but you would need to decide a strategy for how they should save each recording and send you a copy.

As in all research activities, it is essential to contact – and preferably to meet – the people who will be giving up their time, so that you can explain the purpose of the exercise fully, discuss any possible difficulties and, if possible, resolve them. Reluctant diarists will rarely provide usable data, so preliminary consultation is of the utmost importance. As with any other form of data collection, some form of check with diary-keepers is often desirable and sometimes essential if interest is to be maintained.

Representativeness

In any diary exercise, there can be problems regarding representativeness. Was this day of the week typical of others or is Monday always the crisis day? Is this week exceptional? Oppenheim draws attention to this problem and reminds us that:

> "The respondents' interest in writing up the diary will cause them to modify the very behaviour we wish them to record. If, for instance, they are completing a week's diary of their television viewing behaviour, this may cause them to engage in 'duty viewing' in order to 'have something to record', or they may view 'better' types of programmes in order to create a more favourable impression."
>
> (Oppenheim 1992: 252)

This may well be true, but many other methods of data collection can also have an influence on normal behaviour, as many researchers have discovered during the course of their investigations.

The diary-interview method

There are many different ways in which diaries are used. They can be stand-alone methods of data collection or be part of a larger study incorporating interviews, questionnaires and observation. In 1977, Zimmerman and Wieder used diaries in their ethnographic study of the counter-culture in the USA as a preliminary to interviewing in cases where it was not at first clear what were the right questions to ask. In an article on their diary-interview method, they discussed the role of diaries as 'an observational log maintained by subjects which can then be used as a basis for intensive interviewing' (Zimmerman and Wieder 1977: 481).

The potential for diaries as question-generating devices is clear, but Zimmerman and Wieder took this process a step further. They viewed the use of a diary, in conjunction with the diary interview, as an approximation to the method of *participant observation*, including: the length of time involved; the fact that any observer, even a participant, may have an effect on normal behaviour; and, in some studies, moral, legal or ethical constraints. They proposed the use of the diary-interview method 'for those situations where the problems of direct observation resist solution, or where further or more extended observation strains available resources' (Zimmerman and Wieder 1977: 481).

Zimmerman and Wieder asked their respondents to record in chronological order the activities in which they engaged over a seven-day period, following the formula what/when/where/how? The 'what?' involved a description of the activity or discussion recorded in the diarists' own categories. The 'when?' involved reference to the time and timing of the activity, with special attention to recording the actual sequence of events. The 'where?' involved a designation of the location of the activity, suitably coded to prevent identification of individuals or places. The 'how?' involved a description of whatever logistics were entailed by the activity (Zimmerman and Wieder 1977: 486).

Clearly, diarists must be of a certain educational level to understand the instructions, let alone complete the diary. They must also have time. If you are asking colleagues to cooperate by completing diaries, be clear that the diary is the best way of obtaining the information you need and that you can convince your diarists that what they are doing is likely to be of some use.

Piloting returns forms and instructions to participants

No matter how pressed for time you are, it's essential that you pilot your returns forms and the instructions to respondents. If you can't get hold of trial respondents similar to those you hope to be able to include in the real diary exercise, ask, cajole or even bribe (!) anyone who is willing to give you time to complete a few days of the selected diary. Decide what the instructions should include – and you can be confident that friends and family will make it quite clear if your instructions are incomprehensible, insufficient, badly written or generally useless. That's what friends and family are for. However, before you begin to distribute draft returns documents and instructions to your pilot group, there is work to be done.

As in every research exercise, do nothing until you have decided exactly what information (or enlightenment) you need from your respondents. It might be something vague like 'wanting to find out what people do at work'. But do you mean everything, from the time people hang up their coat when they arrive to when they switch off the lights as they leave? Well, could be, but perhaps not for someone working on a limited-time project. So, begin to make the move from the general to the specific.

If you decide to follow Zimmerman and Wieder's (1977) 'what/when/where/how?' approach, start with the 'what' – what are you hoping to learn from respondents? Write down everything you can think of that might come into the 'what' category. Then do the same with 'when' and 'where'. Do you need to know the time and place when respondents made their entries? This might be important if you want to know what time of day they took certain medication. And it might sometimes be important to know where they took it – in a meeting, on the bus, when they woke up, at a fixed time every day, any old time? Leave the 'how' until you're sure you have dealt with the what, when and where because only then can you decide which type of data collection instrument will suit your purposes best. It might be a diary in which entries will 'record what an individual considers relevant and important and may include events, activities, interactions, impressions and feelings' (Alaszewski 2006: 2). Is that what you want? If you are only interested in a record of what happened on a certain day at a certain time, without any comments, would a log suffice? But if you need to know what critical incidents, if any, occur during working days, you will need to be quite sure that your and your participants' understanding of what a critical incident is are the same – and that might be harder than it at first seems.

When all this preparatory work is completed, give or send your instructions and recording forms to your volunteers, and perhaps suggest a possible date for returns. When all (or at least almost all) are returned to you, take note of what they say about the design of your form and the clarity (or lack of clarity) of your instructions, redesign both and then give some thought to how you will be able to analyse future returns and present the data in your final report.

There are many variations in the way diaries are structured, the time over which they are conducted and the detail required, so before you begin your diary exercise, take time to read the following five short extracts from diary studies conducted by five experienced researchers. They give some interesting insights into the approaches they adopted.

Five case studies

The primary pupils' food diary

Burgess (2002) incorporated diaries as a method of data collection in many of the research projects he conducted over the years. In his chapter 'On diaries and diary keeping' (1994), he discusses two very different diary studies: the first, by Morrison and Burgess (1993), and the second, by Burgess and Morrison (1993), both related to a food diary study of primary pupils. They adopted Zimmerman and Wieder's (1977) 'what/when/where/how?' approach and the pupils were asked:

> "What did you eat and drink today?
> When did you eat and drink today?
> Where did you eat and drink today? (at school, home, somewhere else?)"
>
> (Burgess and Morrison 1993: Appendix)

Other items were added, namely, whether they had enjoyed a celebration, like a birthday, on any day and whether they liked what they had eaten or had to drink. As the diary was to be completed by children, a specific approach had to be devised:

> "First, it was important to talk with pupils to explain what it is that had to be done. Secondly, the time period over which a diary would be kept was limited to one week including a weekend ... Inside the diary there were a series of instructions which were included in a covering letter addressed to each pupil."
>
> (Burgess 1994: 304)

The supply teachers' diary and time log

In the second study, Burgess worked on a very different and far more detailed diary study concerning the experience of and relationship among teachers, supply teachers and pupils when regular teachers were unable to take a timetabled class. A three-column grid was devised, with 'time' in the first column, 'main activities' in the second column, and 'other' in the third column. The purpose of this **time grid** or **time log** was to provide a framework within which supply teachers could record what happened and when, but which also gave them freedom to develop their ideas. The researchers felt that this format allowed the diary writers to 'place limits on the extent to which they give access to their world and their work' (Burgess 1994: 308).

The general practitioners' time log

Sutherland and Cooper also used a time log as part of their investigation into ill-health and job dissatisfaction among general practitioners (GPs) working in the UK. GPs were asked to complete what amounted to a detailed record of how they spent their day, in order to identify the amount of time spent on various activities, the necessity (or otherwise) and purpose of those activities. The log consisted of six columns, with the headings of 'start time', 'duration', 'activity', 'time problem (who/what/why?)', 'outcome' and 'feelings/reaction/further action' (Sutherland and Cooper 2003: 184). After three or four days of entries, or when the log was completed, the doctors were asked to rank the importance of the activities, which could well have been the most difficult part of the log exercise for professionals who might have found everything they did important.

Busy doctors were being asked to complete full-day records of their activities, to include reasons for any time problems, what happened as a result of time delays, how they felt about the delays (angry/frustrated/pleased?) and what action was taken. It had to be a log that could be 'easily completed with minimum effort' (Sutherland and Cooper 2003: 66) and no doubt the diarists had to be convinced there was some purpose to the exercise. In fact, the diary exercise was designed to: 'highlight interruptions, failure to delegate, and the ways in which other people disrupted your schedule. Ultimately, it should be possible to use your time log to identify the source of disruptions and enable you to prioritize key activities' (Sutherland and Cooper 2003: 67). It was anticipated that identification of problem areas would enable doctors to produce an action plan to improve their time management behaviour and to learn how to 'work smarter not harder' (p. 69). Perhaps at least some stressed GPs might feel that the possibility of an improved, less stressful professional life would be worth the effort of completing the log.

The asthma treatment diary

Bowling reports on two interesting but different diary studies conducted by Hyland and Crocker (1995) and by Hyland (1996), who carried out diary-with-questionnaire studies into the impact of asthma treatment on patients. Patients were asked to complete 'quality of life' diaries over a six-month period but in short time slots. The first asked patients to complete daily diaries over a two-week period. This was followed by a request to produce a diary for the first week of every month for six months, before finally the researchers distributed questionnaires three and six months after treatment. They concluded that 'the diaries proved to be better longitudinal correlations with the physiology of the respondents in comparison with the questionnaires, while the questionnaires had better cross-correlations with physiology' (Bowling 2002: 426).

So, as always, the selection of data collection instruments depends on the purpose of the study, the type of information needed, *and* the willingness of respondents to spend the necessary time completing diaries, logs, questionnaires or being interviewed.

The heads of department critical incidents and problem-portfolio logs

In many ways, the **critical incidents technique** adopts the same – or similar – processes used by Burgess in his supply teachers' study and by Sutherland and Cooper in their GP time log. Both studies attempted to identify essential and important aspects of work behaviour and both were concerned with which tasks were 'critical' and which were 'non-critical'. Oxtoby also used a job diary/log in his study of how heads of department (HoDs) in further education colleges in England and Wales spent their time, and initially considered asking diarists to identify 'critical incidents' in their working day. He defined a critical incident as being a task or an incident that makes the difference between success and failure in carrying out important parts of the job. He wrote:

> "The idea is to collect reports as to what people do that is particularly effective in contributing to good performance and then to scale the incidents in order of difficulty, frequency and importance to the job as a whole. The technique scores over the use of diaries in that it is centred on specific happenings and on what is judged to be effective behaviour. But it is still laborious and does not lend itself to objective quantification."
>
> (Oxtoby 1979: 239–40)

The use of job diaries/logs is perhaps the most simple and widely accepted way of finding out how time is spent in any group or institution, but as Oxtoby discovered:

> "Self-recording can be inaccurate – many of the shorter episodes tend to get omitted – and compiling a detailed diary is usually a tiresome and onerous business. Although it is undoubtedly valuable in terms of enabling people to make more effective use of their time, a diary does not provide much reliable information about the skills or qualities developed. Moreover, the prospect of using diaries to compare differences between large numbers of staff and their jobs is extremely daunting, if only because of the difficulties in handling the data. There are snags, therefore, in employing job diaries to analyse the diversity of HoD activities."
>
> (Oxtoby 1979: 240)

Eventually, Oxtoby decided on a *problem portfolio* approach originally advocated by Marples (1967) in which respondents were asked to record information about how each problem arose, methods used to solve it, difficulties encountered, and so on.

As will be apparent from the above, there can be problems in the use of diaries as a method of gathering evidence, not least the time respondents need to complete the forms. However, diaries can produce a wealth of interesting data and are relatively simple to administer – at least if there are only a few diarists. Analysis of completed forms is not so simple, however, so, as always, you will need to consider how responses will be analysed *before* your respondents begin filling in the diaries. If you are considering using diaries as part of your project, you may wish to consult the checklist at the end of this chapter before you distribute them.

The ethics of diary use

Burgess expresses concern about the extent of intrusion into diary writers' lives and urges researchers to be aware of this. For example, in the food diary, he asked researchers to consider the extent to which the exercise constituted intrusion into the lives of the children and their families before selecting the diary approach. He draws our attention to the fact that if the purpose of the supply teacher diary is 'to gain access to material that would otherwise be hidden from the researchers' view ... to what extent is such a device intrusive on the lives and work of teachers?' (Burgess 1994: 308). I suppose it can equally be said that interviews, questionnaires and observations can also intrude. Researchers frequently use diaries as one of several methods of data collection in their investigations. All I can say is that the impact of our research on the respondents must always be considered before decisions are made about which approach to adopt and that the same ethical considerations should apply to diary studies as for any other method or technique.

A final word of warning

Before you make a final decision about whether or not to select a diary approach, it might be useful to consider Alan Alaszewski's admirable summary of the advantages and disadvantages of diaries as one method of data collection. He writes:

> "Diaries are flexible: they can form part of a variety of research designs, including experimental and survey designs, historical research

and ethnographic or naturalistic research, and can be used in combination with other methods of data collection. They are particularly effective in accessing information which is difficult to access in other ways. However, it is also important to note that diaries have limitations. They can be expensive to use and they may introduce a selection bias into the research. They need to be used with care."

(Alaszewski 2006: 115)

A friendly word of warning!

The impact of your research on the respondents must always be considered. The same ethical considerations should apply to diary studies as for any other method or research technique.

Blogs

Helene Snee, drawing on an excellent article by Hookway (2008), explains that social researchers have used blogs both as a source of data, including content analysis of gender and language use, and as a focus for research in ethnographic studies of why, how and when blogs are used by communities (http://www.methods.manchester.ac.uk/methods/blog-analysis/index.shtml). In a video on the website, Snee describes her own research study, which explored travel blogs as a documentary resource. She raises some methodological and ethical issues that can arise when researchers are considering analysing blogs. She raises the following questions:

- As blogs are self-published and are usually open access, are they 'fair game' for researchers to analyse or should permission be sought from the author?
- How can we guarantee authorship of a blog? Have other people contributed to it?
- What is public information and what information should be treated sensitively? For example, people have written blogs about their terminal illness, wanting to leave a record of how they coped with their impending death for their family and other sufferers so that they might learn from and understand their experience. Although these blogs are accessible by anyone searching the Internet, you might take the view that the content is so sensitive and personal that it should not be discussed or analysed in public.

Less common are accounts of blogs being used as a diary or log to record everyday experience from which the researcher can extract information as a primary resource, as described below. This is because the kind of diary research participants are asked to keep is normally private and anonymous whereas blogs are public and their authorship acknowledged. There is no reason why one of your research participants shouldn't keep a blog to provide you with data, but all the safeguards about permission, confidentiality and anonymity raised in Chapter 3 should be observed. My advice is simple and straightforward: if you are in doubt whether you can use unpublished data, whether public or otherwise, ask the author. He or she can only say no – if so, you shouldn't have been using the data without permission anyway.

Diaries, Logs, Critical Incidents and Blogs Checklist

1. Make sure you are clear about the purpose of your diary study.	Consider precisely what you wish to find out and which diary format will be likely to give you the information you need.	
2. Decide whether a diary, log or critical incidents checklist is the best way of obtaining the information.	But before you get too enthusiastic about carrying out a diary exercise, remember to get permission to approach your diarists. Never assume 'it will be all right'. It might not be.	
3. No matter how busy you are, you must pilot your diary. If you are as confident as you can be that	Make sure all your respondents will be able to understand what is required and allow time at the planning stage to discuss what is	

the diary approach will be appropriate for your purposes, ask friends, family and/or colleagues to act as guinea pigs by completing the form/checklist for a few days.	involved. Instructions must be precise – and don't use jargon. Ask them to comment on the design of the response form. Was there enough space, or too much? Would another format be better? Ask how long it took them to complete the form. Did anyone think some of your questions were offensive?	
4. When you have looked at the returned forms from your 'volunteer' respondents, you will have a good idea about what changes, if any, will need to be made to your instructions and to your response form.	Pilot respondents (particularly family members) will certainly let you know if your instructions are confused, inadequate or even incomprehensible. Even though you will have received only a few returns, begin to think about how responses from a much larger group might be analysed.	
5. Redesign your returns form(s) and, if necessary, reword your instructions.	Contact your main diarists and agree dates for the receipt and return of completed forms. Decide what you will do with non-returners *before* you distribute the documents to your respondents.	
6. Remember that the same ethical considerations should apply to diary studies as for any other method or technique.	Diary completion will be an intrusion into the diarists' lives. If some entries give very personal insights into their daily lives, never divulge information you know to be indiscrete.	

7. Make sure respondents know *why* they are being asked to carry out this chore and what you plan to do with the information.	Will responses be destroyed when the project is completed? Who will see them? Will they be anonymous? And will your understanding of 'anonymous' be the same as that of your respondents'?	☑
8. Try to find time to check progress with the diarists.	If you are asking people to carry out this task for more than one day, evidence seems to indicate that a solicitous inquiry about how things are going may help them to keep on with the task.	☑
9. Write up your findings as soon as you can.	If you have only a small number of respondents, it may be all right to wait until all the returns are with you. However, if you have more than 20 respondents, I would start writing under possible headings as soon as the first arrive. However, that's just me, so decide whether you are a writer or a waiter. Whatever suits you best.	☑
10. Completing a diary is a chore. Don't forget to thank your respondents.	Give them feedback if you can, but don't promise anything if you are unlikely to have time to do it.	☑

Further reading

Alaszewski, A. (2006) *Using Diaries for Social Research*. London: Sage.

Alaszewski gives us detailed discussions of a wide range of diary use in experimental, survey and many other research designs and strategies. He discusses the development and use of diaries, how to get started, finding diarists, collecting the data, analysing diaries and, finally, exploiting the potential of research diaries.

Bowling, A. (2009) *Research Methods in Health: Investigating Health and Health Services* (3rd edn). Maidenhead: Open University Press.
Ann Bowling, writing about the use of diaries with patients, refers to two major diary exercises relating to a trial of asthma treatments. See Hyland, M.E. and Crocker, G.R. (1995) Validation of an asthma quality of life diary in a clinical trial, *Thorax*, 50: 724–30. See also Hyland, M.E. (1996) Diary assessments of quality of life, *Quality of Life Newsletter*, 16: 8–9.

Burgess, R.G. (1994) On diaries and diary keeping, in N. Bennett, R. Glatter and R. Levaćič (eds) *Improving Educational Management through Research and Consultancy*. London: Paul Chapman, in association with the Open University.
In this chapter, Burgess discusses the use of logs, diaries and journals, and includes examples of the supply teacher project considered there as well as an interactive video use diary. He includes ethical questions relating to intrusion into the lives of respondents.

Hart, E. and Bond, M. (1995) *Action Research for Health and Social Care: A Guide to Practice*. Buckingham: Open University Press.
On pages 201–4, there are two extracts from diary studies, one relating to outpatients' clinic experiences, the other an extract from a log.

Hayes, N. (2000) *Doing Psychological Research: Gathering and Analysing Data*. Buckingham: Open University Press.
Chapter 9, 'Analysing documents' (pp. 147–55), provides useful guidance about the advantages, disadvantages, design and analysis of diary studies.

Morrison, M. (2007) Using diaries in research, in A.R.J. Briggs and M. Coleman (eds) *Research Methods in Educational Leadership and Management* (2nd edn). London: Sage.
This chapter provides examples of extracts from several diaries and includes sections on researchers' and research informants' diaries, the design and analysis of diaries, and combining diaries with interviews.

Sutherland, V. and Cooper, C.L. (2003) *De-stressing Doctors: A Self-management Guide*. London: Butterworth Heinemann.

12 Observation

INTRODUCTION

This chapter provides an overview of observation as a data-gathering technique. Put simply, observation is the process of watching someone carry out a task or series of actions in order to gather data about specific aspects of behaviour, content, processes or interactions. This could be observing students in a learning environment such as a classroom, observing engineers on a construction site, or nurses in a healthcare setting. It can be used to better understand individuals or groups in any setting that is relevant to your research topic. There are, however, certain criteria you should follow to ensure your findings are reliable and valid. This chapter addresses:

- What observation is, how it can be used effectively, what its limitations are and the risks involved as a data-gathering technique.
- The differences between unstructured observation, structured observation and participant observation.
- How to create observation schedules or grids for recording what you observe.
- How to ensure your observations are well-run and that your valuable research time is used efficiently.

Key terms

No doubt you will think it unnecessary to remind you, once again, that before you begin to consider observation as one of your data collection techniques, you need first to decide *what* you wish to observe, *what* your main areas of interest are and *why* you think observation will produce the information you need. Is it to be one of several data-gathering methods or the only one? Are you considering observation as a form of validating other evidence? Do you really need evidence from observation, because considerable skill is required. Careful planning and piloting are essential, and it takes practice to get the most out of this technique. However, once mastered, it can reveal characteristics of groups or individuals that would be impossible to discover by other means. Interviews, as Nisbet and Watt (1978: 13) point out, provide important data, but they reveal only how people *perceive* what happens, not necessarily what actually happens. Observation can be useful in discovering whether people do what they say they do, or behave in the way they claim to behave. However, observation also depends on the way people perceive what is being said or done.

On occasions, I have been to meetings and after discussing what happened with colleagues, I have begun to wonder whether I was at the same meeting. We had very different recollections of who said what and what decisions were made. If three or four people stand at a window overlooking a busy street, observing what is going on for five minutes or so, and then write up what they have seen, the accounts are likely to vary. The observers will have their own focus and will interpret significant events in their own way. As observers, we 'filter' the material we obtain from observation, which can lead us to impose our own interpretations on what is observed and so fail to understand 'what an activity means for those who are involved in it' (Darlington and Scott 2002: 75–6).

The fact that we are all fallible does not mean there is little point in including observation as one of our data collection techniques, but it does mean that we have to be particularly aware of the dangers, do our best to eliminate preconceived ideas and prejudices, and constantly look out for possible signs of *bias*.

Solo observers are always in danger of accusations of bias or misinterpretation and especially if you are researching in your own professional area, try to persuade a friend, colleague or fellow student to join you for as many observation sessions as possible. Observation can be *structured* or *unstructured*, *participant* or *non-participant*. Each approach has some advantages but also disadvantages. All require a degree of expertise but if you have, after careful thought, decided to include observation as one of your data collection instruments, then you will need to decide which approach to adopt – and why.

Unstructured observation

Researchers who decide to adopt an **unstructured approach to observation** generally do so because although they may have a clear idea of the purpose of the observation, they may not be so clear about the detail. The researcher:

> "does not use predetermined categories and classifications but makes observations in a more natural open-ended way . . . The logic here is that categories and concepts for describing and analysing the observational data will emerge later in the research, during the analysis, rather than be brought to the research, or imposed on the data, from the start."
>
> (Punch 2005: 179–80)

As in grounded theory, the researcher will 'postpone definitions and structures until a pattern has been observed . . . and then continues with the fieldwork in order to elaborate these while the data are still available for access' (Bowling 2002: 367).

Unstructured observation can be useful to generate hypotheses, but it is not easy to manage. If the nature of your research points you in the direction of unstructured observation, read as widely as you can, ask colleagues and friends if they know of anyone who successfully adopted this approach, and consult your supervisor before you commit yourself to this – or for that matter any other – approach.

Participant observation

Some of the disadvantages of unstructured observation may also apply to **participant observation**, which involves the researcher participating in the daily life of an individual, group or community and listening, observing, questioning and understanding (or trying to understand) the life of the individuals concerned. In some cases, researchers may have been involved for months or even years in a community in order to become generally accepted as part of the group.

Cohen and colleagues draw attention to some of the criticisms levelled at participant observation:

> "The accounts that typically emerge from participant observations echo the criticisms of qualitative data . . . being described as subjective, biased, impressionistic, idiosyncratic and lacking in the precise

> quantifiable measures that are the hallmark of survey research and experimentation. While it is probably true that nothing can give better insight into the life of a gang of juvenile delinquents than going to live with them for an extended period of time, critics of participant observation will point to the dangers of 'going native' as a result of playing a role within such a group."
>
> (Cohen *et al.* 2011: 468).

Experienced participant observers are well aware of the danger of bias but it is difficult to stand back and adopt the role of objective observer when all the members of the group or organization are known to you. If you are researching in your own organization, you will be familiar with the personalities, strengths and weaknesses of colleagues, and this familiarity may cause you to overlook aspects of behaviour that would be immediately apparent to a non-participant observer seeing the situation for the first time.

Bias is not the only danger in participant observation, particularly if 'total' participation is attempted. Denscombe draws our attention to the fact that 'those being studied will not be aware of the research or their role in it. They can hardly give informed consent' (Denscombe 2010a: 209). However, he considers that:

> "First, if it can be demonstrated that none of those who were studied suffered as a result of being observed, the researcher can argue that certain ethical standards were maintained. Second, and linked, if the researcher can argue that the identities of those involved were never disclosed, again there is a reasonable case for saying that the participant observation was conducted in an ethical manner."
>
> (Denscombe 2010a: 209)

In spite of the difficulties and criticisms, participant observation can yield valuable data. Researchers are able to observe changes over time. Rather than having to depend on one-off observations or at best observations carried out over a limited period of time, the participant observer is able to share in the lives and activities of other people; to learn their language and interpret their meanings; to remember actions and speech; and to interact with people in their own environment (Burgess 1982: 45). By listening and experiencing, 'impressions are formed and theories considered, reflected upon, developed and modified' (May 2011: 189).

May, however, acknowledges that:

> "participant observation is not an easy method to perform, or to analyse, but despite the arguments of its critics, it is a systematic and disciplined study which, if performed well, greatly assists in

understanding human actions and brings with it new ways of viewing the social world.″

(May 2011: 189)

I agree, but in 100-hour projects, it might be unwise to undertake participant *or* unstructured observation unless you are already experienced, have the time and are very familiar with the techniques involved. To derive worthwhile information from the data, you will probably need to adopt a more structured approach and devise some form of coding in order to identify aspects of behaviour that you have determined beforehand as being of likely relevance to the research. More of this later in the chapter.

Structured observation and keeping records

The **structured approach to observation** can also be criticized as being subjective and biased: you have decided on the focus rather than allowing the focus to emerge. However, you will already have formulated a hypothesis or identified the objectives of your study and the importance of observing some aspect of behaviour will have become apparent.

Whether your observation is structured or unstructured and whether you are observing as a participant or a non-participant, your role is to observe and record in as objective a way as possible. The fact that different observers can, and do, produce different accounts of situations is worrying for all researchers who hope to include observation as one of their means of data collection. In Denscombe's opinion:

> ″It is precisely this problem which is addressed by systematic observation and its use of an *observation schedule*. The whole purpose of the schedule is to minimize, possibly eliminate, the variations that will arise from data based on individual perceptions of events and situations. Its aim is to provide a framework for observation which *all* observers will use.″

(Denscombe 2010a: 199; emphasis in original)

Observation schedules can take the form of a checklist, a diary, chart, time or critical incidents log – or whatever approach suits your purpose. Spradley (1980), Williams (1994), Denscombe (2010a) and Bowling (2009) all provide examples of charts, grids, categories and other methods of recording that will give you a range of useful ideas for devising schemes of your own. The sad fact is that, despite all the tried and tested methods that have been employed by researchers over the years, there never seems to be an example that is quite right for a particular task. Inevitably, you will find you have to adapt or to devise a completely new approach, and all new systems need careful piloting and refining in the light of experience. If you have access to only one group or one meeting, you must be quite sure that your selected method of recording is going to work. You will probably need to devise your own system of shorthand symbols and these will have to be memorized because you can't always be consulting your notes during the course of a meeting or observation of a group. You will need to decide beforehand how often to record what is happening (all the time?, every three seconds?, every five minutes?, every twenty minutes?) and with whom (the group?, individuals?).

Preparation is all-important. Charts and seating plans have to be prepared. You will need to discuss with whoever is in charge where it would be best to sit. Opinions vary. In a lecture room, there is some merit in sitting where the students can see you. At least that way they are not always turning round to see what you are doing, but if participants have other views, listen – and conform. An observer can never pass entirely unnoticed, but the aim is to be as unobtrusive as possible so that observed behaviour is as close to normal as possible.

It is impossible to record everything, so you need to be clear whether you are interested in the *content* or *process* of a group or meeting, in *interaction* between individuals, in the *nature of contributions* or in *some specific aspect* such as the effectiveness of questioning techniques. Once you have decided what you wish to find out and have satisfied yourself that you need this information to further your research, then you will be in a position to consider what methods of recording will best suit your purposes.

Recording behaviour

One common method of recording behaviour is based on a system of interaction-process analysis originally devised by R.F. Bales in 1950. He devised a method of classifying or coding under one of twelve headings, which enabled the observer to make a record of the behaviour of individuals in groups. Examples of his *categories* of behaviour include 'shows tension release', for which he then identified indicators of tension release (jokes, laughs, shows satisfaction), and 'shows antagonism' (deflates others' status, defends or asserts self).

Since 1950, many different types of approach have been devised, some relatively simple and others extremely complicated. The Flanders system, which was derived from the Bales method of classifying behaviour, is one of the best known. Flanders (1970) devised ten categories of teacher/student behaviour (the Flanders Interaction Analysis Categories), which the observer used as a basis for categorizing and recording what took place in the classroom. Observers were required to record what was happening every three seconds and to enter the appropriate category number on a prepared chart. The problem about Flanders-type systems is that the categories are quite complex, have many sub-sections and inevitably involve the observer making some value judgements as to which category is closest to the particular types of behaviour.

The requirement to record every three seconds means that the observer has to be fully conversant with categories and criteria and to recall instantly the number assigned to particular aspects of behaviour. This takes a considerable amount of practice. The more complicated (and so more thorough) the system of categories, the harder it is to manage.

I have to confess that the one time I tried to use the 'every three seconds' approach was a miserable failure. Trying to keep track of the time and at the same time observing and classifying activities under Flanders-type headings became impossible and so a simpler system had to be devised. I had to go back to basics and to ask myself again why I was observing the meeting. What exactly did I want to find out? What was feasible to record? And only then was I able to eliminate any irrelevances and begin to simplify the categories.

Most researchers I know have devised their own system of categories, and limited them to about three or four. Are you interested in who is aggressive, time-wasting, positive in moving forward the business of the meeting, disagreeing about much (or all) that is being proposed – or none of those things? Ask yourself whether you are more concerned with the *behaviour* of individuals or the *content* of what is being said. Or perhaps you might be interested only in how long each individual speaks and who is silent throughout. If one of your categories happened to be 'disagreement', participants may not need to speak. A lot can be deduced from facial expressions, nods, scowls or signs of dissent from the 'silent' individuals. It's up to you to decide on your categories and, once having decided, to devise ways of recording.

The way in which observations are recorded is a matter of personal preference. If you are observing a meeting, it is helpful to have a table plan before the meeting starts, as shown in Figure 12.1. Each of the categories is given a number and you will know which number applies to which category. In Figure 12.1, if category number 1 deals with aggressive behaviour, you would put '1' underneath or at the

Figure 12.1 Table plan recording individual behaviour according to categories

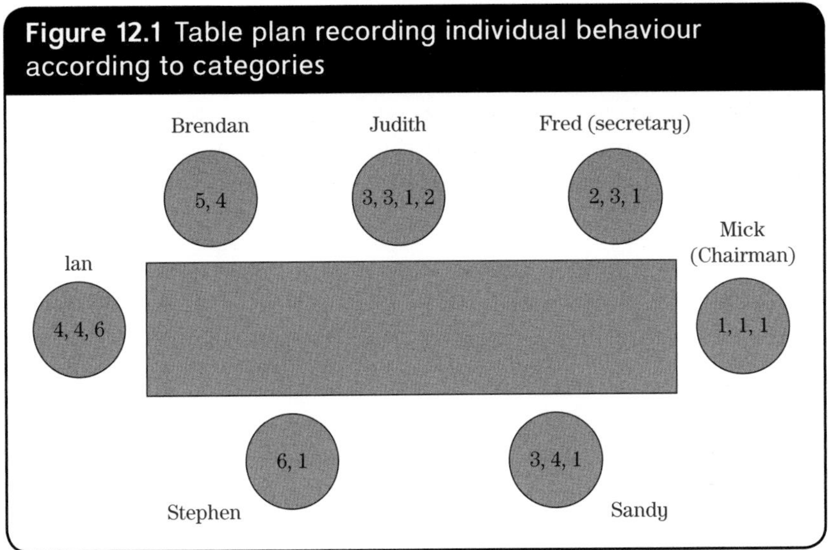

Figure 12.2 Chart recording total number of entries for each category

Participants	Categories						
	1	2	3	4	5	6	Totals
Chairman (Mick)	✓✓✓						3
Secretary (Fred)	✓	✓	✓				3
Judith	✓	✓	✓✓				4
Brendan				✓	✓		2
Ian				✓✓		✓	3
Stephen	✓					✓	2
Sandy	✓		✓	✓			3
Totals	7	2	4	4	1	2	

side of each participant for each indication of such behaviour. Or you could record behaviour in a chart, as in Figure 12.2.

Contributions might also be plotted on a graph or presented in some way that clearly illustrates the nature of the contributions made. And always bear in mind that it will not be enough merely to present the information as observed. Commentary on the significance (or lack of significance) will also be necessary.

Content

The analysis of the content of a meeting or group discussion may be rather more straightforward. If the main interest is in who makes most contributions and spends most time speaking (not necessarily the same thing), then a simple chart along the lines of that shown in Figure 12.3 might be constructed. In this case, a vertical line would indicate that the named person spoke for a set time (say half

Figure 12.3 Example of a chart recording speaking contributions of individuals

Participants	
Mick	///=
Fred	
Judith	/≡//
Brendan	//
Ian	////=/≡
Stephen	//
Sandy	/=//
Multiple speaking	///

a minute or less). A following horizontal line would indicate that the same person continued to speak for longer than the set period.

The above examples appear to be fairly simple to manage and should produce useful, though limited, information. If all you need to know is who spoke most or which topics took up most time, then they will suffice, and adaptations to these charts have been used to good effect in many different situations. However, if you wish to find out who says most about what, then a more complex system is needed, and it may be best to make fuller notes during the course of the observation and then transfer them to a summary chart.

Do your best to get some observation practice to try out your recording skills. If you have the opportunity (and obtain permission) to attend a formal meeting as an observer, ask if you might see an agenda beforehand. Sometimes this will be granted, sometimes not. It's a great help if you are able to see what items are to be considered, so it's worth asking.

If you are unable to attend any meetings, group sessions or classes, try out your recording skills on a television programme. Political discussions are good, because they often degenerate into arguments, with everyone speaking at the same time. Select no more than three categories, such as 'dissent', 'aggression' and 'agreement', but make sure you are clear about how you define each of these categories. What are the indicators of 'aggression' (shouting, pointing of a finger, sneering, what else?). Devise your own chart and see if you can record the contributions. Ten minutes should be enough to show you how complex recording can be, even when your categories seem to be perfectly clear. You may discover that categories can sometimes overlap, contributions to the discussion can come thick and fast and you have to concentrate, to look at contributors' expressions, to listen for mixed messages *and* to put your number in the right place at the right time. Your first shot at a chart may not suit you and so you will need to devise one or two different designs to see which you find easiest for recording, analysis and interpretation after the event.

A few words of warning – again

At the beginning of this chapter, I said that observation can often reveal characteristics of groups or individuals that would be impossible to discover by other means. This has been demonstrated in many research studies that made extensive use of observation techniques, but the greatest care has to be taken to ensure that you get the most out of your periods of observation. You are unlikely to have three years in which to begin an investigation with an entirely open mind and to evolve hypotheses and methods as you go along. It is likely you will only have one opportunity to observe a meeting, group or class and so you will need to be quite clear about the purpose of your observation and why you are observing that particular group or individual. You may discover that unforeseen and interesting information emerges during the course of your observation, but you will be mainly dependent on the decisions taken before you begin your period of observation for the type of data you eventually gather. If you make a decision before a meeting that your main interest is the content of the meeting, then charts, grids or checklists have to be devised with that aim in mind. It will be too late to record interactions. If your main interest is process, then other methods will have to be found to record how a class or a meeting is conducted. As you select and refine your methods, keep constantly in mind the same old questions: What do I need to know? Why do I need to know it? And what shall I do with this information when I have it?

Pilot exercises and practice in recording will answer some of these questions and will point to weaknesses in technique. When you begin your one-off observation exercise, you need to be as sure as you can that you are prepared and ready.

You only have one shot at any observation. Avoid trying to make a record of too many aspects of the behaviour you are observing.

After the event

The task is not complete when the observation has taken place and records have been made. If you were observing a meeting and felt at the end of it that it was rather ineffectual, you would need to analyse the reasons. Was the process altogether too formal? Did the chair (or someone else) speak for 80 per cent of the time? Were contributions from some people dismissed? Some forms of interaction analysis can help you to classify process and content, but whatever methods of recording you have selected, it is essential to consider the event as a whole, as soon after the event as you can. Review in your mind what took place and decide whether any conclusions can be drawn that might be of interest in your study.

Observation Checklist

1. Decide exactly what you need to know.	List all topics/aspects about which information is required.	☑
2. Consider why you need this information.	Examine your list and remove any item that is not directly associated with the task.	☑
3. Is observation the best way of obtaining the information you need?	Consider alternatives.	☑
4. Decide which aspects you need to investigate.	Are you particularly interested in content, process, interaction, intervention – or something else?	☑
5. Request permission to observe.	Clear official channels and discuss what is involved with the individuals concerned.	☑
6. Devise a suitable grid, checklist or chart.	Consult published examples, adapt where necessary – and acknowledge the source. Decide on your categories.	☑
7. Consider what you will do with the information.	Is it likely to produce anything of interest? Will the data be sufficiently complete to enable you to come to any conclusions?	☑
8. Pilot your method and revise if necessary, and invite someone to observe with you. Compare notes afterwards to see if you saw the same things.	Memorize categories. Devise your own system of shorthand (symbols, letters, etc.). Practise recording until you are confident you can cope.	☑

9. Prepare carefully before the observation.	Draw a plan of the room, indicating seating arrangements and layout. Make sure you have enough copies of grids or checklists. Consult minutes of previous meetings, agendas, schemes of work, and so on.	☑
10. Discuss where you will sit with whoever is in charge and with the people who will be observed.	You want to be as unobtrusive as possible. Exactly where you sit will depend on your own preferences and the views of participants.	☑
11. Remember that no grid, no matter how sophisticated, will tell the full story.	Try to place the event in its organizational context. Obtain as much information about the organization/institution/committee or group before the observation.	☑
12. Always write up field notes as you go along, add items to your summary sheet and write your thoughts down about significant events.	If you wait until later, you will forget important items.	☑
13. Analyse and interpret the data. Do your best to eliminate bias or misinterpretation.	Statements about what has been observed are only part of the task. Consider what the facts indicate or imply. Make quite sure that none of the individuals you observe will suffer as a result of being observed, and make equally sure that their identities will never be disclosed.	☑

14. Don't forget to thank the people who have allowed you to observe.	You may need their help again!	

Useful though grids, forms and checklists are, they all have limitations. They cannot take account of emotions, micropolitical processes behind some of the interactions, the influence of certain key members of the group, and the effect they can have on the way meetings and discussions are conducted and decisions reached.

The work that goes into recording and adding up the numbers of committee or group members who showed aggression, agreement, dissent or who spoke for a specified period of time is important, but it is even more important to place what you observe in its organizational and/or curricular context, to look beyond the event itself and to be able to identify important moments in the interaction.

Further reading

Bowling, A. (2009) ***Research Methods in Health: Investigating Health and Health Services*** **(3rd edn). Maidenhead: Open University Press.**
Chapter 15, 'Unstructured and structured observational studies', provides useful information about participant observation, gaining access, establishing validity and reliability (reducing observer bias), structured and unstructured observations, and analysis and categorization of data.

Darlington, Y. and Scott, D. (2002) ***Qualitative Research in Practice: Stories from the Field.*** **Buckingham: Open University Press.**
Chapter 4, 'Observation', is helpful and well worth consulting. The authors provide guidance about the observation process, including useful reminders about the ethics of observation.

Denscombe, M. (2010) ***The Good Research Guide for Small-scale Social Research Projects*** **(4th edn). Maidenhead: Open University Press.**
Chapter 11, 'Observation', in this excellent book is well worth a read. Denscombe covers the advantages and disadvantages of systematic

observation; observation schedules; types of events and behaviour to be recorded; suitability for observation; the advantages and disadvantages of participant observation; making field notes (and the dangers of fieldwork), and ethics.

Jorgensen, D.L. (2008) *Participant Observation: A Methodology for Human Studies* (2nd edn). London: Sage.

Moyles, J. (2002) Observation as a research tool, in M. Coleman and A.R.J. Briggs (eds) *Research Methods in Educational Leadership and Management* London: Sage.

Punch, K.F. (2005) *Introduction to Social Research: Quantitative and Qualitative Approaches* (2nd edn). London: Sage.
Pages 178–84 consider structured and unstructured approaches to observation, recording observational data and participant observation.

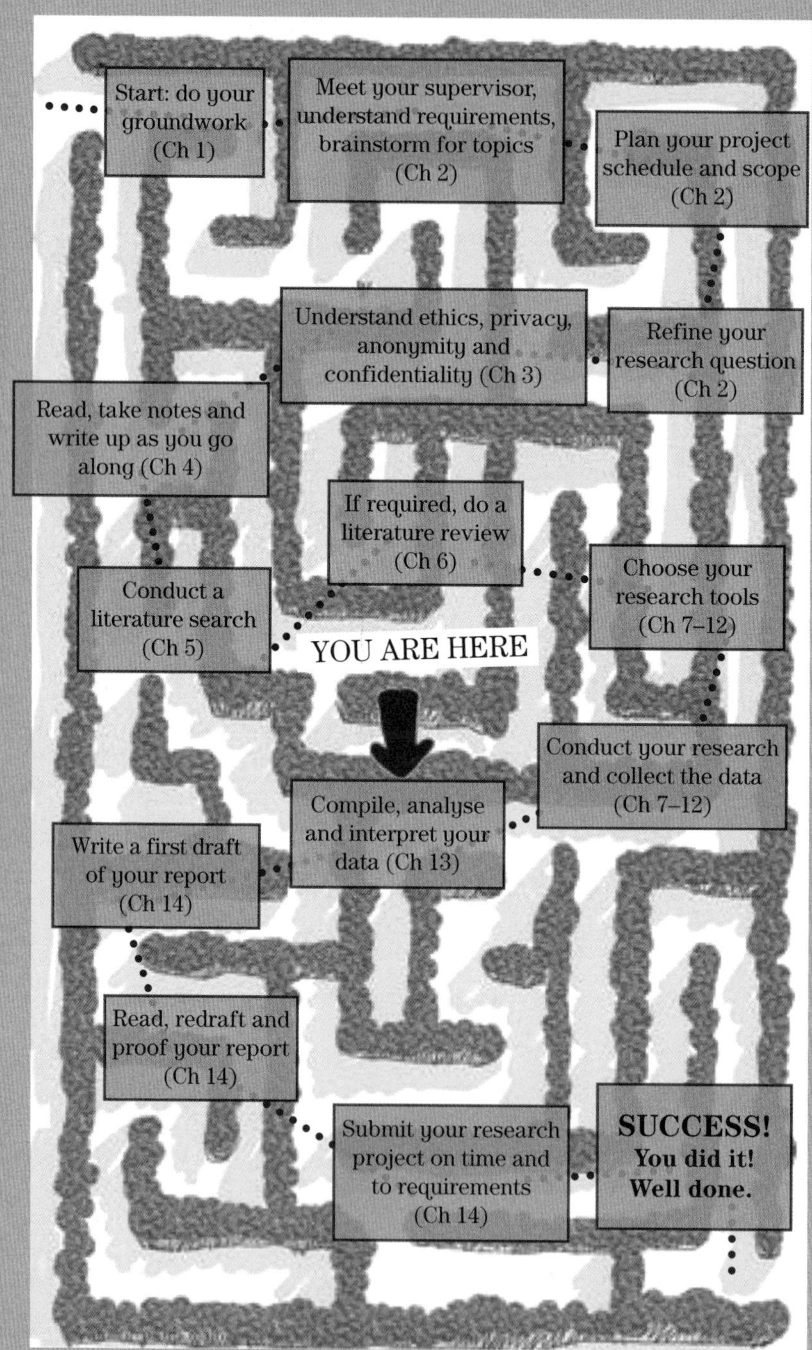

Start: do your groundwork (Ch 1)
Meet your supervisor, understand requirements, brainstorm for topics (Ch 2)
Plan your project schedule and scope (Ch 2)
Understand ethics, privacy, anonymity and confidentiality (Ch 3)
Refine your research question (Ch 2)
Read, take notes and write up as you go along (Ch 4)
If required, do a literature review (Ch 6)
Conduct a literature search (Ch 5)
Choose your research tools (Ch 7–12)
YOU ARE HERE
Conduct your research and collect the data (Ch 7–12)
Compile, analyse and interpret your data (Ch 13)
Write a first draft of your report (Ch 14)
Read, redraft and proof your report (Ch 14)
Submit your research project on time and to requirements (Ch 14)
SUCCESS! You did it! Well done.

PART III

Interpreting the Evidence and Reporting the Findings

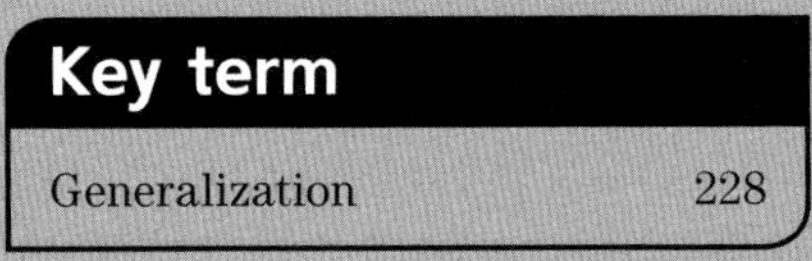

Key term

Generalization 228

Data collected by means of questionnaires, interviews, diaries or any other method mean very little until they are analysed and evaluated. Gathering large amounts of information in the hope that something will emerge is not to be recommended in any small or smallish investigation, especially not for new researchers. As I said in the introduction to this book, those of you who have a limited statistical background cannot attempt highly complex surveys involving advanced statistical techniques, but that does not mean that a worthwhile study cannot be carried out. It is all a case of working within your level of expertise, selecting research methods which are suitable for the task and which can be readily analysed, interpreted and presented.

If at some stage you decide to carry out a large quantitative study, then you will need to get to grips with statistical procedures and, if appropriate, with statistical analysis software. Every institution of higher education will have specialists to advise you. Make use of them. They will keep you on the straight and narrow and will ensure you do not waste valuable time following false trails.

In many projects and theses, it will be sufficient to understand simple arithmetical procedures such as averages and percentages. If your data collection instruments are well devised and have been well-piloted, you will have already done the groundwork for the collection, analysis and presentation of information.

Before you begin your study of the next two chapters, there are a number of issues that already have been raised but which need to be reiterated. In Chapter 1, I briefly discussed the question of *generalization*. Bassey (1981: 85–6) drew attention to the problems of generalizing from insufficient data, and made a strong case for individual researchers working to a limited timescale to produce research structured in response to an existing or potential problem so that the results might be of use to the institution. Such research, he felt, might go some way to solving a particular problem or lead to informed discussion of how a particular problem might be tackled. He commended the descriptive and evaluative study of single pedagogic events and (writing about education case-study methods) concluded that:

> "An important criterion for judging the merit of a case study is the extent to which the details are sufficient and appropriate for a teacher working in a similar situation to relate his decision-making to that described in the case study. The relatability of a case study is more important than its generalizability."
>
> (Bassey 1981: 85)

I raise this issue again here because in the analysis, interpretation and presentation of data, care has to be taken not to claim more for the results than is warranted, and equally care has to be taken not to attempt generalizations based on insufficient data. In relatively small projects, generalization may be unlikely, but relatability may be entirely possible. Well-prepared, small-scale studies may inform, illuminate and provide a basis for policy decisions. As such, they can be invaluable. There is no need to apologize about inability to generalize, but there would be every need to apologize if data was manipulated in an attempt to prove more than could reasonably be claimed.

13 Interpreting the Evidence and Reporting the Findings

INTRODUCTION

This chapter takes a detailed look at a critical stage in your research. Now you have gathered all your data, what do you do with it? This chapter examines how you should analyse your data, and provides some important tools for dealing with quantitative information and presenting data clearly in your findings. In this chapter, you will learn:

- How to compile summary sheets of data from your responses.
- How to calculate mean and median values and deal with dispersion of data in measures such as interquartile range and standard deviation.
- How to present your data in tables, bar charts, pie charts and histograms.

Key terms

Arithmetic mean	233	Standard deviation	235
Median	234	Coding	239
Mode	234	Ordinal scale	241
Range	234	Grids	242
Interquartile range	234	Scales	243

Raw data taken from questionnaires, interview schedules, checklists, and so on need to be recorded, analysed and interpreted. A hundred separate pieces of interesting information will mean nothing to a researcher or to a reader unless they have been categorized and interpreted. We are constantly looking for similarities and differences, for groupings, patterns and items of particular significance.

You may have ideas about categories before the data are collected. Your informed hunch tells you that the likelihood is that responses will tend to fall into any one of six or seven main categories. There can be dangers in placing too much reliance on preconceived ideas, not least the possibility that your line of questioning may direct respondents to reply in certain ways. However, assuming you have been able to eliminate bias of this kind, your first-thoughts categories will give you a start in the process of collating the findings. Others will undoubtedly emerge as your research proceeds but start with broad categories, and only move to more detailed examples when it becomes apparent that they merit a label of their own.

In Chapter 9, we saw that Michael Youngman (1982, 1994) suggested that in questionnaires, it is helpful to identify question types and to work out ways in which responses can be analysed and presented. You will recall that he listed seven question types (list, category, quantity, ranking, grid, scale and verbal). In this chapter, some of these question types will be used to illustrate ways in which responses might be interpreted and presented.

List questions

Let us say you wish to find out what qualifications your mature students possessed before they registered for a course. You produce a list that invites respondents to tick appropriate boxes. They may well tick more than one box and so you will need to be ready to deal with multiple responses. In Question 13.1, categories have already been selected (None, Professional qualification, Successful completion of Access or Return to Study course, A level or equivalent, and Other).

You may have been using an online survey tool such as Survey Monkey for your questionnaire, in which case it is likely that the respondents' data has been collated for you. By using the reporting tab, you can access the raw data or use the functions in the survey tool to create tables or graphs. It is important, however, when relying on these tools that you understand how to analyse the data it produces and what the data reveals. It is not enough to copy and paste the graphs from Survey Monkey into your report without explaining what the data means in relation to the research question or issue you are attempting to address. We will therefore run through the process

Question 13.1: Qualifications before entry

What qualifications did you have before you started your degree course?

None	☐	Professional qualification*	☐
Successful completion of Access or Return to Study course	☐	A level or equivalent*	☐
Other*	☐		

Please specify*____

____

____

of analysing and presenting data manually, using some research examples.

If you are collating survey data by hand, a summary sheet needs to be prepared for all items before questionnaires are distributed, so that returns can be entered as they come in. We all have our own ways of recording returns, but if you decide to record question by question, the following is probably as simple a way as any.

Summary sheet for Question 13.1: Qualifications before entry

None	Professional	Access/Return to Study	A level	Other
~~1111~~	~~1111~~	~~1111~~	~~1111~~	~~1111~~
1	~~1111~~	~~1111~~	~~1111~~	~~1111~~
	~~1111~~	~~1111~~	11	~~1111~~
	~~1111~~	~~1111~~		1
	~~1111~~	~~1111~~		
	111	~~1111~~		
		11		
6	28	32	12	16

Once the summary sheet is complete, you will begin to have a picture of the types of qualifications the students had before beginning their degree course. The information can be presented in a variety of

Table 13.1 Qualifications of mature students before entry to their course

None	A level	Professional	Access/Return to Study	Other
6	12	28	32	16

ways. A simple table followed by commentary highlighting any items of interest is one option (see Table 13.1).

The full list of 'Other' qualifications will need to be recorded on a separate sheet and if sufficient recurring types of qualifications emerge, then reference can be made to them in the commentary.

A vertical bar chart would be another option (see Figure 13.1). The variable (qualification/s) would be on the horizontal axis and the frequency (number of students) on the vertical axis. (Note that n = number of participants in the study.)

Which of the two is clearer – the table or the bar chart? Any data that tells you nothing of significance may as well be abandoned, but

Figure 13.1 Qualifications of students before entry to their degree course

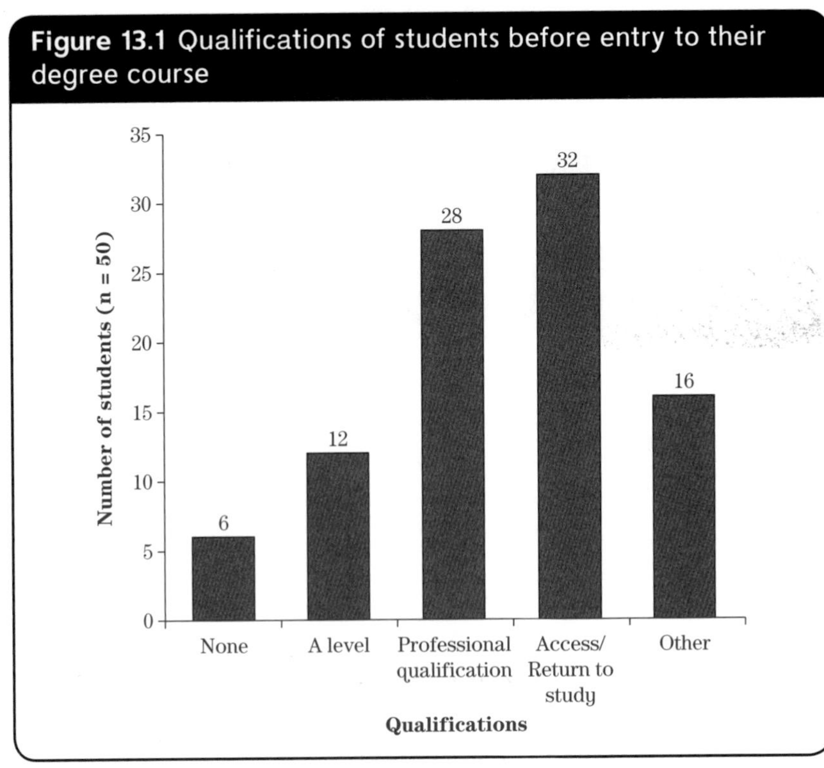

there are interesting features here. Thirty-two of the 50 students in our sample (64%) took Access/Return to Study courses, whereas only 12 (24%) had A levels or equivalent. It might be interesting to discover which group performed better in examinations. Six students (12%) had no qualifications at all on entry. How, then, had they prepared themselves for their undergraduate studies? Are they coping? It might be useful to follow up these and similar issues in interviews.

Quantity and category questions

What Michael Youngman described as quantity and category questions are, at first sight, simpler to deal with. They require one answer only. The response to a quantity question is a number (exact or approximate), giving the amount of some characteristics. The response to a category question is one only of a given set of categories. For example, if age categories are provided (20–29, 30–39, and so on), the respondents can only fit into one category.

In the mature students' study, you will probably need to know students' ages. If you have spent time on question wording and have refined the focus of each question, you will have decided whether you want to know students' ages at the time they registered, at the time they completed the questionnaire or at some other stage. You decide to ask a straight question.

Question 13.2: Age distribution of students at initial registration

> How old were you when you first registered for your degree course?

What will you do with responses? *What exactly do you want to know?* The average age of students? If so, you will need to decide what sort of average (or measure of central tendency) will suit your purpose – *the arithmetic mean, the median* or *the mode.*

Measures of central tendency

The **arithmetic mean** is simple – it is obtained by adding together each item (or value) and dividing by the total number of items (values). So, if we take 12 respondents (Group A) whose ages are 26, 26, 27, 28, 29, 30, 30, 31, 32, 33, 34 and 34, and add those values together, we get 360. Divide 360 by 12. The mean is 30. Another group of 12 (Group B) might have a different range of ages, for example 21, 22, 24, 25, 25, 29, 31, 31, 32, 35, 40 and 45. The mean is also 30 but, in these two cases, there is a clear difference in the dispersion (measures of spread) of the results.

The **median** allows us to find the middle value. This is particularly useful when there are extremes at both ends or at either end of the range that may affect the mean to a significant extent. To find the median, values must be listed in order – which in this case has already been done. If we had an odd number of values, the middle value would be the median. Where we have an even number, as in Group A, the average of the two middle values (30 + 30) is taken and so the median is 30. The fact that in this case the mean and the median are the same is because there are no extreme values at either end. There is an age progression, but if the ages were 21, 22, 29, 29, 30, 30, 33, 33, 33, 36, 39 and 84, then the differences would become apparent. The mean of these values is 34.9, whereas the median (i.e. the average of the middle points) is 31.5. You would need to decide which of the median and mean provides a more realistic picture.

The **mode**, which is not often used in small studies, relates to the most frequently occurring value. In this last example, the modal score is 33.

Each of these measures of central tendency has different uses. As always, it depends on what you need to know and why.

Look at the Group A and Group B examples again. The two groups have a very different spread of age. In Group A, the range is from 26 to 34 and so ages are close to the mean and the median. In Group B, they range from 21 to 45 and so are not clustered around the mean age. Is that worthy of comment? If so, ways have to be found of dealing with dispersion. Commonly used measures are the range, interquartile range and standard deviation.

The **range** is simply the difference between the highest and lowest values measured. For Group A, the range is 8 years, but for Group B it is 24 years. The range is not a particularly good measure of dispersion, as it can be influenced by one high and/or one low value and takes no account of the numbers of responses in the middle of the group.

The **interquartile range** gives a more accurate picture and reduces the importance of the extreme ends of the range. It is derived from the median. The highest and the lowest quarter of the measures are omitted and the interquartile range of the middle 50 per cent of the values is quoted. For Group A, the top three values (34, 34 and 33 – one-quarter of the twelve values) are omitted, as are the lowest three values (26, 26 and 27). This gives an interquartile range of 28–32, or 4 years. For Group B, the values 45, 40 and 35 are omitted, as are 21, 22 and 24. This gives an interquartile range of 25–32, which is 7 years. Is that worth commenting on? In some cases, it certainly will be. If the median has been selected as providing the best indication of the average of a set of data, then the interquartile range will indicate the extent to which data vary.

If the mean has been selected, then the standard deviation has to be used to summarize dispersion:

> "In statistics and probability theory, standard deviation ... shows how much variation or dispersion exists from the average (mean), or expected value. A low standard deviation indicates that the data points tend to be very close to the mean; a high standard deviation indicates that the data points are spread out over a large range of values."
>
> http://en.wikipedia.org/wiki/Standard_deviation

Standard deviation uses values for the group as a whole rather than for a section, whereas other measures do not. Any book on statistics will give the mathematical expression for standard deviation and how it can be calculated. Carrying out the calculations by hand can be tedious, particularly for a large group. However, the calculation is written into most computer programs so that the standard deviation is automatically produced in association with the mean. In our example, the standard deviation for Group A is 2.8 and for Group B it is 7.

In the case of these two groups, all the measures – the range, interquartile range and standard deviation – indicate that Group B has a wider spread than Group A. Used on their own, means and medians may not be sufficiently descriptive to provide a complete picture of the data. You will need to decide whether one of these measures of dispersion is also necessary when you analyse and interpret your data.

It was a straightforward matter to determine the mean and the median of data derived from Question 13.2. However, you might decide you do not wish to ask participants to say how old they are. Perhaps you consider it would be more sensitive to ask them to tick a box or circle a number to indicate the age category into which they fit. Decide whether you wish to have categories (or class intervals) of five (20–24, 25–29) or ten (20–29, 30–39). How important is it to have the groups of five? If the answer is 'not very', then take the wider span. It will be easier to manage.

Make sure your instructions are clear. In the Alternative Question 13.2, respondents would be asked to circle the number (1–5) under the appropriate age category. A respondent of 32 would circle the number 2 underneath the 30–39 age category. Take particular care to ensure that the likely full age range of your respondents is provided.

Alternative Question 13.2: Age when you first registered for your degree

20–29	30–39	40–49	50–59	60+
1	2	3	4	5

If you wished to find the arithmetic means of respondents' ages from the class intervals, this is still straightforward. Take the mid-point of each class interval and multiply that age by the number in each class. That is, mid-point × frequency, as in Table 13.2.

Dividing 1495 by the number of respondents (50) gives a mean of 29.9. The first class interval (20–29) includes those who entered higher education on their twentieth birthday and also those who entered the day before their thirtieth birthday. The interval therefore covers almost 10 years, with the exception of the final class (60). Usually, it is anticipated that only a small number of responses will fall into the final class. In the above example, the one respondent could be any age from 60 upwards and so it is necessary to assign an arbitrary mid-point. For the purpose of this exercise, the age 60 was selected.

You would then need to decide how to present the information in a way that best illustrates the age balance of the sample. You have several options. You could provide a simple chart (Figure 13.2) derived straight from your summary sheet (Table 13.3).

Table 13.2 Arithmetic mean of respondents' ages

Age	Frequency	Mid-point	Frequency × Mid-point
20–29	34	25	850
30–39	10	35	350
40–49	4	45	180
50–59	1	55	55
60+	1	60	60
Total	50		1495

Figure 13.2 Age distribution of mature students at initial registration

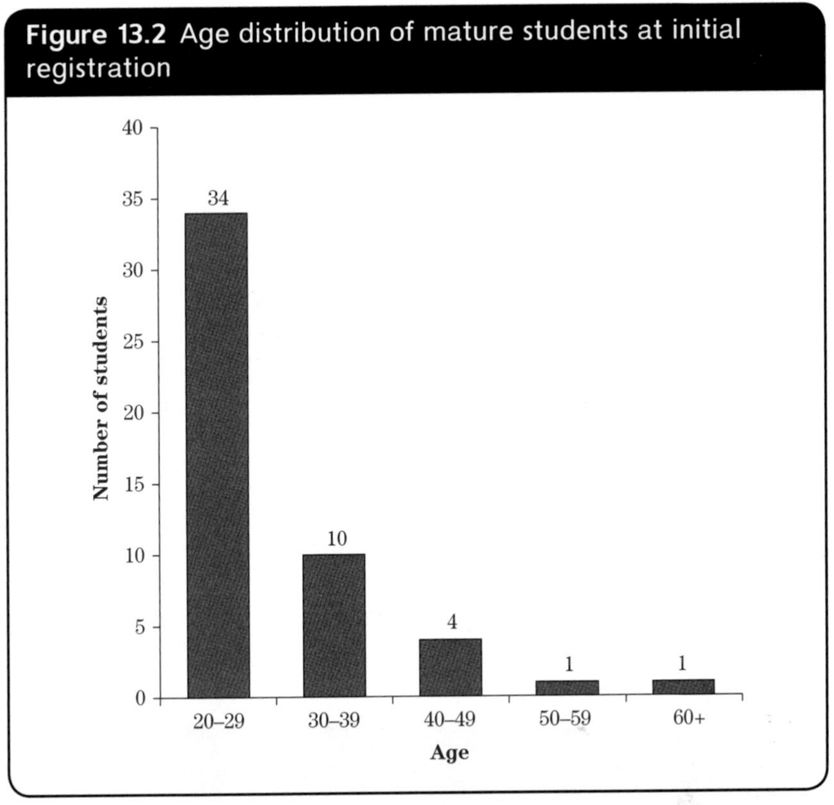

Table 13.3 Age distribution of students at initial registration

Age	Number of students
20-29	34
30-39	10
40-49	4
50-59	1
60+	1
Total	50

The same data could be represented by a histogram. A histogram is the same as a bar chart, but in the case of a histogram the bars touch, to reflect the continuous nature of the variable, which in this case is 'age'.

Alternatively, you might decide a pie chart would represent a clearer (or different) picture. Pie charts are useful, particularly if you wish to illustrate the *proportion* of students who fall into the different age groups. In this case, frequencies are changed to percentages. The 30–39 age range accounts for 20% of the total sample. The circumference of a circle is 360° and so 1% will be 3.6°. Multiplying 20 by 3.6 gives an angle of 72°. It becomes immediately apparent from Figure 13.3 that if numbers are small, percentages can be misleading, so if at all possible, include numbers with the percentages.

Do the table, histogram or pie chart provide any interesting findings? You might comment on the skewed age distribution, to the effect that few students over the age of 39 had committed themselves to the three-year full-time undergraduate course. But why would that be interesting? Subsequent interviews might provide further information about motives. Would you have expected the age distribution to be weighted at the younger end? When you examine the university records for the full mature student population (assuming you have permission to access the records), does your sample follow the same pattern, or is it different? If it is significantly different, then that

Figure 13.3 Age distribution of students at the start of their course

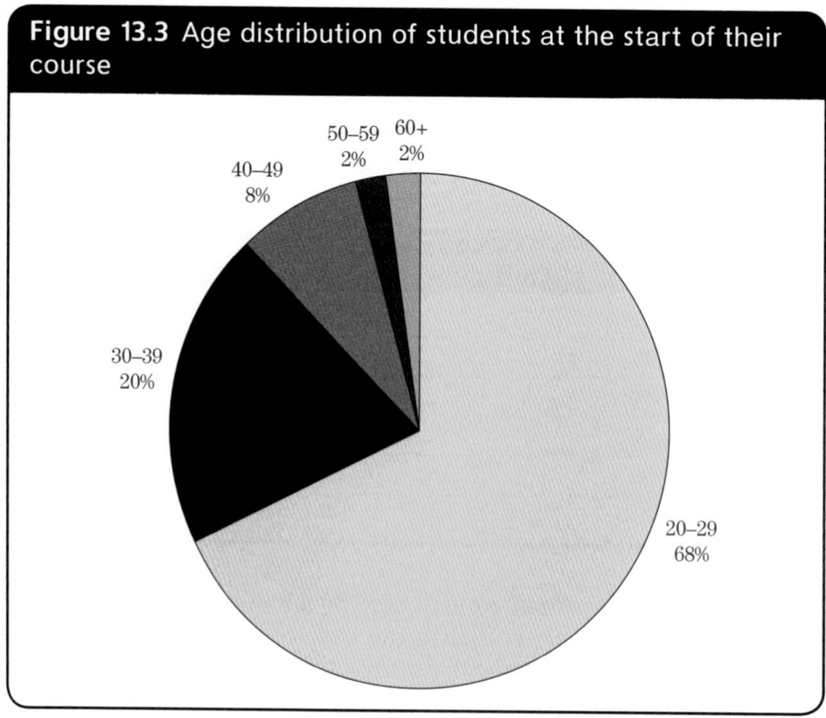

might indicate that further study is needed to try to find out why. Do university records indicate a gradual (or sudden) change in the age profile of students? What about the balance of women to men?

Would it be helpful to know whether most of the younger students are women? If you have asked students to indicate whether they are male or female, you would be able to find that out, but if you have not, it will be too late once the questionnaires are returned. Your pilot and trial collation and presentation of data should give you clues as to which information is likely to be of interest and at that stage there is still time to make adjustments to your data collection instruments. The trials will also allow you to prepare the types of summary sheets that will suit your purpose – and for that, you may need to code your data.

Coding

Writing about qualitative data analysis, Miles and Huberman state that:

> "*Codes* are tags or labels for assigning units of meaning to the descriptive or inferential information compiled during a study. Codes are usually attached to 'chunks' of varying size – words, phrases, sentences or whole paragraphs, connected or unconnected to a specific setting."
>
> (Miles and Huberman 1994: 56)

They take the view that it is not the words themselves that matter, but their *meaning*.

> "Codes are used to retrieve and organize the chunks . . . The organizing part will entail some system for categorizing the various chunks, so the researcher can quickly find, pull out, and cluster the segments relating to a particular research question, hypothesis, construct, or theme. Clustering, and . . . display of condensed chunks then sets the stage for drawing conclusions."
>
> (Miles and Huberman 1994: 57)

So, **coding** allows you to 'cluster' key issues in your data and take steps towards 'drawing conclusions'. The data you have collected mean very little until you have identified your clusters and can begin to understand what it all means.

If you plan to enter your data directly into a software package, you will need to use numerical labels, as in:

Question 13.1: Qualifications before entry

None	1
Professional qualifications	2
Access/Return to Study	3
A level or equivalent	4
Other	5
No reply	9

You might decide to break down the 'Professional qualifications' returns, if you have sufficient items, and possibly to indicate 'degree in another subject', 'nursing qualification', 'engineering qualification' or 'forestry management qualification'.

In **Alternative Question 13.2**, codes for 'age' could be allocated in the same way:

20–29	1
30–39	2
40–49	3
50–59	4
60+	5
No response	9

These numbers are *nominal scales* that have no numerical significance and so any numbers could have been used. Remember that there must be no overlapping categories. This may be obvious with the age example because a respondent could not be classified as being in the 20–29 and the 30–39 category, but especially when dealing with open or verbal responses and invariably with qualitative rather than quantitative analysis, it can be quite difficult to select guaranteed non-overlapping categories.

If you are involved in a very small project and only need basic information, such as additions or percentages, you may decide you don't need to go to the lengths of using statistical analysis software, unless you are using the exercise as a trial for a larger investigation. However, you will still need to prepare a coding frame, which is your classification system, and your key. In questionnaires, you will have a good idea of many, or even most, of the categories and so will be able to plan your coding frame at the same time as you design your questionnaire. Even so, it's unlikely you will have covered all possibilities, so wait until you have returns from your pilot studies, and again after a number of returns from the main distribution, before you begin to complete your coding frame. It's irritating if you find you were wrong originally and you have to adjust codes and to go through all the returns again.

Open questions may well produce unexpected items. Collate all the responses and then try to identify any recurring items. They will form the basis of your coding system, but remember that quite often two or three identical – or similar – responses may give you too many categories. Particularly in a small project, there is likely to be a limit to how many are reasonable. You will always need an 'odds and ends' category and remember to allow for a 'no response' category. The number '9' is often used for 'no response' and if this number suits you, keep it for all 'no response' items. If you don't need numerical codes, then use 'NR' because there is considerable merit in adopting letters, or even words, instead of numbers. Letters and words are easily identified, whereas numbers have to be checked against your coding frame.

As described in Chapter 9, you can use an **ordinal scale**, such as a Likert scale (named after the man who devised it in 1932 – Rensis Likert). Likert scales ask respondents to indicate strength of agreement or disagreement with a given statement or series of statements, generally over a 5-point or 7-point range, by circling the appropriate number. Answers are then scored, generally from 1 ('strongly disagree') to 5 or 7 ('strongly agree') and a measure of respondents' feelings can be produced. The coding frame would follow the same numerical approach, namely:

Strongly disagree	Disagree	Neutral	Agree	Strongly agree
1	2	3	4	5

Of course, if you are not entering the data into a statistical software program, you could equally well decide to use the easily recognized letters SD, D, N, A and SA. At least with the letters you are not constantly referring back to the coding frame to make sure you have the right number.

There are no set ways of coding. It is a case of deciding on a system that will suit your data and your way of managing it. Try out different summary sheets and coding frames. Keep things as simple as possible. If you are concerned mainly with a quantitative study and wish to make use of software to analyse your returns, prepare as well as you can before you finalize your data collection instruments. As I've said before (but it's sufficiently important to repeat here), find out if there is anyone in your department or institution whose job it is to help students to organize and code data and to select suitable software that is within your level of expertise. I hope that long before you have reached this stage of interpreting the evidence and reporting the findings, you will have attended courses offered by your faculty, IT department or library. Try out imaginary returns from your questionnaire and see if your program can cope with them. Better to find out you asked the questions in the wrong way as soon as possible, rather than when all returns are received.

Time to move on to grids, scales and verbal questions.

Grids

The simple types of response questions such as list, quantity and category are relatively easy to deal with. **Grids** require a little more care. A grid (or table) question will ask students to provide answers to two or more questions at the same time.

Go back to the question about students' qualifications before they started their degree course. Instead of merely asking whether they had 'no qualifications', a 'professional qualification', 'A level or equivalent', 'successful completion of an Access or Return to Study course' or 'other' qualification, you might decide it would be more useful to learn about study carried out after the age of 18. If so, a grid question could be devised (**Question 13.3**). Here there are two dimensions – years of study and type of study. Students might have spent one year on an Access course, two years on an A level course, four on a professional qualification, three on some other course. In that case, ticks would be placed in three of the boxes.

Question 13.3: Since the age of 18, how many years have you spent on the following? (Ignore periods of less than one academic year.)

	1–2 years	3–4 years	5–6 years	More than 6 years
Professional qualification				
GCE A Level or equivalent				
Access/ Return to Study course				
Other (please specify)				

Figure 13.4 Years spent on study since the age of 18

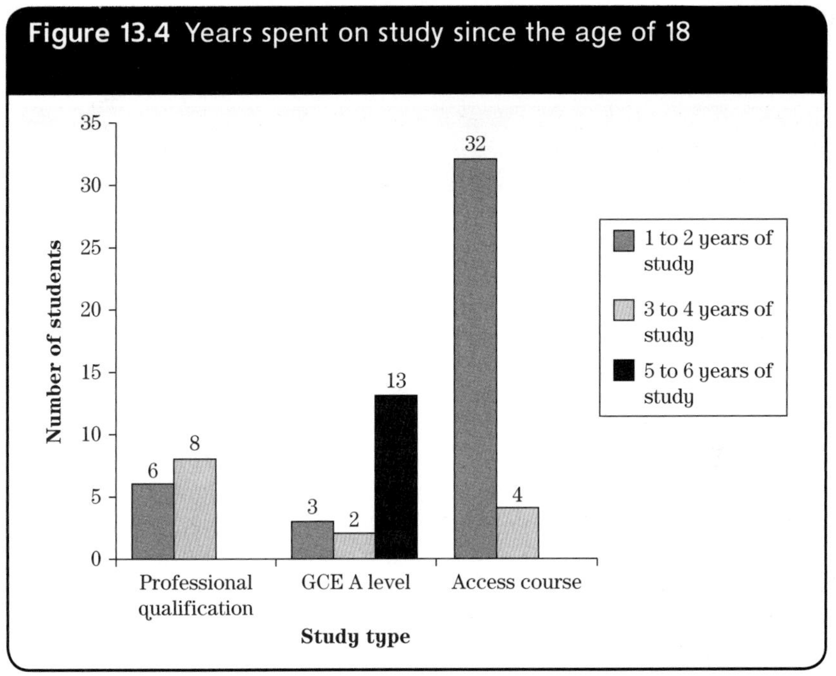

The returns could be presented in table form in much the same style as the original question, but it would also be possible to produce a compound bar chart that compares numbers of students with years of study spent on different courses (see Figure 13.4).

Scales

Scales are devices to discover strength of feeling or attitude. There are many different types of scale, including the Likert scale, some of which require quite complex construction and analysis. Thurstone (Thurstone and Chave 1929) and Guttman (1950) scales in particular require careful handling.

A simplified Likert scale might be used with **Question 13.4**.

Question 13.4: I consider my chances of doing well in finals are good

Strongly disagree	Disagree	Neutral	Agree	Strongly agree
1	2	3	4	5

Table 13.4 Levels of agreement among mature students that chances of success in finals are good

Strongly disagree	Disagree	Undecided	Agree	Strongly agree	Totals
10 (20%)	7 (14%)	6 (12%)	16 (32%)	11 (22%)	50 (100%)

Responses could be presented as shown in Table 13.4. A bar chart would also illustrate the range of responses, as in Figure 13.5. It is clear from Table 13.4 and from the bar chart (Figure 13.5) that more than half the students (54%) are optimistic about their results, but what about the rest? Will these percentages be influenced by the faculty to which students belong? It would be interesting to find out.

Early findings from the pilot study may have alerted you to the likely importance of the faculty dimension. If so, you would have been able to ask students to complete a combined Likert scale/grid question, which might produce the results shown in Table 13.5.

Figure 13.5 Levels of agreement among mature students ($n = 50$) that chances of success in finals are good

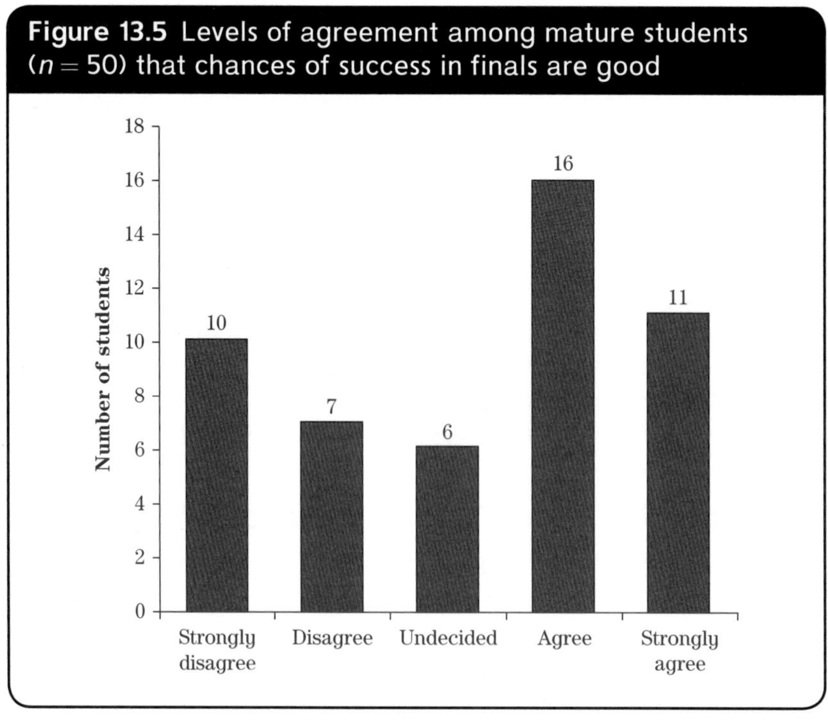

Table 13.5 Levels of agreement among mature students that chances of success, by faculty, are good

Faculty	Strongly disagree	Disagree	Undecided	Agree	Strongly agree	Total
Maths	4	0	0	0	0	4
Science	6	6	2	0	0	14
Social Science	0	0	4	16	0	20
Humanities	0	1	0	0	11	12
Totals	10	7	6	16	11	50

Presenting this data in tabular form is perfectly acceptable, but ask yourself whether other methods of presentation would illustrate the position more clearly. In this case, numbers may not present the same picture as would percentages, although as I've pointed out before, in small studies it is dangerous to use percentages without the associated numbers. They can be misleading and give the impression that the sample is bigger than it in fact is. However, if you decide it is likely to be important to discover the proportion of students who disagree or agree with the statement *by faculty*, then frequencies can be converted to percentages and a percentage component bar chart produced (Figure 13.6).

Does Figure 13.6 illustrate the position better? You will need to decide. What does emerge is that the table and the bar chart make it clear that there are major differences in the perceptions of Maths and Science students compared with Social Science and Humanities. The percentage component bar chart demonstrates the extent of the differences. So, what is happening in Maths and Science? Were the students inadequately prepared? Are there lessons to be learnt from this data? Or are the students unnecessarily pessimistic about their prospects? All these questions could be followed up in interviews with students and with tutors.

The table and bar chart illustrate the extent to which there is a relationship between the faculty's and the students' perceptions of chances of success in finals. Data plotted onto a scattergram (or scattergraph) may also indicate a relationship between two variables. As part of your investigation, you may have hypothesized that first-year coursework scores will be the same as the first-year

Figure 13.6 Percentage of students by faculty who feel their chances of doing well in finals are good

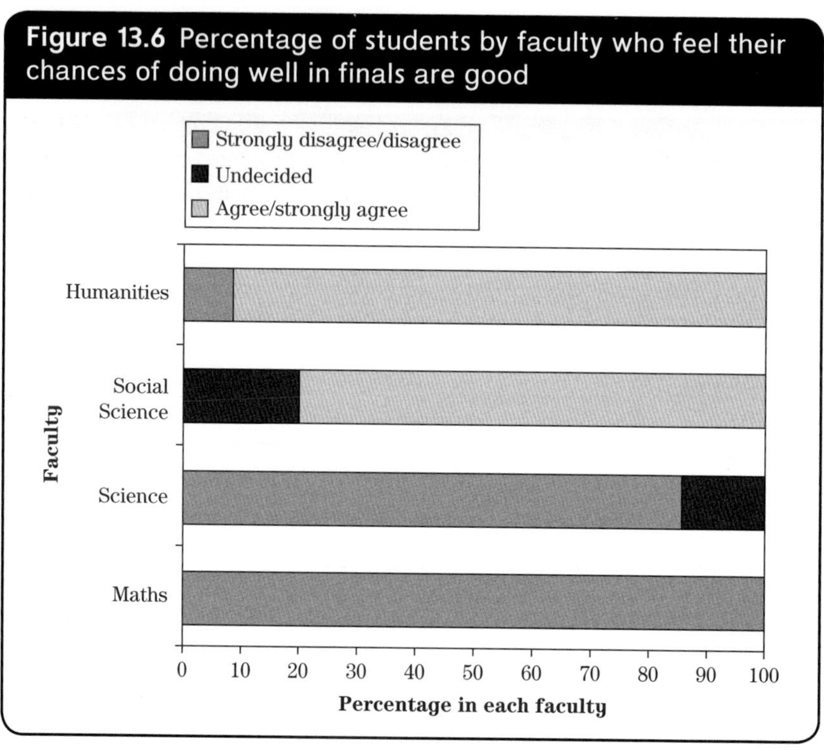

examination scores. Unlikely though that would be, let's say that the results support your hypothesis. You discover that first-year examination scores are indeed the same as coursework scores. If you produce the figures in a table, they will be the same as in Table 13.6.

Table 13.6 First-year examination and coursework scores

Student number	Examination score	Coursework score
1	30	30
2	35	35
3	40	40
4	45	45
5	50	50
6	55	55
7	60	60
8	65	65
9	70	70

It is clear that the values of the two scores match exactly, although I imagine a few questions might be asked at examination board meetings if such results were produced! However, never mind. These figures are merely used to illustrate how a 'perfect' positive correlation, which is what we have here, might be presented. Ask.com explains a correlation as '. . . a relation that exists between two things or mathematical values that tend to vary or occur together in a way not expected on the basis of chance. For example, there is a correlation between working hard in school and entering college.' Thus in Table 13.6, there is a 100% correlation between the scores of first-year students and their coursework marks, as the two are identical.

If these data were to be plotted on a graph, with the examination score on the horizontal axis and the coursework score on the vertical axis, then a perfect straight line would be produced, as in Figure 13.7.

Another sample might produce different data, as in Table 13.7. This data, transferred on to a graph (Figure 13.8), demonstrates once more that the correlation is 'perfect', but this time, as the examination score increases, the coursework decreases, and vice versa. There is therefore a negative relationship between the two variables. In reality, such relationships are rare. More realistic data might be in the third example (Table 13.8).

Figure 13.7 Positive relationship between examination and coursework scores

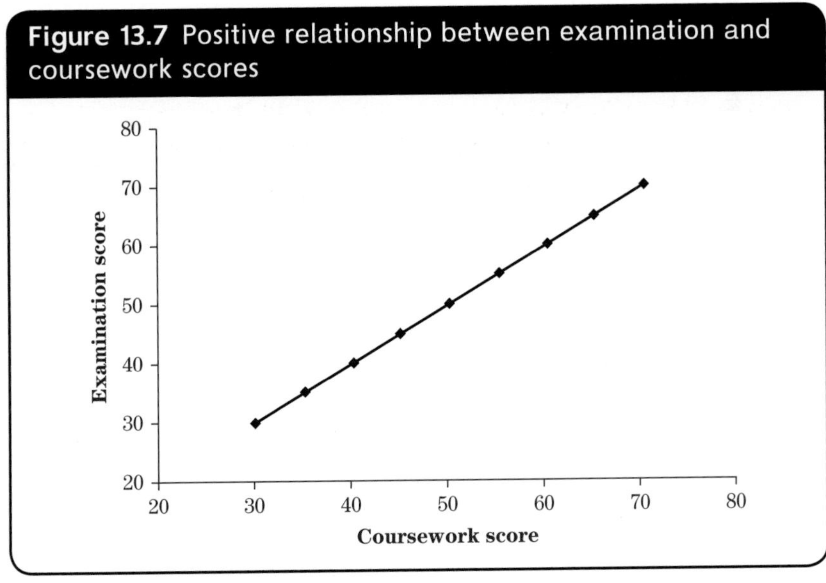

Table 13.7 First-year examination and coursework scores

Student number	Examination score	Coursework score
1	30	70
2	35	65
3	40	60
4	45	55
5	50	50
6	55	45
7	60	40
8	65	35
9	70	30

Figure 13.8 Negative relationship between examination and coursework scores

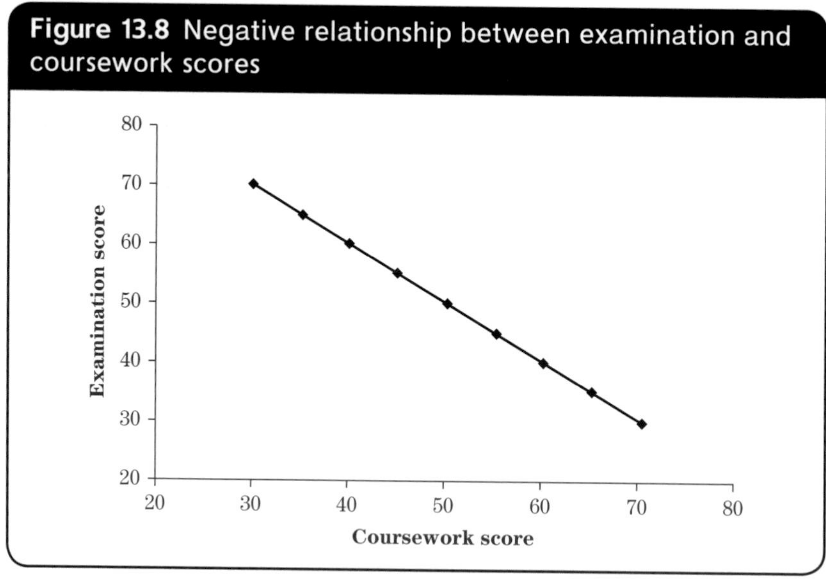

When the points are plotted on the graph, the resulting figure (Figure 13.9) shows whether there is a general trend in the results and indicates the scatter of results. In this case, since the general trend is for an increase in examination score associated with an increase in coursework score, a positive relationship exists, but it is not perfect. (The line drawn here is merely to illustrate the extent to which the scatter points relate to the perfect relationship.)

Table 13.8 First-year examination and coursework scores

Student number	Examination score	Coursework score
1	37	45
2	42	40
3	46	44
4	53	68
5	54	60
6	59	50
7	63	55
8	72	85
9	74	75

Some data, when plotted on a scattergram, may be completely random, with no discernible pattern. In this case, it is reasonable to assume that there is little or no relationship between variables. In other cases, there may be clusters, or groups of points on the scattergram, suggesting that within the total sample there are smaller groups within which the individuals have similar characteristics. Take care though. Unless calculations for **correlation coefficients**

Figure 13.9 Positive (though not perfect) relationship between examination and coursework scores

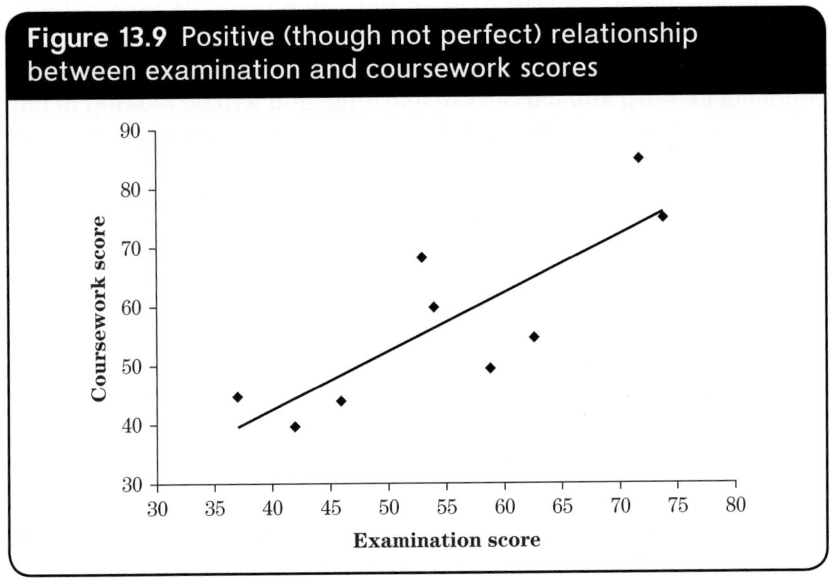

are carried out, only inferences can be drawn – not direct causal relationships. A question and answer page on Yahoo at http://answers.yahoo.com/question/index?qid=20090912141927AArnxbc defines a correlation coefficient as

> "a number between +1 and −1 that describes the type of relationship an independent variable has with a dependent variable. A coefficient of +1 means a perfect positive relationship, a coefficient of 0 means no correlation, and a coefficient of −1 means a perfect negative correlation. For example, if a study was performed on the effects of exercise on people's happiness and there was a correlation coefficient of +0.8, it would mean that exercise is a good indicator of people's happiness."

If you feel correlation coefficients are required, then you will have to become familiar with the necessary statistical techniques or to make use of software such as IBM's SPSS Statistics or whatever package your supervisor suggests.

Verbal questions

A study of responses to verbal (or open) questions will often provide useful pointers to the types of issues it may be worthwhile following up in interviews. These questions are often included on questionnaires to allow respondents to draw attention to anything about which they feel strongly. Referring to such responses is often a way of starting an interview.

The usual practice is to write or type each response on a separate sheet. This allows all items to be organized to see whether there are any recurring themes. If you are interested in discovering whether students identify any barriers to learning, you will be looking in particular for statements that relate to problems with study, tutor support, and so on. Some of the responses will probably provide useful quotations to illustrate certain points in the report – although the temptation to give greater emphasis to statements that happen to support your particular point of view has to be resisted.

Some form of content analysis may be necessary to deal with such material. If so, follow the same content analysis procedures as would be applied for the study of documents (see Chapter 7). As always, you will be looking for categories and for common criteria, if any.

Conclusions

Only the simplest methods of presentation have been considered in this chapter. They provide a starting point. The tables and charts are easy to manage. You may be able to devise different question types and different methods of analysis and presentation. The advantage of familiarizing yourself with a range of question types is that, once you have experimented with different formats and know how to produce tables, charts and graphs, you will be able to draw on whichever format suits the data and the purpose. A diagram can often simplify quite complex data that could take a paragraph or more to explain.

When you move on to larger and more complex investigations, you will need to familiarize yourself with more complex methods of analysis and with the use of statistical software programs. Try out some of the programs, using data with which you are familiar, possibly data that has been collated, analysed and presented 'by hand' in connection with one of your 100-hour projects. This will allow you to understand the principles and get to grips with the practicalities of the software.

Decide what data you need to collect for your research topic before deciding how you will present the findings, rather than choosing to collect data that will fit a method of presentation.

Interpreting the Evidence and Reporting the Findings Checklist

1. Data must be recorded as soon as it is available.	Make sure you prepare and pilot summary sheets before the main data collection begins.	
2. Look for similarities, groupings, clusters, categories and items of particular significance.	100 separate pieces of interesting information will mean nothing to a researcher or a reader until they are analysed and interpreted.	

3. First-thoughts categories will be a start in the process of collating findings.	You may find you have to amend them after your pilot studies and when your data is assembled.	☑
4. Prepare final summary sheets.	Your pilot studies will show you whether they are appropriate for your purposes.	☑
5. Experiment with different ways of presenting findings. Tables, bar charts, histograms. Other diagrams or graphs?	If you plan to use computer statistical packages, find out what help is available before you begin your pilot studies and try out possible packages.	☑
6. If you need to discover the average of certain values, decide whether the mean, median or mode is the most suitable.	Remember that each of these measures of central tendency has different uses.	☑
7. Used on their own, means and medians may not be sufficiently descriptive to provide a complete picture of the data.	A measure of dispersion may be required – range, interquartile range or standard deviation.	☑
8. Try out codes for your data. If you plan to use computer statistical packages, you will require numerical codes. If not, letters will suffice.	Do not attempt complex statistical techniques unless you have the expertise to cope. It is perfectly possible to produce a worthwhile investigation without an in-depth knowledge of statistics. However, if you can familiarize yourself sufficiently well with statistical software packages,	☑

	they can save you many hours and produce good-looking charts, tables and figures – once you know how.	
9. All data requires interpretation.	It is not enough only to describe.	☑
10. Don't claim more for your research than your evidence will support.	And watch out for possible bias.	☑

Further reading

There are many good books that deal with basic statistical techniques. However, if you consider yourself to be statistically challenged and that you need to learn more, ask your supervisor and the library staff for information about courses dealing with statistical techniques and computer analysis – and make sure you attend. If any of the following are on your library shelves, you might wish to consult the introduction, contents pages and indexes of one or more of them to see whether your understanding of 'basic' is the same as that of the authors.

Alaszewski, A. (2006) *Using Diaries for Social Research*. London: Sage.
If you have selected diaries as one type of data collection, then Chapter 5 of this book is useful. Alaszewski addresses the analysis of narrative, conversational, and other qualitative research; identifying themes in text – and coding (converting data into numbers).

Bryman, A. and Cramer, D. (2011) *Quantitative Data Analysis with IBM SPSS 17, 18 and 19: A Guide for Social Scientists*. London: Routledge.

Cramer, D. (2003) *Advanced Quantitative Data Analysis*. Buckingham: Open University Press.
This book considers a variety of techniques used to analyse quantitative data. Useful examples are provided, together with a glossary of key concepts. Some previous basic statistical knowledge would be helpful.

Denscombe, M. (2010) ***Ground Rules for Good Research: Guidelines for Good Practice*** **(2nd edn). Maidenhead: Open University Press.**
Chapter 10 of this very readable book deals with issues relating to generalization, including criteria for the selection of samples and case studies, generalizability and transferability, and guidelines for good practice.

Gibbs, G.R. (2008) ***Analysing Qualitative Data*****. London: Sage.**
Gibbs outlines how to select the most appropriate tool for analysing data, and reminds us of various challenges in interpreting data generated in qualitative research.

Hardy, M.A. and Bryman, A. (eds) (2004) ***Handbook of Data Analysis*****. London: Sage.**
This is a very good guide to basic issues in data analysis.

Miles, M.B. and Huberman, A.M. (1994) ***Qualitative Data Analysis*** **(2nd edn). Thousand Oaks, CA: Sage.**
This book has since been updated but everything in this second edition is worth reading and noting. I particularly like Chapter 3, 'Focussing and bounding the collection of data', which includes 'Linking qualitative and quantitative data', 'Management issues bearing on analysis' and 'Data management', and in Chapter 4, 'Early steps in analysis', which considers issues relating to codes and coding – and, of course, much more.

Opie, C. (ed.) (2004) ***Doing Educational Research: A Guide for First-time Researchers*****. London: Sage.**
Chapter 7 by Clive Opie considers the statistical analysis of quantitative and qualitative data. Chapter 8 by Ann-Marie Bathmaker outlines the use of the NUD-IST (Non-Numerical, Unstructured Data Indexing, Searching and Theorising) software for analysing qualitative data. Chapter 9 by Michael Pomerantz discusses the ATLAS.ti computer software application, which allows the user to study and analyse interview transcripts. Opie ends the book with a glossary of terms used in quantitative analysis.

Pallant, J. (2013) ***SPSS Survival Manual: A Step by Step Guide to Data Analysis using IBM SPSS*** **(5th edn). Maidenhead: Open University Press.**
Pallant provides examples of ways of choosing the right data analysis techniques, formulating the right questions, analysing data and reporting results, using IBM SPSS Statistics.

Punch, K.F. (2014) ***Introduction to Social Research: Quantitative and Qualitative Approaches*** **(3rd edn). London: Sage.**
Chapter 7 deals with the analysis of qualitative data and Chapter 10 discusses the analysis of quantitative data.

Rugg, G. (2007) *Using Statistics: A Gentle Introduction*. Maidenhead: Open University Press.
This very readable book guides the reader gently through the field of statistics, with few calculations and fewer equations.

Ten Have, P. (2007) *Doing Conversation Analysis* (2nd edn). London: Sage.
This book provides researchers with practical suggestions for conducting conversation analysis research.

14 Writing the Report

INTRODUCTION

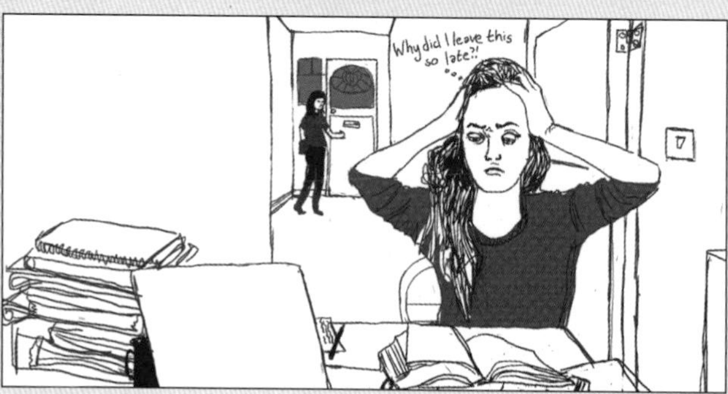

This chapter covers the final stage of your research project – the writing of the report itself. After all your hard work planning your research topic, using research tools to gather information and analysing your data, you now need to shape this into a written report that summarizes your findings and does justice to your efforts. This can seem daunting. This final chapter shows you how to approach the task of writing your report step-by-step and includes:

- Advice on the practicalities of writing – getting into good habits, finding a productive time and place for you to focus, and devising an approach to writing that works best for you.
- How to structure the report – step-by-step guides to its key components from title page to appendices, including advice on the main sections such as the abstract, analysis, discussion, and the all-important summary and conclusion.
- Working through drafts, anticipating the number of revisions, taking a critical view of your research and knowing when to stop.

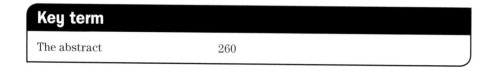

Key term

Getting started

When all the hard work of gathering and analysing evidence is complete, you will need to write the final report. Bodgan and Biklen, writing about the problems of getting started, offer the following advice:

> "Many writers are big procrastinators. We find countless reasons not to get started. Even when we finally get ourselves seated at our desks, we always seem to find diversions: make the coffee, sharpen the pencil, go to the bathroom, thumb through more literature, sometimes even get up and return to the field. Remember that you are never 'ready' to write; writing is something you must make a conscious decision to do and then discipline yourself to follow through."
>
> (Bogdan and Biklen 2003: 205)

But this is easier said than done. However, remember that a study is not finished until it is written up and, in your original planning I hope you allowed time for writing – and rewriting. I always have a sense of impending doom when a student says, 'All I have to do now is to write the project report/dissertation/thesis and I should be able to finish it in a week or two.' However, enough doom! I'm confident you will have followed some of the earlier advice in this book, that your bibliographical records, *and back-up copies*, will be in good order, with notes and useful quotations to guide your writing. I'm similarly confident that you will not have started your project unless your objectives were clear (though you may have amended them as your investigation developed). If you adopted the principle of 'writing-as-you-go' throughout your research, you will already have some drafts; and even if they are rough, it's always better to face badly written and incomplete drafts than a blank page or screen.

The final writing task

Writing requires discipline, and even the most experienced of researchers need to impose some sort of self-control to ensure that the writing task is completed on time. There are no hard and fast rules about when and how to write. We all have different ways of working and what suits one person may not suit another. Some colleagues are firm that it is best to write according to a strict schedule (always between 8 and 10 p.m. on weekdays; always between 6 and 8 a.m. every day). I've tried to do that, but I just don't seem able to keep to such a regular pattern. Things, and sometimes people, get in my way. Ideally, I have to be quiet and alone to write, with all my source material around me. Other people say they can't write in silence. They need the radio or music in the background, while others are unable to concentrate without the use of headphones.

Some writers and researchers are convinced it's a good idea to aim for a certain number of words in every writing session, and I did know one person who could produce 1000 words of good quality writing most days, but only one. I've never managed to achieve that, although I do make plans to complete particular sections or even paragraphs at one sitting. And if I'm in the middle of a good writing session and come across an incomplete reference, I now *don't stop to look it up*. I make a note or highlight it, and then return to it later. If I try to correct it immediately, the time it takes might break my concentration. I might then feel I need a break anyway and that it is absolutely the right time to make a cup of tea, tidy up the kitchen, do some cleaning. On second thoughts, abandon the cleaning and let somebody else tidy up the kitchen. One job might lead to another – and then that's the end of the writing session.

As far as I can, I try to work to an agenda and if I can achieve more than one item, I feel full of virtue and have even been known to give myself time off for such good behaviour. We all have to have our little treats in life.

I try to set aside writing days or half days when I know I can be more or less alone and free from distractions, but I only write for two hours at a time. I've learnt that if I press on hour after hour, I begin to write rubbish. I don't know it's rubbish at the time but when I read it after it has 'gone cold' the next day or next week, then I most certainly do. After two hours or so, assuming I've reached a stage from which it will be easy to move on, I can then have a cup of tea (or even something stronger), wander around, check my messages, deal with that irritating, incomplete reference, take the dog for a walk – anything to give myself a break before I move on to the next stage.

I'm regularly told by colleagues that I have bad writing habits and perhaps I do. However, I am quite disciplined in a number of ways. My index and reference systems are generally quite good, so I can find what I need most of the time. Bitter experience has taught me that keeping notes, transcripts, references and rough drafts in what Miles and Huberman (1994: 56) describe as an 'alpine collection of information' is a thoroughly bad idea. Experience has also taught me to print on one side of the paper only, and in the early drafts, to try to keep to one or two paragraphs to a page. And yes, I know researchers who still handwrite all drafts. That approach suits them and that's fine. I know that my early drafts won't be good enough, so I need to be able to move paragraphs and even sentences around – and so I find it better to use Word from the start. We all have our own ways of doing things and that's good, *as long as we each have some system and plan of our own that enables us to write to and keep to an agenda* (more or less).

Just one more thing (or, to be more precise, one or two more things) before I move on to the structure of your report. Never throw away or delete early drafts. Open a junk file. Call it what you like – a dump, junk or something-else file. Tidy up before you make a start on your final writing task. Make sure you name and date each item before you dump it. You never know what might come in handy at some later stage. I have found that saving a draft of my writing at the end of each day in a folder named with the title or topic of my research and dating it is invaluable. While it means that I amass a number of files of the report in date order, I can go back to an earlier draft if necessary, for example to retrieve a reference I have accidentally deleted or to re-read a section that I have altered and have had second thoughts about.

Structuring the report

Institutions and departments almost always provide guidelines about the way the final report should be presented and, if they do, it goes without saying that they should be followed to the letter. If for any reason they are not provided, something on the following lines will generally be acceptable.

1 Title page

Include the title of your study, your name and the date. The title should accurately reflect the nature of your study and should be brief and to the point. A subtitle may be provided if it clarifies the purposes of the study.

2 Acknowledgements

You may (or may not) wish to acknowledge the help given to you throughout your research. If you do, then acknowledgements and thanks generally come after the title page.

3 Contents

The contents page will be produced when your report is completed.

4 The abstract

In most cases, an **abstract** will be required, though practices vary, so consult the 'house' rules. It is quite difficult to say in a few words what your investigation set out to do, the methods employed and what conclusions were reached. The following example is one way in which the task might be approached:

> "This project attempts to identify effective teaching and learning strategies and any barriers to learning as perceived by mature students at Bramhope University. Data were gathered from questionnaires, interviews and observation of, and participation in, lectures, seminars and tutorials. The report concludes that there is scope for consideration of more varied approaches to the delivery of the curriculum and for consultations with mature students about ways in which changes might be introduced."

If you are allowed more space, you will be able to develop this abstract to provide the reader with more information, but for short reports, something along the above lines will generally suffice. Get into the habit of looking at abstracts usually placed at the beginning of journal articles. Ask yourself whether they give a good idea of what the article is about, how data were collected and what conclusions were reached.

5 Aims and purpose of the study

This should be a brief explanation of the purpose of the research. Explain the research problem in a few sentences. State aims/objectives/hypotheses. Provide any background to the study in order to place it in its context.

Draw attention to any *limitations of the study* at this stage. An individual researcher with only 100 hours or so to complete a project can neither hope to become involved in complex sampling techniques nor to interview hundreds of people. You cannot do everything in a small study, and your supervisor will know that, but in this section you should make it clear that you know what the limitations of the study are. Be honest.

6 Review of the literature

Not all reports will require a review of previous research, though for Master's and Doctoral studies a review will normally be expected. In a short project, and subject to your supervisor's agreement, you may have decided to use your reading mainly to support or to reject arguments throughout the report, but the value of a review to the reader is that it explains the context and background of the study. Remember Haywood and Wragg's warning in Chapter 6, that critical reviews can too often turn out to be uncritical reviews – 'the furniture sale catalogue, in which everything merits a one-paragraph entry no matter how skilfully it has been conducted' (Haywood and Wragg 1982: 2). A selection has to be made, and only books and articles that relate directly to the topic should be included.

The review, if required, can be written first and, if you have managed to discipline yourself sufficiently well to write up sections and sub-sections as you have completed them, much of the work of this section will be ready for revision before you begin to collect data. You may find that you need to adapt your original version, but you should not need to start from the beginning by reading through notes to decide what should be included and what left out.

7 Methods of data collection

An alternative heading might be 'Some considerations of method' – or any other title that in your view describes the content of the section well. This section explains how the problem was investigated and why particular methods and techniques were employed. Accounts of the procedure, size of sample, method of selection, choice of variables and controls, and tests of measurement and statistical analysis, if any, should be provided. Consult your supervisor about how much detail is required. Point out that it is unnecessary to describe in detail any tests or procedures that are well known and frequently used, but if you have devised any of your own systems of measurement, it is likely that full information will be needed.

Important terms should be defined precisely and any deficiencies in the methods mentioned. It is important to bear in mind that, in certain kinds of investigation, the research needs to be repeatable, and a fellow researcher should be able to obtain enough information from this section to make this possible.

8 Statement of results

This is the heart of the report and will consist of text and, if necessary, tables or figures, depending on the nature of the project. The way results are presented is important. Tables, charts, graphs and other figures should illustrate and illuminate the text. If they do not, then there is no point in them taking up space. The text, which should be written after the results are prepared, should not duplicate information in the tables and figures but should highlight significant aspects of the findings so that all relevant facts are presented in a way that draws attention to what is most important. It is quite an art to achieve this balance, and you may find you need several drafts before you are satisfied.

All tables and figures should be numbered, given a title and carefully checked before you submit your report. Tables are generally numerical presentations in lists or columns, though there can be tables of names or other items. Figures are other types of presentation of data. It is customary for the number and title of a table to appear above the table, and those for a figure below the figure. It is quite a good idea to look at the way other students have presented them – and take care to follow any institutional guidelines.

9 Analysis and discussion

It is often best to start this section with a restatement of the problem before discussing how the results affect existing knowledge of the subject. If your research aimed to test certain hypotheses, then this section should demonstrate whether they were or were not supported by the evidence. Any deficiencies in the research design should be mentioned, with suggestions about other approaches that perhaps might have been more appropriate.

Most researchers find it best to write sections 6, 7 and 8 in sequence to ensure continuity and logical progression. It is quite feasible to write some sections as discrete units at different times, but these three sections need to be considered as a whole. If you have to take a break from writing, make sure you re-read everything that has gone before when you return, in order to ensure a smooth continuation – and to avoid repetition.

10 Summary and conclusions

The main conclusions of the report that have been discussed in section 8 should be summarized here, briefly and simply. Only conclusions that can be justifiably drawn from the findings should be made. That sounds (and is) obvious, but there is often a great temptation to include an opinion for which no evidence is provided in the report. Take care or you may spoil a good report by including an unsubstantiated comment.

Before you write this section, read through the whole report and make a note of key points. Readers who want a quick idea of what your research is about will look at the abstract, possibly the introduction and almost certainly at the summary and conclusions. This final section should be sufficiently succinct and clearly expressed to enable readers to understand quite clearly what research has been done and the conclusions that have been drawn *from the evidence*.

11 List of references

It is worthwhile at this stage in your writing to refer to Blaxter and colleagues' guidance on the use and abuse of references. They write that references should not be included to 'impress your readers with the scope of your reading', or to 'replace the need for you to express your own thoughts' but they should be used to:

- 'justify and support your arguments
- allow you to make comparisons with other research ...
- demonstrate your familiarity with your field of work.'

(Blaxter *et al.* 2010: 130).

You are not in the business of producing the longest list of references ever known and it would be a pity to spoil a good report with irrelevant references, so check carefully that each one is there for a purpose.

Opinions vary as to whether a full bibliography or a list of references, or both, should be included. My view is that only items that have been cited in the report should be included. However, some institutions also require a bibliography, which includes all sources consulted during the preparation of the investigation. You will need to consult your supervisor about institutional practice.

If you adopted the Harvard method of referencing, which I have recommended in this book, then references will appear in alphabetical order, which simplifies the process and avoids overlap. The amount of time it takes you to produce a bibliography, list of references, or both, will depend on how meticulous you were when you first recorded your sources. This is the time when all your hard work and systematic recording will really pay off.

12 Appendices

Copies of any data collection instruments (questionnaires, interview schedules, and so on) that have been used should be included in an appendix, unless you have been instructed otherwise. Your tutor will not wish to receive all the completed questionnaires but one copy of any data collection instrument that has been used is generally required.

13 Length

Your supervisor will offer you guidance on length and many institutions have their own rules about this. If you have not been told what length is expected, then ask. If a maximum number of words is stipulated, try not to exceed that number. You may have plus or minus 10 per cent of the word count to play with. Ensure you keep within the limits or you may be penalized. I confess that, sometimes against institutional rules, I was not willing to mark down an outstanding piece of work because it was too long. My view was that outstanding work was outstanding work, whatever the length. However, best to ignore me. Just make sure you know what your department/institution/supervisor require and do your best to conform.

14 Quotations

All quotations must, of course, be acknowledged. Remember that your tutor has probably read the same books, so is likely to recognize the source. As I said in Chapter 4, if you are quoting only a few words or one sentence, it will be sufficient to indicate this by using inverted commas in the main text, with the source in brackets. For example: As Laws (2013: 306) says, 'The *title* should be of immediate interest to the reader, as with a newspaper headline.'

If the quotation is longer, indent it, with the author, date of publication and page number at the end, as in the following:

> "Your style should be determined by your own natural way of expressing yourself and the needs of your audience. However, while some audiences might be impressed by a complex way of writing, the main purpose of the exercise is to convey information … Clear and simple expression will help people to make sense of the material you present, and therefore to act on it."
>
> (Laws 2013: 288)

As I'm sure you know, the three full stops (ellipsis) indicate an omission.

15 Presentation

Reports are generally typed using double line spacing. Pages should be numbered. Print on one side of the page only, leaving a left-hand margin of one and a half inches.

Check your institution's rules about presentation. For a short project report, it will generally be enough to provide a title page but rules will vary significantly for dissertations and theses. Some institutions require them to be bound; others do not, so once again, check what is required.

The need for revision

I've never known anyone who has been able to produce a perfect first draft, so don't convince yourself that you will be the exception. You won't. You may find you need two, three or even more drafts before you are satisfied with the final result, so time must be set aside for this writing and refining process.

One problem about spending so much time on drafts is that parts of them may seem right, simply because you have read them so often. Another is that you may be so familiar with the subject that you assume something is understandable to the reader when it is not. Time will give you a better perspective on your writing, so you should put the script aside, for several days if you can, so that you can return to it with a more critical eye. This will help you to identify repetitive passages, errors of expression and lack of clarity.

Work through your first draft section by section to ensure its sense, accuracy, logical sequencing and soundness of expression. If you wrote or typed only one paragraph on one side of each sheet, as suggested earlier, this correcting and reordering stage will be relatively straightforward and this will make cutting and pasting much easier. Check spelling. Spell checks help, though remember that most use American spelling and most do not check spelling in context. So homophones (words that sound the same but are spelled differently) will go unnoticed (e.g. 'there' and 'their'). Check quotations, punctuation, references, repetition, consistency of tenses and the overuse of certain terms. *Roget's Thesaurus of English Words and Phrases* may help you to find alternative forms of expression.

Remind yourself as you read that whatever structure has been selected, your readers will wish to be quite clear why you carried out the investigation, how you conducted it, what methods you used to gather your evidence and what you found out. *It is not enough to describe: you will be expected to analyse, to evaluate and, if the evidence merits it, to make recommendations.*

If research findings are to be put into practice, they have to be presented in a way in which practitioners and policy-makers can understand them. There is no special academic language that should be used in academic papers and as I keep saying, good, clear English remains good, clear English, whatever the context. Technical language may well save time when you are talking to colleagues with a similar background to your own, but it rarely translates well on to paper, and your readers (and your examiner) may become irritated by too much jargon or obscure language.

The need for revision and rewriting was emphasized in a radio interview, when a world-famous economist who had many scholarly books to his credit, was complimented by the interviewer on his style of writing. 'It must be a great advantage', said the interviewer, 'to be able to write so freely and so easily. How do you do it?' The economist revealed his secret as follows:

> "First, I produce a draft and then I leave it alone. I go back to it after a few days and decide it has been written by an ignoramus, so I throw it away. Then I produce a second draft and leave it alone for a few days. I read it and decide there are the germs of a few good ideas there but it is badly written, so I put it to one side. After a few days, I write a third draft. When I read it again, I discover the ideas are developing, that there is some coherence to my arguments and that the grammar is not too bad. I correct this draft, change paragraphs around, insert new thoughts, remove overlapping passages and begin to feel progress is being made. After a few days, I read through this fourth draft, make final corrections and hand over the fifth draft to the typist. At this stage, I find I have usually achieved the degree of spontaneity for which I have been striving."

You may not need five drafts. Three may be enough if you write well, but rest assured that no one gets away with one or two – and many of us take four or five.

When you have completed the writing to the best of your ability, try to enlist the help of someone who will read your draft to look for any remaining errors. My partner is particularly good at locating errors, repetition, omissions, conclusions from insufficient evidence, sections that make no sense and several dozen other sins. Sometimes I accept the corrections and sometimes I don't, but it's amazing how many times I have read a script and never noticed some obvious omission or repetition. Another pair of eyes is always helpful, even if your reader knows nothing about your specialist area. And if you cannot find anyone willing to read and comment on your draft, you might read it out loud, though make sure you are alone or your family might think the strain has been too much for you! Reading aloud is particularly useful for detecting the need for better linking passages and, perhaps surprisingly, it can sometimes reveal awkward wording that you had not noticed before.

You will not be able to write your report first time round. Leave time to write several drafts. Before you submit your report, leave a few days between finishing your final draft and proofreading it. That way you are more likely to notice mistakes or aspects of your writing that you could improve.

Any possibility of plagiarism?

In Chapter 4, I discussed the issue of plagiarism but this is sufficiently important to repeat here. You are plagiarizing if you copy someone else's words and claim them as your own and you cannot use other people's data or their ideas unless you provide adequate acknowledgement. I'm confident your institution will have guidelines on plagiarism, so make sure you read them. Excuses such as 'Nobody ever told me I couldn't take assignments or answers to exam questions off the Internet without acknowledgement' or 'Everybody else does it, so why not me?' are not acceptable, and if it is discovered that you have committed plagiarism, you could be suspended or even expelled from your course. So, take great care to ensure that you have been meticulous in recording sources, making it clear in your notes which are direct quotations, your paraphrasing or merely your own thoughts.

There has been sufficient publicity to ensure that all researchers know, or should know, what plagiarism means and what the penalties for infringements are. Some unfortunate, well-publicized cases have brought discredit to the individuals and the institutions concerned, and this issue is not going to go away. Make sure you are absolutely clear about what is permissible and what is not.

Evaluating your own research

There are no universally accepted criteria for judging research reports but if you were asked to review a piece of research conducted by someone else, you would need to decide how you would judge it. Look at a journal article, or a novel, assuming you have had time to read a novel recently, and ask yourself, 'Is this a good report/novel?' If you consider it is good – or bad, try to decide how you came to that conclusion. Then, read your own draft. Do you think it is good? Are some parts better than others? Why? It's not easy to make such judgements about your own work, but better that you should identify areas of weakness yourself, while there is time to correct them, rather than leaving it to the examiner. So, before you hand over what you hope will be your final draft, ask yourself:

1. Is the meaning clear? Are there any obscure passages?
2. Is the report well-written? Check tenses, grammar, spelling, overlapping passages, punctuation, jargon.
3. Is the referencing well done? Are there any omissions? Are any references incomplete?
4. Does the abstract give the reader a clear idea of what is in the report?
5. Does the title indicate the nature of the study?
6. Are the objectives or purposes of the study stated clearly?
7. Are the objectives or purposes of the study fulfilled?
8. If hypotheses were postulated, are they proved or not proved?
9. Has a sufficient amount of literature relating to the topic been studied?
10. Does the literature review, if any, provide an indication of the state of knowledge in the subject? Is your topic placed in the context of the area of study as a whole?
11. Are all terms clearly defined?
12. Are the selected methods of data collection accurately described? Are they suitable for the task? Why were they chosen?
13. Are any limitations of the study clearly presented?
14. Have any statistical techniques been used? If so, are they appropriate for the task?
15. Are the data analysed and interpreted or merely described?
16. Are the results clearly presented? Are tables, diagrams and figures well-drawn and labelled?
17. Are conclusions based on evidence? Have any claims been made that cannot be substantiated?
18. Is there any evidence of bias? Any emotive terms or intemperate language?
19. Is the data likely to be reliable? Could another researcher repeat the methods used and have a reasonable chance of getting similar results?
20. Are recommendations, if any, feasible?
21. Are there any unnecessary items in the appendix?
22. Would you give the report a pass if you were the examiner? If not, perhaps an overhaul is necessary.

Writing the Report Checklist

1. Set deadlines.	Allocate provisional dates for sections, sub-sections and the whole report. You may need to make adjustments, but the handover date is fixed, so work towards it. Keep an eye on your schedule. Make a note in your diary, put dates on the wall of your study or somewhere obvious so that it will be a regular reminder of where you should be on certain dates.	☑
2. Write up sections according to your time plan, if possible. Stop at a point from which it is easy to resume writing.	Don't bother too much about perfect writing at this stage. Better to settle for a rough draft rather than run over time with constant correction and rewriting. There will be time for refinement later on.	☑
3. Create a rhythm of work, if at all possible.	If your writing is going well, or even if it isn't, don't stop to check references. Highlight or underline them or insert stickers on sections and/or pages where more work is needed and return to this task later.	☑
4. Make a start on your literature review.	If you have been sufficiently disciplined to write a draft literature review when most of your main reading was complete, then the task of literature writing at this stage will be – well, not exactly easy, but much less difficult.	

5. Leave space for revisions, additions or good ideas.	Just face the fact that you won't manage a first, perfect draft, so make it easy to insert (or delete, if necessary). Print on one side of the page.	☑
6. Publicize your plans and your timescale.	You may need a little help from your family and friends to meet deadlines.	☑
7. Check that all essential sections have been covered.	Abstract, outline of the research, review of previous work, statement of the scope and aims of the investigation, description of procedures, statement of results, discussion, summary and conclusions, and references. Anything else?	☑
8. Check length and format meet institutional requirements.	You don't want to be failed on a technicality.	☑
9. Don't forget the title page. Does your title reflect the contents of your report?	If you are preparing a dissertation or thesis, make sure you know what your institution's rules are regarding binding or not binding.	☑
10. Any acknowledgements and thanks?	If so, they usually come at the start of the report, but practice varies, so check what the local rules say.	☑
11. Include headings where possible and where appropriate.	Anything to make it easier for readers to follow the structure will help. And it helps you to ensure you are following a logical pattern.	☑
12. Number tables and figures, and provide titles.	Put numbers and titles above tables, but below figures.	☑

13.	Make sure all quotations, authors' good ideas, your paraphrases of authors' work, and so on are suitably acknowledged.	Check that quotations are presented in a consistent format and omissions indicated by ellipsis (...).	☑
14.	Appendices should only include items that are required for reference purposes. Do not clutter the report with irrelevant items.	Unless instructed otherwise, one copy of each data collection instrument should be included.	☑
15.	Provide a list of references. Check that you have used a consistent system and that there are no incomplete references.	Unless instructed otherwise, include only items to which reference is made in the report.	☑
16.	Remember to leave sufficient time for revision and rewriting – even at this late stage.	Check that you have written in plain but good English and without unnecessary jargon.	☑
17.	Try to get someone to read your almost-final draft report.	Fresh eyes will often see errors you have overlooked.	☑
18.	Take note of any comments from your readers.	And thank him/her/them. It takes time to read a long, or even a short, report.	☑
19.	Read your report aloud.	Sometimes, readers are too embarrassed to point out relatively small errors but reading aloud will quite often identify any dubious wording, punctuation and poor linkages.	☑

20. Check through the 22 questions at the end of this chapter for a last time. Are you sure you have dealt with each one honestly?	When you are satisfied your report is as good as you can make it, it's time to type it up. Check that you are conforming to any departmental/institutional rules about format.	

Finally, it's done! Congratulate yourself on an excellent job completed **on time**. Hand in your report, dissertation or thesis and give yourself a night off! But don't throw away any drafts until your examiner tells you that you have passed with flying colours.

Further reading

Creme, P. and Lea, M.R. (2008) ***Writing at University: A Guide for Students*** **(3rd edn). Maidenhead: Open University Press.**
This is a guide to university writing skills for undergraduates, postgraduates and for large and small projects. It deals with report and thesis writing, journals and the Internet.

Denscombe, M. (2010) ***The Good Research Guide for Small-scale Social Research Projects*** **(4th edn). Maidenhead: Open University Press.**
Chapter 15, 'Writing up the research', goes through the procedures involved, what should be included, style and presentation.

Hall, G. and Longman, J. (2008) *The Postgraduate's Companion*. **London: Sage.**
This book sets out to provide support and guidance for anyone undertaking a research degree. However, much of the guidance applies equally to students embarking on a 100-hour research project. It includes the supervisory relationship, writing your thesis, research training, completion and, where appropriate, the Viva.

Hyatt, D. (2004) Writing research, in C. Opie (ed.) ***Doing Educational Research: A Guide to First-time Researchers*****. London: Sage.**
In this chapter, Hyatt discusses what is required for student academic writing, academic writing conventions, structuring a research-based assignment and 'Some advice I've been given (or wish I'd been given!)'.

Laws, S. with Harper, C. and Marcus, R. (2013) ***Research for Development: A Practical Guide*** **(2nd edn). London: Sage.**
Chapter 14, 'Writing effectively', also includes guidance about what must be included in a research report (and what must be left out), and warnings about common pitfalls.

Levin, P. (2011) ***Excellent Dissertations!*** **(2nd edn). Maidenhead: Open University Press.**
A useful guide to doing research – and writing it up.

Maimon, E. and Peritz, J. (2009) *A Writer's Resource: MLA Update*. **Buckingham: Open University Press.**
This interesting book addresses many of the problems facing researchers, particularly as they write assignments, research papers, theses – and reviewing and editing what has been written. American, so take care with differences in spelling and grammar.

Miles, M.B. and Huberman, A.M. (1994) ***Qualitative Data Analysis*** **(2nd edn). Thousand Oaks, CA: Sage.**
Chapter 12, 'Producing reports', provides brief but good advice about structuring a report, under the headings of 'Voices, genres, and stances (How do we speak to the reader?)', 'Style', 'Formats' and 'Structures'.

Murray, N. and Hughes, G. (2008) ***Writing Up Your University Assignments and Research Projects*****. Maidenhead: Open University Press.**
A handbook for research students who feel they need help in writing essays, dissertations and other research projects. It includes what the authors describe as a 'toolkit' with help on punctuation, and a glossary of key terms.

Murray, R. and Moore, S. (2006) ***A Handbook of Academic Writing: A Fresh Approach*****. Maidenhead: Open University Press.**
This book is written mainly with Master's and Doctoral students in mind, though the advice given can equally be applied to writing up any research project.

Oliver, P. (2014) ***Writing your Thesis*** **(3rd edn). London: Sage.**
Considers strategies for organizing your work as you write and discusses techniques of academic writing.

Wolcott, H.F. (2009) ***Writing Up Qualitative Research*** **(3rd edn). London: Sage.**
In Chapter 2, I said that everything Wolcott has written is worth reading and this book in particular is excellent. I still go back to it, particularly if I am stuck and just can't get going. His chapter headings are 'Get going', 'Keep going', 'Linking up', 'Tightening up' and 'Finishing up'.

Glossary

(The) Abstract A short paragraph that explains concisely what an investigation sets out to do, the methods employed, the main conclusions reached and recommendations for action as a result of the findings. It is usually found on the front of the research report or, if the research is presented in a journal article, at the top of the first page.

Academic research community website A location on the web where members upload their ideas or research to share their findings and to ask fellow academics to comment on their drafts, offer advice or review research studies they have completed. The site usually allows members to search for relevant research papers that have been uploaded. Belonging to a research community is very useful if you are researching alone.

Action research An approach that is appropriate where 'a problem involving people, tasks and procedures cries out for solution, or where some change of feature results in a more desirable outcome' (Cohen *et al.* 2011: 344). It is applied research, carried out by practitioners who have identified a need for change or improvement, sometimes with support from outside the institution; other times not. The aim is 'to arrive at recommendations for good practice that will tackle a problem or enhance the performance of the organization and individuals through changes to the rules and procedures within which they operate' (Denscombe 2010b: 12).

Anonymity '*Anonymity* is a promise that even the researcher will not be able to tell which responses came from which respondents' (Sapsford and Abbott 1996: 318–19). Sapsford and Abbott make a distinction between anonymity and confidentiality (see definition below).

Arithmetic mean The arithmetic mean is obtained by adding together each item (or value) and dividing by the total number of values. So, if we take 12 respondents (Group A) whose ages are 26, 26, 27, 28, 29, 30, 30, 31, 32, 33, 34 and 34 and add those values together, we get 360. Divide 360 by 12. The mean is 30.

Bias A careful selection of data to present a particular point of view. A writer can set out to deliberately influence or mislead by producing biased accounts, or may be unaware that they are presenting a particular viewpoint and not providing an objective account.

Blogs The word 'blog' is a shortening of 'web logs'; a blog therefore is a log – a kind of diary, record or journal – published on the web. It consists of entries ('posts'), usually of up to 1000 words, published in date order with the most recent posts appearing at the top of the page.

Case study A case is a real-life situation that can be studied. Researchers identify an 'instance', then evidence on the 'instance' is collected systematically, the relationship between variables studied (a variable being a characteristic or attribute) and the investigation methodically planned. Though observation and interviews are most frequently used in case study research, no method is excluded. Case studies may be carried out to follow up and to put flesh on the bones of a survey. Most, however, are carried out as free-standing exercises.

Coding Codes are tags or labels for assigning units of meaning to the descriptive or inferential information compiled during a study. Codes are usually attached to 'chunks' of varying size – words, phrases, sentences or whole paragraphs, connected or unconnected to a specific setting. To paraphrase Miles and Huberman (1994), codes are used to organize the chunks so the researcher can quickly find, pull out and cluster the segments relating to a particular research question, hypothesis, construct or theme. Coding allows you to 'cluster' key issues in your data and take steps towards 'drawing conclusions'. The data you have collected mean very little until you have identified your clusters and can begin to understand their implications.

Confidentiality Sapsford and Abbott (1996: 318–19) define confidentiality as a promise that respondents will not be identified or presented in identifiable form. They make a distinction between confidentiality and anonymity (see definition above).

Content analysis Stemler (2001) defines content analysis as 'a systematic, replicable technique for compressing many words of text into fewer content categories based on explicit rules of coding'. Essentially, it is a research tool with which to analyse the frequency and use of words, terms or concepts in a document, with the aim of assessing the meaning and significance of a source. Content analysis can be used for television, film and websites as well as for written documents (Brett Davies 2007: 181–2).

COPAC Consortium of University Research Libraries Online Public Access Catalogue. Copac is a free online catalogue that combines most of the major university research libraries in the UK and Ireland with other specialist libraries, including the British Library. It has over 35 million records.

Critical incident A critical incident is a task or an event that makes the difference between success and failure in carrying out important parts of a job (Oxtoby 1979: 230). Flanagan, who devised the Critical Incident Technique (CIT) of research, describes it as follows: 'any specifiable human activity that is sufficiently complete in itself to permit inferences and predictions to be made about the person performing the act. To be critical the incident must occur in a situation where the purpose or intent of the act seems fairly clear to the observer and where its consequences are sufficiently definite to leave little doubt concerning its effects' (Flanagan 1954: 327). A critical incident does not have to be a dramatic event to be considered worthy of investigation. One example would be the 'handover' from the night nursing staff to day staff – a routine daily procedure. A researcher might observe the process and report back the behaviour and actions of the two teams and the analysis might lead to greater efficiencies.

Crowdsourcing One definition of crowdsourcing is as follows: 'the practice of obtaining needed services, ideas, or content by soliciting contributions from a large group of people, and especially from an online community, rather than from traditional employees or suppliers. This process is often used to subdivide tedious work or to fund-raise start-up companies and charities, and can also occur offline. It combines the efforts of numerous self-identified volunteers or part-time workers, where each contributor of their own initiative adds a small portion to the greater result' (http://en.wikipedia.org/wiki/Crowdsourcing).

Deliberate sources These sources are produced for the attention of future researchers. These include autobiographies, memoirs of politicians, medical practitioners or educationalists, diaries or letters intended for later publication, and documents of self-justification (Elton 2002). They involve a deliberate attempt to preserve evidence for the future, possibly to ensure that someone is not blamed for events or actions at the time or for reputation enhancement.

Diaries These are personal reflections or private records of events. For example, someone might keep a diary on a cruise to record not only where the cruise liner has been but also personal thoughts and emotions related to the journey.

Document 'Document' is a general term for an impression left on a physical object by a human being. Research can involve the analysis of images, films, videos and other non-written sources, all of which can be classed as documents, but the most common kinds of documents in educational and medical research are written as printed or manuscript sources. Increasingly, records are kept in electronic format but the scholarly approach to both online and offline documents is the same (see Chapter 7 by Brendan Duffy).

Ethics committees A group of people appointed by an institution or organization to assess the ethics of research. They play an important part in ensuring that no badly designed or harmful research is permitted and are usually comprised of academic staff from the institution where it is proposed that the research be carried out. Darlington and Scott (2002: 22–3) consider that ethics committees have 'a duty to consider all possible sources of harm and satisfy themselves that the researcher has thought through all the relevant issues prior to granting permission to proceed'.

Ethnography Brewer (2000: 6) defines ethnography as 'the study of people in naturally occurring settings or "fields" by means of methods which capture their social meanings and ordinary activities, involving the researcher participating directly in the setting, if not also the activities, in order to collect data in a systematic manner but without meaning being imposed on them externally' (Brewer 2000: 10).

Experiment An experiment is a scientific procedure undertaken to make a discovery, test a hypothesis or demonstrate a known fact. It is undertaken in an environment where the researcher has as much control of the variables as possible. An experiment in social science research will often compare a control group (which is unaffected by the experiment) with a group of participants affected by it. The two are compared to assess the impact on the participants affected by the experiment.

External criticism External criticism aims to discover whether a document is both genuine (not forged) and authentic (it is what it purports to be and truthfully reports on its subject) (Barzun and Graff 2003: 69). For example, an observer could write a report of a meeting he had never attended. His report would be genuine, because he actually wrote it, but it would not be authentic because he was not present at the meeting.

Focus group The purpose of a focus group is to concentrate discussion on a particular issue. They can be formal or informal gatherings of a varied group of people who may not know each other, but who might be thought to have a shared interest, concern or experience. Focus groups can be structured, where there are pre-prepared questions and checklists, or unstructured, where intervention by the researcher is minimal. The intention is that participants will interact with each other, will be willing to listen to all views, perhaps to reach consensus about some aspects of the topic or to disagree about others. The researcher acts as a moderator or facilitator.

Framework A theoretical framework is an explanatory device or a means of making sense of an idea, which explains the main things to be studied and the key factors, variables and presumed relationships between them. Polit and Hungler (1999: 110) state that: '**A framework** is the conceptual underpinnings of a study . . . In a study based on a theory, the framework is referred to as the **theoretical framework**; in a study that has its roots in a specified conceptual model, the framework is often called the **conceptual framework** (although the terms conceptual framework and theoretical framework are often used interchangeably).'

Grids A grid (or table) question will ask respondents to provide answers to two or more questions at the same time by filling in a table, providing a number of answers across columns and rows. See Chapter 9 for more about question types.

Grounded theory The grounded theory approach to qualitative data analysis was developed by Glaser and Strauss in the 1960s during the course of a field observational study of the way hospital staff dealt with dying patients (Glaser and Strauss 1965, 1968). Strauss (1987) tells us that a piece of grounded theory research is approached 'without any particular commitment to specific kinds of data, lines of research, or theoretical interests' and as such is a style rather than a specific method. It has a number of distinct features, 'such as theoretical sampling, and certain methodological guidelines, such as the making of constant comparisons and the use of a coding paradigm, to ensure conceptual development and density' (Strauss 1987: 5). The theory is not pre-specified in the research but emerges as the research proceeds. Over the years, there have been some adjustments to the original 1960s approach to grounded theory, but the principle remains much the same, which is that theory evolves during research by means of the analysis of the data. For more on grounded theory, see Chapter 1.

Harvard method of referencing A frequently used system in the academic community to indicate where ideas, theories, quotes, facts and any other evidence and information can be found. It is also known as the Author and Date system.

Hypothesis Many research projects begin with the statement of a hypothesis, defined by Verma and Beard (1981: 184) as: 'A tentative proposition which is subject to verification through subsequent investigation. It may also be seen as the guide to the researcher in that it depicts and describes the method to be followed in studying the problem. In many cases, hypotheses are hunches that the researcher has about the existence of relationship between variables.'

Inadvertent sources Inadvertent sources are sources used by researchers for some purpose other than that for which they were originally intended. For example, a report by the government on poverty, intended to show that fewer people are below the poverty line than five years previously, could be used by a researcher to show that the definition of poverty has changed, such that it makes the figures meaningless.

Informed consent Consent by an individual to participate in some form of research after receiving full and clear information about the research and of any risks involved. Full details of the research project and how information gained from it will be used and reported should have been sent in advance and the participant's agreement secured in writing. This protects the participant and also reduces the legal liability of the researcher.

Intellectual property Intellectual property is something you create that is unique and can be an idea, concept or physical entity. The creator or their organization usually owns the intellectual property. It includes copyright, patents, designs and trademarks, and can include new products, their design or appearance, brands, logos, written work online or in print, photos, illustrations, film or audio recordings, musical compositions or software.

Internal criticism Subjecting the contents of a document to rigorous analysis. It is more likely to be used in small-scale educational research.

It seeks to answer important questions about the document's origins, characteristics and authorship. See Chapter 7 for more on internal criticism.

Interquartile range An accurate picture of a range that reduces the importance of the extreme ends of the range. It is derived from the median. The highest and the lowest quarter of the measures are omitted and the interquartile range of the middle 50 per cent of the values is used as a measurement.

Keyword A word or phrase that captures what your search is looking for and which will be recognized and accepted by a database or search engine. Keywords focus on the essential contents of a topic.

Likert scale A device to discover strength of feeling or attitude towards a given statement or series of statements. Originally devised by R. Likert in 1932, it is most frequently used in questionnaires. The statements are usually on a 3-, 5- or 7-point scale and ask respondents to indicate rank order of agreement or disagreement by circling the appropriate number. Individuals or objects are arranged from the highest to the lowest. For more on Likert scales, see the sections on questionnaires in Chapter 9.

Literature review Aveyard (2010: 5) defines a literature review as 'a comprehensive study and interpretation of literature that relates to a particular topic. When you undertake a literature review you identify a **research question**, then seek to answer this question by searching for and **analyzing** relevant literature using a systematic approach.' It aims to broaden your understanding of a topic, to identify what work has been done in the area and how it has been researched, and helps you identify key issues for your own research (Hart 2001: 1). For more on literature reviews, see Chapter 6.

Logs Whereas diaries are usually personal reflections or private records of events (see above), logs are intended to be read more widely by a group of people requiring a permanent and more objective record of events. A ship's log, for example, is a detailed record of the distance travelled, ports visited, weather encountered, and so on.

Median The middle value. This is particularly useful when there are extremes at both ends or at either end of the range, which may affect the mean to a significant extent. To find the median, values must be listed in order. If there is an odd number of values, the middle value is the median. Where there is an even number of values, the average of the two middle values is the median.

Mode The mode, which is not often used in small studies, relates to the most frequently occurring number in a range of numbers.

Model A model is a visual representation of a process or concept. Models are often characterized by the use of analogies to give a more graphic representation of a particular phenomenon.

Narrative enquiry/stories Narrative enquiry involves the collection and development of stories, either as a form of data collection or as a means of structuring a research project (Gudmunsdottir 1996: 295). It might include autobiography or life stories that add meaning and can illustrate a theme developed by the researcher. For more, see Chapter 1.

Observation schedule An Observation schedule is a framework that all observers use to ensure consistency in approach to an observation. It can take the form of a checklist, a diary, chart, time or critical incidents log that you use to 'minimize, possibly eliminate, the variations that will arise from data based on individual perceptions of events and situations' (Denscombe 2010a: 199).

Operationalizable This refers to 'the rules we use to link the language of theory (concepts) to the language of research (indicators)' (Rose and Sullivan 1996: 12–13). An example of this is the concept of social class, which is unobservable. If we use the value of a house to act as an indicator of social class, we are operationalizing.

Ordinal scale A scale that shows data in order of magnitude since there is no standard of measurement of differences. For instance, a squash ladder is an ordinal scale since one can say only that one person is better than another, but not by how much.

Parameter Factor decided before you carry out a literature search and used to define what you include in the search. This could be a keyword, the language the source was written in and where and when it was published.

Participant observation Involves the researcher participating in the daily life of an individual, group or community and listening, observing, questioning and trying to understand the life of that individual, group or community. In some cases, researchers have been involved for months or even years in a community in order to become generally accepted as one of the group.

Plagiarism Plagiarism is using other people's written words and ideas as if they are your own.

Primary sources Documents or evidence that came into existence during the period of the research (for example, the minutes of a hospital's governing body).

Problem-oriented approach Investigates what has already been discovered about a subject before establishing the focus of the study and then researching the relevant primary sources. As the research progresses, a much clearer idea of what sources are relevant will emerge and more questions will occur to the researcher as their knowledge of the subject deepens (Tosh 2010).

Protocol A carefully structured, written plan to ensure the smooth running and successful conclusion of a clinical trial but also to gain the compulsory agreement of an ethical committee. An essential part of research in a medical setting, the term has also been widely adopted by other research disciplines.

Qualitative Researchers adopting a qualitative perspective are more concerned to understand individuals' perceptions of the world. They doubt whether social 'facts' exist and question whether a 'scientific' approach can be used when dealing with human beings. Punch (2005: 28) draws our attention to an important characteristic of qualitative research, in that it 'not only uses non-numerical and unstructured data but also, typically, has research questions and methods which are more general at the start, and become more focused as the study progresses'.

Quantitative Quantitative researchers collect facts and study the relationship of one set of facts to another. They use 'numerical data and, typically . . . structured and predetermined research questions, conceptual frameworks and designs' (Punch 2005: 28). The data is subjected to statistical analysis, using techniques that are likely to produce quantified and, if possible, generalizable conclusions.

Range The difference between the highest and lowest values measured.

Research diary Written by researchers to record the progress of their research, including their personal thoughts and reflections. It is invaluable when they are describing the process of their research in their final report.

Scales Devices to discover strength of feeling or attitude. There are many different types of scale, including the Likert scale (see above), some of which require quite complex construction and analysis. The Thurstone (Thurstone and Chave 1929) and Guttman (1950) scales in particular require careful handling.

Secondary sources Interpretations of events of a period based on primary sources. An example is a document relating to the history of a hospital's development (primary source) and the minutes of a discussion between clinicians and managers of the future development of the hospital (secondary source) based on it.

Social networking The organization of like-minded individuals into specific groups. Although social networking occurs in the workplace, universities and high schools, it is most popular online due to the ease with which individuals who are looking to meet other people can gather and share first-hand information and experiences. Social websites function as an online community of Internet users where members may share common interests or contacts. Once you are granted access to a social networking website you can begin to socialize, reading the profile pages of other members and contacting them online.

Source-oriented approach When embarking on a study using documents, it is possible to have two different approaches. One has been called the source-oriented approach in which the nature of the sources determines the research project and helps to generate questions for your research. The feasibility of the project is determined by the nature of existing sources so that a particularly full collection of material, for example on the restructuring of a college or hospital, would lead to an investigation of that area. Rather than bringing predetermined questions to the sources, the research is led by the material they contain.

Standard deviation 'In statistics and probability theory, standard deviation ... shows how much variation or dispersion exists from the average (mean), or expected value. A low standard deviation indicates that the data points tend to be very close to the mean; a high standard deviation indicates that the data points are spread out over a large range of values' (http://en.wikipedia.org/wiki/Standard_deviation). Standard deviation uses values for the entire group rather than for a section. The calculation is written into most statistical software so that the standard deviation is automatically produced in association with the mean.

Structured interview A standardized interview that is a quantitative research method commonly used in survey research. The aim is to ensure that each interview is conducted with exactly the same questions in the same order, guaranteeing that answers can be reliably collected and that comparisons can be made with confidence between respondents or between different survey periods.

Structured observation A systematic method of data collection where there is considerable pre-coding. The observation takes the form of recording when, how often or for how long the pre-coded behaviours occur. Observing usually means both watching and listening, although it may entail either watching or listening.

Supervisor A key person in a student researcher's academic life, the principal role of the supervisor is to help students achieve their academic potential. The supervisor will provide reasonable commitment, accessibility, professionalism, stimulation, guidance, respect and consistent encouragement to the student. For more about supervision, see Chapter 2.

Survey A general term meaning to examine or look at something comprehensively. In the context of research, it has a number of different interpretations, but is most often used to describe the task of asking people a series of questions in order to gather information about what they do, or how they think about a particular topic. Moser and Kalton (1971: 1) make it clear that 'the term and the methods associated with it are applied to an extraordinarily wide variety of investigations'.

This could be a census of an entire population or a short opinion poll. For more on surveys, see Chapter 1.

Theory Theory has been defined as being 'a set of interrelated abstract propositions about human affairs and the social world that explain their regularities and relationships' (Brewer 2000: 192); or 'theory at the lowest level can be an ad hoc classification system, consisting of categories which organise and summarise empirical observations' (Bowling 2002: 139). However, theory can be, and often is, merely taken to refer to the current state of knowledge in a subject derived from the published literature.

Unstructured interview A formally agreed interview where the interviewer has a clear plan for the exchange with a goal in mind but no guide or set questions. The interviewer instead elicits responses by building a rapport with the interviewee, using open questions. It does not offer the interviewer the control afforded by a structured interview.

Unstructured observation In unstructured observation, the researcher 'does not use predetermined categories and classifications but makes observations in a more natural open-ended way ... The logic here is that categories and concepts for describing and analysing the observational data will emerge later in the research, during the analysis, rather than be brought to the research, or imposed on the data, from the start' (Punch 2005: 179–80).

Unwitting evidence Underlying assumptions unintentionally revealed by participants in the language they use in a document or account. So, a teacher being interviewed by a researcher about misbehaviour in the classroom may use the term 'offenders', unintentionally comparing misbehaving learners to prisoners and thereby revealing the teacher's opinion of the learners.

Witting evidence The information that the original author of the document intended to impart. If, for example, a government minister made a speech announcing a proposed educational reform, the 'witting' evidence would be everything that was stated in the speech about the proposed change.

References

Alampi, A. (2012) *Social media is more than simply a marketing tool for academic research* [Online]. Available at http://www.theguardian.com/higher-education-network/blog/2012/jul/24/social-media-academic-research-tool [Accessed 14 March 2014].

Alaszewski, A. (2006) *Using Diaries for Social Research.* London: Sage.

Aldridge, A. and Levine, K. (2001) *Surveying the Social World: Principles and Practice in Survey Research.* Buckingham: Open University Press.

Arguadiola (2012) *Tips for writing a literature review article* [Online video]. Available at http://www.youtube.com/watch?v=SfxrrMVzXK0 [Accessed 14 March 2014].

Atkinson, P. and Coffey, A. (2011) Analysing documentary realities, in D. Silverman (ed.) *Qualitative Research* (3rd edn). London: Sage.

Aveyard, H. (2010) *Doing a Literature Review in Health and Social Care: A Practical Guide* (2nd edn). Maidenhead: Open University Press.

Bales, R.F. (1950) *Interaction Process Analysis: A Method for the Study of Small Groups.* Reading, MA: Addison-Wesley. Reprinted 1976 by The University of Chicago Press, Chicago, IL.

Baltes, P.B., Dittmann-Kohli, F. and Dixon, R.A. (1984) New perspectives on the development of intelligence in adulthood, in P.B. Baltes and O.G. Brim, Jr. (eds) *Life-span Development and Behavior* (Vol. 6). Orlando, FL: Academic Press.

Barbour, R. (2008) *Doing Focus Groups.* London: Sage.

Barzun, J. and Graff, H.F. (2003) *The Modern Researcher* (6th edn). Belmont, CA: Wadsworth.

Bassey, M. (1981) Pedagogic research: on the relative merits of the search for generalization and study of single events, *Oxford Review of Education*, 7 (1): 73–93.

Bassey, M. (1999) *Case Study Research in Educational Settings.* Buckingham: Open University Press.

Bassey, M. (2007) Case study, in A.R.J. Briggs and M. Coleman (eds) *Research Methods in Educational Leadership and Management* (2nd edn). London: Sage.

Bell, J. (1996) *An investigation into barriers to completion of post-graduate research degrees in three universities.* Unpublished report funded through the Leverhulme Emeritus research fund.

Bell, J. and Opie, C. (2002) *Learning from Research: Getting More from Your Data*. Buckingham: Open University Press.

Bell, J. and Woolner, P. (2012) Developing and using questionnaires', in A.R.J. Briggs, M. Coleman and M. Morrison (eds) *Research Methods in Educational Leadership and Management* (3rd edn). London: Sage.

Best, J.W. (1970) *Research in Education* (2nd edn). Englewood Cliffs, NJ: Prentice-Hall.

Blaxter, L., Hughes, C. and Tight, M. (2006) *How to Research* (3rd edn). Maidenhead: Open University Press.

Blaxter, L., Hughes, C. and Tight, M. (2010) *How to Research* (4th edn). Maidenhead: Open University Press.

Blendtec (2010) *Will it blend?* [Online video]. Available at http://www.youtube.com/watch?v=lAl28d6tbko [Accessed 6 January 2014].

Bogdan, R.C. and Biklen, S.K. (2003) *Qualitative Research for Education: An Introduction to Theory and Methods* (4th edn). New York: Pearson.

Bowen, G.A. (2009) Document analysis as a qualitative research method, *Qualitative Research Journal*, 9 (2): pp. 27–40.

Bowling, A. (2002) *Research Methods in Health: Investigating Health and Health Services* (2nd edn). Maidenhead: Open University Press.

Bowling, A. (2009) *Research Methods in Health: Investigating Health and Health Services* (3rd edn). Maidenhead: Open University Press.

Brett Davies, M. (2007) *Doing a Successful Research Project: Using Qualitative or Quantitative Methods*. Basingstoke: Palgrave Macmillan.

Brewer, J.D. (2000) *Ethnography*. Buckingham: Open University Press.

Bruce, R. and Mertens, M. (2013) *Academics will need both the physical and virtual library for years to come* [Online]. Available at http://www.theguardian.com/higher-education-network/blog/2013/jun/19/academic-publishing-print-digital-libraries.

Bryman, A. and Cramer, D. (2011) *Quantitative Data Analysis with IBM SPSS 17, 18 and 19: A Guide for Social Scientists*. London: Routledge.

Burgess, R.G. (ed.) (1982) *Field Research: A Sourcebook and Field Manual*. London: George Allen & Unwin.

Burgess, R.G. (1994) On diaries and diary keeping, in N. Bennett, R. Glatter and R. Levaćič (eds) *Improving Educational Management through Research and Consultancy*. London: Paul Chapman, in association with the Open University.

Burgess, R. (2002) *Biographical Research*. Buckingham: Open University Press.

Burgess, R.G. and Morrison, M. (1993) Teaching and learning about food and nutrition in school, in *The Nation's Diet Programme: The Social Science of Food Choice*, report to the ESRC.

Burton, N., Brundrett, M. and Jones, M. (2008) *Doing Your Education Research Project*. London: Sage.

Busher, H. and James, N. (2007) Ethics of research in education, in A.R.J. Briggs and M. Coleman (eds) *Research Methods in Educational Leadership and Management* (2nd edn). London: Sage.

Caldicott Committee (1997) *Report on the Review of Patient-identifiable Information*. London: Department of Health [Online]. Available at http://static.oxfordradcliffe.net/confidential/gems/caldrep.pdf [Accessed 14 March 2014].

Cann, A., Dimitriou, K. and Hooley, T. (2011) *Social Media: A Guide for Researchers*. London: Research Information Network.

Charmaz, K. (2008) Grounded theory methods in social justice research, in N.K. Denzin and Y.S. Lincoln (eds) *Strategies of Qualitative Inquiry* (3rd edn). London: Sage.

Charmaz, K. (2011) Grounded theory methods in social justice research, in N.K. Denzin and Y.S. Lincoln (eds) *The Sage Handbook of Qualitative Research* (4th edn). London: Sage.

Chartered Institute of Public Relations (2011) *CIPR Social Media (#ciprsm) Best Practice Guide*. London: CIPR.

Clandinin, D.J. (2007) *Handbook of Narrative Inquiry: Mapping a Methodology*. Thousand Oaks, CA: Sage.

Clough, P. (2002) *Narratives and Fictions in Educational Research*. Maidenhead: Open University Press.

Cohen, L., Manion, L. and Morrison, K. (2000) *Research Methods in Education* (5th edn). London: RoutledgeFalmer.

Cohen, L., Manion, L. and Morrison, K. (2011) Case studies, in *Research Methods in Education* (7th edn). Abingdon: Routledge.

Cramer, D. (2003) *Advanced Quantitative Data Analysis*. Buckingham: Open University Press.

Crang, M. and Cook, I. (2007) *Doing Ethnographies*. London: Sage.

Creme, P. and Lea, M.R. (2008) *Writing at University: A Guide for Students* (3rd edn). Maidenhead: Open University Press.

Cryer, P. (2006) *The Research Student's Guide to Success* (3rd edn). Maidenhead: Open University Press.

Darlington, Y. and Scott, D. (2002) *Qualitative Research in Practice: Stories from the Field*. Buckingham: Open University Press.

Data Protection Registrar (1998) *The Data Protection Act 1998: An Introduction* [Online]. Available at http://www.open.gov.uk/dpr/dprhome.htm [Accessed 14 March 2014].

D'Cruz, H. and Jones, M. (2004) *Social Work Research: Ethical and Political Contexts*. London: Sage.

Delamont, S., Atkinson, P. and Parry, O. (2004) *Supervising the Doctorate: A Guide to Success*. Maidenhead: Open University Press.

Denscombe, M. (2010a) *The Good Research Guide for Small-scale Social Research Projects* (4th edn). Maidenhead: Open University Press.

Denscombe, M. (2010b) *Ground Rules for Good Research: Guidelines for Good Practice* (2nd edn). Maidenhead: Open University Press.

Duffy, B. (1998) Late nineteenth-century popular educational conservatism: the work of coalminers on the school boards of the North-East, *History of Education*, 27 (1): 29–38.

Eggleston, J. (1979) The characteristics of educational research: mapping the domain, *British Educational Research Journal*, 5 (1): 1–12.

Eley, A. and Jennings, R. (2005) *Effective Postgraduate Supervision: Improving the Student–Supervisor Relationship*. Maidenhead: Open University Press.

Elton, G.R. (2002) *The Practice of History* (2nd edn). Oxford: Blackwell.

Evans, R.J. (2000) *In Defence of History* (2nd edn). London: Granta Books.

Fan, G. (1998) *An exploratory study of final year diploma in nursing students' perceptions of their nursing education*. Unpublished MEd dissertation, University of Sheffield.

Farrell, A. (ed.) (2005) *Ethical Research with Children*. Maidenhead: Open University Press.

Field, A. (2013) *Discovering Statistics Using IBM SPSS Statistics* (5th edn). London: Sage.

Fielding, N.G., Lee, R.M. and Blank, G. (2008) *The Sage Handbook of Online Research Methods*. London: Sage.

Flanagan, J.C. (1954) The critical incident technique, *Psychological Bulletin*, 51 (4): 327–58.

Flanders, N.A. (1970) *Analysing Teaching Behaviour*. Reading, MA: Addison-Wesley.

Fogelman, K. and Comber, C. (2007) Surveys and sampling, in A.R.J. Briggs and M. Coleman (eds) *Research Methods in Educational Leadership and Management* (2nd edn). London: Sage.

Francis, V.M., Vesey, P. and Lowe, G. (1994) The closure of a long-stay psychiatric hospital: a longitudinal study of patients' behaviour, *Social Psychiatry and Psychiatric Epidemiology*, 29 (4): 184–9.

Gerrish, K. and Lacey, A. (2010) *The Research Process in Nursing* (6th edn). Oxford: Wiley-Blackwell.

Gibbs, G.R. (2008) *Analysing Qualitative Data*. London: Sage.

Gillham, B. (2005) *Research Interviewing: A Practical Guide*. Maidenhead: Open University Press.

Glaser, B.G. (1992) *Basics of Grounded Theory Analysis.* Mill Valley, CA: Sociology Press.

Glaser, B.G. and Strauss, A.L. (1965) *Awareness of Dying.* Chicago, IL: Aldine.

Glaser, B.G. and Strauss, A.L. (1968) *Time for Dying.* Chicago, IL: Aldine.

Goodson, I.F. and Sikes, P. (2001) *Life History Research in Educational Settings: Learning from Lives.* Buckingham: Open University Press.

Gray, C. (2011) *Social media: a guide for researchers.* London: Research Information Network [Online]. Available at http://www.rin.ac.uk/our-work/communicating-and-disseminating-research/social-media-guide-researchers [Accessed 10 March 2014].

Gray, J. (1998) *Narrative inquiry.* Unpublished paper, Edith Cowan University, Joondalup, WA.

Gray, J. (2000) *The framing of truancy: a study of non-attendance as a form of social exclusion within Western Australia.* Unpublished doctoral thesis, Edith Cowan University, Joondalup, WA.

Gray, J. (2009) Unpublished paper, Edith Cowan University, Joondalup, WA.

Green, J. and Thorogood, N. (2004) *Qualitative Methods for Health Research.* London: Sage.

Green, J. and Thorogood, N. (2013) *Qualitative Methods for Health Research* (3rd edn). London: Sage.

Greig, A.D., Taylor, J. and Mackay, T. (2012) *Doing Research with Children* (3rd edn). London: Sage.

Gulliver, K. (2012) *10 commandments of Twitter for academics* [Online]. Available at http://chronicle.com/article/10-Commandments-of-Twitter-for/131813/ [Accessed 14 March 2014].

Gutmunsdottir, S. (1996) The teller, the tale, and the one being told: the narrative nature of the research interview, *Curriculum Inquiry,* 26 (3): 293–306.

Guttman, L. (1950) The basis for scalogram analysis, in S.A. Stouffer (ed.) *Measurement and Prediction.* Princeton, NJ: Princeton University Press.

Hakim, C. (2000) *Research Design: Successful Designs for Social Economics Research* (2nd edn). London: Routledge.

Hall, G. and Longman, J. (2008) *The Postgraduate's Companion.* London: Sage.

Hardy, M.A. and Bryman, A. (eds) (2004) *Handbook of Data Analysis.* London: Sage.

Hart, C. (1998) *Doing a Literature Review: Releasing the Social Science Research Imagination.* London: Sage, in association with the Open University.

Hart, C. (2001) *Doing a Literature Search: A Comprehensive Guide for the Social Sciences*. London: Sage.

Hart, E. and Bond, M. (1995) *Action Research for Health and Social Care: A Guide to Practice*. Buckingham: Open University Press.

Hayes, N. (2000) *Doing Psychological Research: Gathering and Analysing Data*. Buckingham: Open University Press.

Haywood, P. and Wragg, E.D. (1982) *Evaluating the Literature*, Rediguide 2. Nottingham: University of Nottingham School of Education.

Holsti, O.R. (1969) *Content Analysis for the Social Sciences and Humanities*. Reading, MA: Addison-Wesley.

Hookway, N. (2008) 'Entering the blogosphere': some strategies for using blogs in social research, *Qualitative Research*, 8 (1): 91–113.

Hyatt, D. (2004) Writing research, in C. Opie (ed.) *Doing Educational Research: A Guide to First-time Researchers*. London: Sage.

Hyland, M.E. (1996) Diary assessments of quality of life, *Quality of Life Newsletter*, 16: 8–9.

Hyland, M.E. and Crocker, G.R. (1995) Validation of an asthma quality of life diary in a clinical trial, *Thorax*, 50: 724–30.

Johnson, D. (1984) Planning small-scale research, in J. Bell, T. Bush, A. Fox, J. Goodey and S. Goulding (eds) *Conducting Small-scale Investigations in Educational Management*. London: Harper & Row.

Jorgensen, D.L. (2008) *Participant Observation: A Methodology for Human Studies* (2nd edn). London: Sage.

Keats, D. (2000) *Interviewing: A Practical Guide for Students and Professionals*. Buckingham: Open University Press.

Keeble, H. and Kirk, R. (2007) Exploring the existing body of research, in A.R.J. Briggs and M. Coleman (eds) *Research Methods in Educational Leadership and Management* (2nd edn). London: Sage.

Klatzky, R.L. (1988) Theories of information processing and theories of aging, in L.L. Light and D.J. Burke (eds) *Language, Memory and Aging*. Cambridge: Cambridge University Press.

Krippendorf, K. (2012) *Content Analysis: An Introduction to its Methodology* (3rd edn). London: Sage.

Kvale, S. (2008) *Interviews: An Introduction to Qualitative Research Interviewing* (2nd edn). London: Sage.

Laws, S. with Harper, C. and Marcus, R. (2013) *Research for Development: A Practical Guide* (2nd edn). London: Sage.

Levin, P. (2011) *Excellent Dissertations!* (2nd edn). Maidenhead: Open University Press.

Likert, R. (1932) *A Technique for the Measurement of Attitudes*. New York: Columbia University Press.

Lomax, P. (2007) Action research, in A.R.J. Briggs and M. Coleman (eds) *Research Methods in Educational Leadership and Management* (2nd edn). London: Sage.

LSE (2013) *Impact of social sciences: maximizing the impact of academic research* [Online]. Available at http://blogs.lse.ac.uk/impactofsocialsciences/ [Accessed 14 March 2014].

Lutz, F.W. (1986) Ethnography: the holistic approach to understanding schooling, in M. Hammersley (ed.) *Controversies in Classroom Research.* Buckingham: Open University Press.

Lutz, F.W. (1993) Ethnography: the holistic approach to understanding schooling, in M. Hammersley (ed.) *Controversies in Classroom Research* (2nd edn). Buckingham: Open University Press.

Maimon, E. and Peritz, J. (2009) *A Writer's Resource: MLA Update.* Buckingham: Open University Press.

Marples, D.L. (1967) Studies of managers: a fresh start, *Journal of Management Studies*, 4: 282–99.

Marwick, A. (2001) *The New Nature of History* (5th edn). Basingstoke: Palgrave.

May, T. (2011) *Social Research: Issues, Methods and Process* (4th edn). Maidenhead: Open University Press.

McCulloch, G. and Richardson, W. (2000) *Historical Research in Educational Settings.* Buckingham: Open University Press.

Medawar, P.B. (1972) The hope of progress, *New Scientist*, June.

Miles, M.B. and Huberman, A.M. (1994) *Qualitative Data Analysis* (2nd edn). Thousand Oaks, CA: Sage.

Miles, M.B. and Huberman, A.M. (2014) *Qualitative Data Analysis* (3rd edn). Thousand Oaks, CA: Sage.

Minocha, S. and Petros, M. (2012) *Handbook of social media for researchers and supervisors: digital technologies for research dialogues* [Online]. Available at http://www.vitae.ac.uk/CMS/files/upload/Vitae_Innovate_Open_University_Social_Media_Handbook_2012.pdf [Accessed 14 March 2014].

Morrison, M. (2007) Using diaries in research, in A.R.J. Briggs and M. Coleman (eds) *Research Methods in Educational Leadership and Management* (2nd edn). London: Sage.

Morrison, M. and Burgess, R.G. (1993) *Chapatis and chips: encountering food use in primary school settings.* Paper prepared at an international conference on Children's Food and Drink: Today's Market and Tomorrow's Opportunities, Chipping Campden Food and Drink Association, Chipping Campden, Gloucester, 10 November.

Moser, C.A. and Kalton, G. (1971) *Survey Methods in Social Investigation* (2nd edn). London: Heinemann.

Moyles, J. (2002) Observation as a research tool, in M. Coleman and A.R.J. Briggs (eds) *Research Methods in Educational Leadership and Management* London: Sage.

Murray, N. and Hughes, G. (2008) *Writing Up Your University Assignments and Research Projects.* Maidenhead: Open University Press.

Murray, R. (2011) *How to Write a Thesis* (3rd edn). Maidenhead: Open University Press.

Murray, R. and Moore, S. (2006) *A Handbook of Academic Writing: A Fresh Approach.* Maidenhead: Open University Press.

National Centre for Social Research, Sage, Oxford Internet Institute (2013) *Blurring the boundaries – New social media, new social science.* Available at http://www.methodspace.com/ [Accessed 14 March 2014].

National Health Service National Patient Safety Agency (undated) [Online]. Available at http://www.npsa.nhs.uk/ [Accessed 6 January 2014].

Neville, C. (2010) *The Complete Guide to Referencing and Avoiding Plagiarism* (2nd edn). Maidenhead: Open University Press.

Neyland, D. (2007) *Organizational Ethnography.* London: Sage.

Nisbet, J.D. and Ross, L. (1980) *Human Inference: Strategies and Shortcomings of Social Judgment.* Englewood Cliffs, NJ: Prentice-Hall.

Nisbet, J.D. and Watt, J. (1978) *Case Study*, Rediguide 26. Nottingham: University of Nottingham School of Education.

Noakes, L. and Wincup, E. (2004) Using documentary evidence in qualitative research, in *Criminological Research: Understanding Qualitative Methods* (pp. 106–20). London: Sage.

Nyberg, L., Backman, L., Erngrund, K., Olofsson, U. and Nilsson, L. (1996) Age differences in episodic memory, semantic memory, and priming: relationships to demographic, intellectual and biological factors, *Journals of Gerontology: Psychological Science*, 51B: 234–40.

O'Dochartaigh, N. (2007) *How to Do Your Literature Search and Find Research Information Online* (2nd edn). London: Sage.

Oliver, P. (2003) *The Student's Guide to Research Ethics.* Maidenhead: Open University Press.

Oliver, P. (2010) *The Student's Guide to Research Ethics* (2nd edn). Maidenhead: Open University Press.

Oliver, P. (2014) *Writing your Thesis* (3rd edn). London: Sage.

Opie, C. (ed.) (2004) *Doing Educational Research: A Guide for First-time Researchers.* London: Sage.

Oppenheim, A.N. (1992) *Questionnaire Design, Interviewing and Attitude Measurement.* London: Continuum.

Oppenheim, A.N. (2000) *Questionnaire Design, Interviewing and Attitude Measurement* (2nd edn). London: Bloomsbury Academic.

Orna, E. with Stevens, G. (1995) *Managing Information for Research.* Buckingham: Open University Press.

Orna, E. and Stevens, G. (2009) *Managing Information for Research: Practical Help in Researching, Writing and Designing Dissertations* (2nd edn). Maidenhead: Open University Press.

Oxtoby, R. (1979) Problems facing heads of department, *Journal of Further and Higher Education*, 3 (1): 46–59.

Pallant, J. (2013) *SPSS Survival Manual: A Step by Step Guide to Data Analysis Using IBM SPSS* (5th edn). Maidenhead: Open University Press.

Patel, S (2011) *10 ways researchers can use Twitter* [Online]. Available at http://www.networkedresearcher.co.uk/2011/08/03/10-ways-researchers-can-use-twitter/ [Accessed 14 March 2014].

Pears, R. and Shields, G. (2013) *Cite Them Right: The Essential Referencing Guide* (9th edn). Basingstoke: Palgrave Macmillan.

Pennink (2013) *The UK Survey of Academics: how academics (re) search* [Online]. Available at http://networkcultures.org/wpmu/query/2013/06/25/the-uk-Survey-of-academics-how-academics-research/ [Accessed 14 March 2014].

Phillips, E.M. and Pugh, D.S. (2000) *How to Get a PhD: A Handbook for Students and their Supervisors* (3rd edn). Buckingham: Open University Press.

Polit, D.F. and Hungler, B.P. (1999) *Nursing Research: Principles and Methods* (6th edn). Philadelphia, PA: Lippincott Williams & Wilkins.

Polit, D.F. and Hungler, B.P. (2004) *Nursing Research: Principles and Methods* (7th edn). Philadelphia, PA: Lippincott Williams & Wilkins.

Poynter, R. (2010) *The Handbook of Online and Social Media Research.* Chichester: Wiley.

Punch, K.F. (2005) *Introduction to Social Research: Quantitative and Qualitative Approaches* (2nd edn). London: Sage.

Punch, K.F. (2014) *Introduction to Social Research: Quantitative and Qualitative Approaches* (3rd edn). London: Sage.

Quinnell, S.-L. (2011) *Academic tweeting: your suggestions and tips* [Online]. Available at http://blogs.lse.ac.uk/impactofsocialsciences/2011/09/30/academic-tweeting-your-suggestions-and-tips-collected/ [Accessed 14 March 2014].

Reason, P. and Bradbury, H. (eds) (2001) *Handbook of Action Research: Participative Inquiry and Practice.* London: Sage.

Richardson, J.T.E. and King, E. (1998) Adult students in higher education: burden or boon?, *Journal of Higher Education*, 69: 65–88.

Richardson, J.T.E. and Woodley, A. (2003) Another look at the role of age, gender and subject as predictors of academic attainment in higher education, *Studies in Higher Education*, 28 (4): 476–93.

Ridley, D. (2012) *The Literature Review: A Step-by-Step Guide for Students* (2nd edn). London: Sage.

Roget, P.M. (2000) *Roget's Thesaurus of English Words and Phrases.* First published in 1982 by P.M. Roget; 2000 edition revised by Betty Kirkpatrick. London: Penguin Books.

Rose, D. and Sullivan, O. (1996) *Introducing Data Analysis for Social Scientists* (2nd edn). Buckingham: Open University Press.

Rugg, G. (2007) *Using Statistics: A Gentle Introduction.* Maidenhead: Open University Press.

Rugg, G. and Petre, M. (2006) *A Gentle Guide to Research Methods.* Maidenhead: Open University Press.

Rumsey, S. (2008) *How to Find Information: A Guide for Researchers* (2nd edn). Maidenhead: Open University Press.

Santafe, I. (2013) *Diary study guide: how to get the best results from diary study research* [Online]. Available at http://www.webcredible.co.uk/user-friendly-resources/web-usability/diary-study-guide.shtml.

Sapsford, R. (2006) *Survey Research* (2nd edn). London: Sage.

Sapsford, R.J. and Abbott, P. (1996) Ethics, politics and research, in R. Sapsford and V. Jupp (eds) *Data Collection and Analysis.* London: Sage.

Sapsford, R.J. and Abbott, P. (2006) Ethics, politics and research, in R. Sapsford and V. Jupp (eds) *Data Collection and Analysis* (2nd edn). London: Sage.

Sapsford, R. and Jupp, V. (eds) (1996) *Data Collection and Analysis.* London: Sage.

Sapsford, R. and Jupp, V. (eds) (2006) *Data Collection and Analysis* (2nd edn). London: Sage.

Scaife, J. (2004) Reliability, validity and credibility, in C. Opie (ed.) *Doing Educational Research: A Guide for First-time Researchers.* London: Sage.

Schaie, K.W. (1996) *Intellectual Development in Adulthood: The Seattle Longitudinal Study.* Cambridge: Cambridge University Press.

Snee, H. (undated) *What is blog analysis* (video) [Online]. Available at http://www.methods.manchester.ac.uk/methods/blog-analysis/index.shtml [Accessed 14 March 2014].

Spradley, J.P. (1980) *Participant Observation.* New York: Holt, Rinehart & Winston.

Stanford, M. (1994) *A Companion to the Study of History.* Oxford: Blackwell. [Online] Available at

StartBlolggingOnline.com (2013) *How to start a blog – step-by-step guide* [Online]. Available at http://startbloggingonline.com/ [Accessed 5 October 2013].

Stemler, S. (2001) *An overview of content analysis.* Available at http://pareonline.net/getvn.asp?v=7&n=17 [Accessed 6 March 2014].

Strauss, A.L. (1987) *Qualitative Analysis for Social Scientists.* Cambridge: Cambridge University Press.

Sundberg, J. (2013) *How to use Facebook for professional networking: 10 useful tips* [Online]. Available at http://theundercoverrecruiter.com/how-use-facebook-professional-networking-10-useful-tips/ [Accessed 6 January 2014].

Sutherland, V. and Cooper, C.L. (2003) *De-stressing Doctors: A Self-management Guide.* London: Butterworth Heinemann.

Ten Have, P. (2007) *Doing Conversation Analysis* (2nd edn). London: Sage.

The Times (2009) News article, 27 May.

Thomas, M. (2012) *Social Media Made Simple: How to Avoid Social Media Suicide.* Berkshire: AppleTree Publishing.

Thurstone, L.L. and Chave, E.J. (1929) *The Measurement of Attitudes.* Chicago, IL: The University of Chicago Press.

Tosh, J. (2010) *The Pursuit of History* (5th edn). Harlow: Longman.

University of Exeter (2013) *Social media guidelines* [Online]. Available at http://www.exeter.ac.uk/staff/web/socialmedia/linkedin/ [Accessed 15 September 2013].

Verhaeghen, P. and Salthouse, T.A. (1997) Meta-analyses of age–cognition relations in adulthood: estimates of linear and nonlinear age effects and structural models, *Psychological Bulletin*, 122: 231–49.

Verma, G.K. and Beard, R.M. (1981) *What is Educational Research? Perspectives on Techniques of Research.* Aldershot: Gower.

Visual.ly (2012) Reaching 50 million users [Online]. Available at http://visual.ly/reaching-50-million-users [Accessed 17 October 2013].

Walsh, M. and Wigens, L. (2003) *Introduction to Research.* Cheltenham: Nelson Thornes.

Wikipedia (undated) *Crowdsourcing* [Online]. Available at http://en.www.wikipedia.org/wiki/Crowdsourcing [Accessed 23 October 2013].

Williams, G.L. (1994) Observing and recording meetings, in N. Bennett, R. Glatter and R. Levaćič (eds) *Improving Educational Management through Research and Consultancy.* London: Paul Chapman.

Wolcott, H.F. (1992) Posturing in qualitative inquiry, in M.D. LeCompte, W.L. Millroy and J. Preissle (eds) *The Handbook of Qualitative Research in Education.* New York: Academic Press.

Wolcott, H.F. (2001) *Writing Up Qualitative Research* (2nd edn). London: Sage.

Wolcott, H.F. (2009) *Writing Up Qualitative Research* (3rd edn). London: Sage.

Woodley, A. (1981) Age bias, in D. Warren Piper (ed.) *Is Higher Education Fair?* Guildford: SRHE.

Woodley, A. (1984) The older the better? A study of mature student performance in British universities, *Research in Education*, 32: 35–50.

Woodley, A. (1985) Taking account of mature students, in D. Jacques and J. Richardson (eds) *The Future of Higher Education*. Guildford: SRHE and NFER-Nelson.

Woodley, A. (1998) Review of McGivney (1996a) *'Staying or Leaving the Course: Non-completion and Retention of Mature Students in Further and Higher Education'*. Leicester: National Institute of Adult Continuing Education.

Woodley, A. and McIntosh, N. (1980) *The Door Stood Open: An Evaluation of the Open University Younger Students' Pilot Scheme*. Barcombe: Falmer Press.

Wragg, E.C. (1980) *Conducting and Analysing Interviews*, Rediguide 11. Nottingham: University of Nottingham School of Education.

Yin, R.K. (1994) Designing single- and multiple-case studies, in N. Bennett, R. Glatter and R. Levaćič (eds) *Educational Management through Research and Consultancy*. London: Paul Chapman.

Yin, R.K. (2012) *Applications of Case Study Research* (3rd edn). London: Sage.

Yin, R.K. (2014) *Case Study Research: Design and Methods* (5th edn). London: Sage.

Youngman, M.B. (1982) *Analysing Questionnaires*, Rediguide 12. Nottingham: University of Nottingham School of Education.

Youngman, M.B. (1994) Designing and analysing interviews, in N. Bennett, R. Glatter and R. Levaćič (eds) *Improving Educational Management through Research and Consultancy*. London: Paul Chapman.

Zimmerman, D.H. and Wieder, D.L. (1977) The diary-interview method, *Urban Life*, 5 (4): 479–99.

Websites referenced in the text

http://answers.yahoo.com/question/index?qid=20090912141927AArnxbc [Accessed 14 March 2014]

http://delicious.com/about [Accessed 14 March 2014]

https://www.dropbox.com [Accessed 14 March 2014]

http://en.wikipedia.org/wiki/Standard_deviation [Accessed 14 March 2014]

www.endnote.com [Accessed 14 March 2014]

www.google.com [Accessed 14 March 2014]

www.mendeley.com [Accessed 14 March 2014]

http://www.methods.manchester.ac.uk/methods/blog-analysis/index.shtml [Accessed 14 March 2014]

www.refworks.com [Accessed 14 March 2014]

http://www.webcredible.co.uk/user-friendly-resources/web-usability/diary-study-guide.shtml [Accessed 14 March 2014]

Index

Note: Key/Glossary terms are in **bold** type.

D

E

Q

R

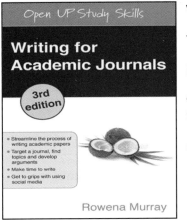